'scuse me while I kiss the sky

50 moments that changed music

'scuse me while I kiss the sky

50 moments that changed music

PAOLO HEWITT

Quercus

CONTENTS

INTRODUCTION

Rock'n'roll has no beginning and no end. There are just rivers of creativity, pouring forth, intermingling, generating new sounds and new styles. Blues, jazz, folk, gospel, pop, rock, heavy metal, rap, house, grime, dubstep – and more to come.

One of those streams was spotted by Sam Phillips. In the 50s he figured out that if he could just find a hip white guy to sing the blues he would clean up. Then Elvis Presley walked into his studio... In later life, Sam would say that the first-ever rock'n'roll record was Ike Turner's 'Rocket 88'. You often see that statement repeated now: rock'n'roll started with 'Rocket 88' because Sam says so. Maybe. But what of those gospel and blues tunes that pre-date Ike but carry distinct rock'n'roll characteristics? Roy Brown's 'Good Rocking Tonight', released in 1947? Or 'Cadillac Boogie', also from 1947, by the wonderfully named Jimmy Liggins and His Drops of Joy. Like I said, streams within streams.

There were earlier clues that a new music was coming. In December 1946 eight of America's leading jazz bands gave up. One of those bands was led by Tommy Dorsey. He and his brother Jimmy went on to host TV shows. In January 1956, they introduced Elvis Presley to the nation. The symbolism could not have been more perfect: rock'n'roll stepped into the spotlight as jazz left the stage.

This happened at a moment of rapid economic growth in America. The nation's youth was expected to rise early and work hard and then go home to the wife and kids and domestic bliss. But some found that the prospect of domestic bliss was not to their liking. The rock'n'roll of people such as Elvis expressed this dissatisfaction. On its arrival kids went crazy. They rioted and they fought and they made out. Rock'n'roll was fresh and thrilling and sexy and dangerous.

And yet by 1960, the year this book begins, America thought rock'n'roll was dead. All its major practitioners – Elvis, Chuck Berry, Jerry Lee Lewis, Little Richard – had found riches or God, or else were languishing in disgrace. Grown-up America breathed a sigh of a relief, but too soon. In Britain, American rock'n'roll was having a huge impact on teenagers such as John Lennon, Paul McCartney, Pete Townshend, Keith Richards, Ray Davies and Steve Marriott. The same with the arrival of rhythm and blues music in Britain. In fact, in the early 1960s the music that was to become soul took over from rock'n'roll as the sound of the teenager. Most up-and-coming British musicians in the early 60s wanted to sing like Ray Charles, with the attitude of Elvis. Ironic then that, by the time bands such as The Beatles took their music back to America, Elvis was a light entertainer, exactly the kind of figure rock'n'roll had set out to destroy.

Seismic changes were also occurring in black music. Many African-American servicemen came back from the Second World War hoping that they would now share in their country's prosperity. When that hope was disappointed, a defiant entrepreneurial spirit sprang up, expressed through black-owned clubs and record labels – most notably Berry Gordy's Motown. The impact of his records plus the work of artists such as Ray Charles cannot be overestimated. In Britain, throughout the early 60s, black music was the driving force behind all the leading bands from The Beatles onwards. And let us not forget Jamaican mento, which begat ska, which begat reggae, and so brought us Bob Marley.

As the 60s progressed, music moved away from its rock'n'soul roots to explore and create other distinct genres such as psychedelia, heavy rock, heavy metal. Again, streams within streams. At first, this music was the force that linked together the youthful, the disenfranchised. Bands were of the people and for the people. In songs and in interviews they stated their desire for freedom. They and their audience didn't want faceless old men telling them what they could wear, listen to or watch.

Yet it was also becoming very apparent that rock music was big business, thus creating a real dichotomy between the performer and the audience. In the 70s the sense of community that drove the idealism of the 60s started to erode. Music became a pursuit of pleasure. It was punk, in the late 70s, that restored rock music's sense of duty to directly challenge the world around it. That gave way to the 80s and a new breed of musicians that made no bones about wanting money and fame. And yet it was this decade that saw Live Aid – the most selfless moment in the history of rock. But in music there is always a reaction. What is dominant one day is replaced by its opposite the next day. Bands such as Primal Scream, Nirvana, Oasis, The Stone Roses and Happy Mondays strove to re-establish rock as rebel music, tied to a lifestyle of defiance.

But rock itself was by this time no longer young. The music had a past, and this book picks up on 50 key moments in its history. The story begins with Elvis and ends with Michael Jackson, two superstars separated by time but not by fate. In between there are moments of absolute genius, moments of true inspiration and outrage, moments of downright stupid behaviour, courageous moments, brilliant moments, outlandish moments and moments of true beauty. All life is here, glorified by the light of stardom and the pursuit of great truths. Some of these 50 moments chose themselves – Cooke, The Beatles, Woodstock, Hendrix, Cobain – others I personally chose in the hope they would illuminate or simply entertain. I am sure you will have your own 50 favourite moments. These are mine.

Paolo Hewitt

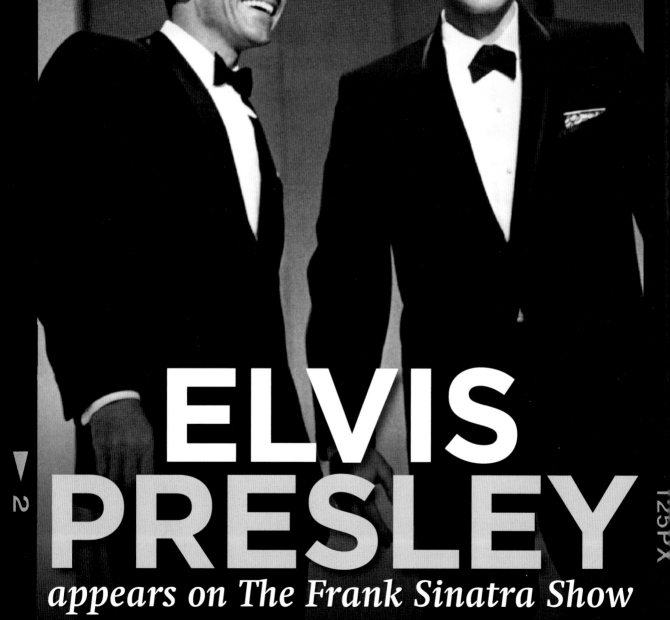

ELVIS PRESLEY
appears on The Frank Sinatra Show

DATE 26 March 1960, Miami Beach

America invented rock'n'roll, and it might as well have set fire to itself. Rock'n'roll corrupted a whole generation. It turned polite young men into surly adolescents who smoked and drank and wore their hair funny. The police called them punks. Tame young girls, destined for motherhood and the kitchen, now became sassy and sexy creatures who would blow any house down. 'We let the devil out,' the singer Carl Perkins once said with a wolfish grin.

There were better singers than Elvis Presley – Little Richard, for example. There were wilder, more dangerous men – Jerry Lee Lewis. And there were far better songwriters and craftsmen – Buddy Holly and Gene Vincent.

But Elvis trumped them because he had the look. Elvis was perfectly built for turning on a generation of girls. He was tall, handsome, continental-looking with his brooding eyes and slicked-back hair. When he danced, he did so without knowing. He was not out to bed his audience with fake moves. He was just himself, swinging his hips, muttering into the microphone, his hair falling over his forehead, his eyes measuring the distance of desire from you to him and back again.

Elvis was like no other. When he walked on stage the girls could not help themselves. They screamed and they rushed towards him and when they couldn't get to him, they rioted. They damaged concert venues and invaded hotels, acted in ways America had not seen. Elvis got to the boys as well. He was their size, their look. It was the perfect formula. Girls wanted to bed him, boys wanted to be him. Jackpot. For two years, everywhere he went, mayhem, craziness, disturbed behaviour. And then the squares hit back.

TAME YOUNG GIRLS, DESTINED FOR MOTHERHOOD AND THE KITCHEN, NOW BECAME SASSY AND SEXY CREATURES WHO WOULD BLOW ANY HOUSE DOWN

They drafted Elvis into the army. He was caught in a trap. If he rebelled, said no way, he would be dubbed unpatriotic, the worst thing you can be called in America. His career would have died on the spot. He had no choice.

It was time to take the uniform, play it low-key. During his two-year stint Elvis was never insubordinate or rebellious. He was the model soldier. Many think that he went that inch further to scotch the idea he was getting special treatment.

In 1960 he was honourably discharged from the US Army, but the world that he knew had changed. Rock'n'roll was dead, finished, *passé*. Jerry Lee Lewis and Chuck Berry had played around with underage girls and could hardly get a gig; Eddie Cochran and Buddy Holly were dead; and Little Richard had decided enough sin was enough, and sought redemption in God. Would Elvis now save the music? Become more rebellious and sneering and even sexier? Or would he bow and say sorry? America got to know the answer when millions tuned into see his first post-army TV performance. The host was none other than Frank Sinatra.

In 1957 Sinatra had told a magazine reporter: 'Rock'n'roll smells phoney and false. It is sung, played and written by cretinous goons... By means of its sly, lewd, dirty lyrics... it manages to be the most martial music of every sideburned delinquent on the face of the earth... [It] is the most brutal, ugly, desperate, vicious form of expression it has been my misfortune to hear.' Now here was Sinatra welcoming Elvis, the king of rock'n'roll, a cretinous goon, on to his TV show with a big handshake and a big smile.

Sinatra, of course, despised Elvis. The fact that Francis Albert was probably more rock'n'roll than Elvis would ever be – with his women and his whisky and his Mafia fixation – never came into it. Sinatra represented clean-cut America, a land of sharp suits and ties, of respect for the law and for women and for the notion of settling down and raising children. Presley had sought to destroy all that, and now here was Frank and here was Elvis, and the two were as one. How sweet. Straight America had finally tamed the beast.

HE WAS THEIR SIZE, THEIR LOOK. GIRLS WANTED TO BED HIM, BOYS WANTED TO BE HIM. JACKPOT. FOR TWO YEARS, EVERYWHERE HE WENT, MAYHEM

What had happened? Although Sinatra hated Elvis's music, he recognized the singer's patriotic leanings, so impressively displayed during the previous two years. And he acknowledged Elvis's great tragedy: the boy lost his mother Gladys in

August 1958. She and Elvis were close, and her passing hurt the kid badly.

For the show, Elvis wore a tux and white shirt. His hair was thick, but painfully styled so as not to cause any offence. After Sinatra's jokey intro – 'I think you only lost your sideburns' – Elvis launched into a very tame song called 'Fame and Fortune'.

He upped the level with his next song, a version of 'Stuck on You'. He clicked his fingers, and at one point swivelled his hips, eliciting screams from the audience. But what once had been subversive was now a party trick. Sinatra then joined Elvis for a duet. Sinatra sang 'Love Me Tender', and Elvis countered with his version of the standard, 'Witchcraft'. At the duet's end, they put their arms around each other. The path ahead was the same for both of them: movies, soundtrack albums, Las Vegas, showgirls, money, paranoia, riches, intemperate behaviour, withdrawal.

Still, both men profited from the show. Frank got to look a little hip and Elvis, with his good manners and willingness to please, placed himself in the mainstream.

The first phase of rock'n'roll was over. But the spirit that Elvis and Buddy and Jerry had whipped up had not died. It had flown across the Atlantic, to Liverpool, and wrapped itself around four teenage musicians. They would take that spirit and conquer the world. When they came to America, the girls – silent for two years – started screaming again. But Elvis didn't hear them. He was fast asleep.

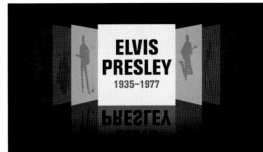

Elvis Aaron Presley was born to Vernon and Gladys Presley in Tupelo, Mississippi, on 8 January 1935. His elder twin brother, Jesse Garon Presley, was stillborn, and Elvis grew up an only child. The family moved to Memphis in 1948, and Elvis graduated from high school in 1953. By then he was obsessed with music, in particular the gospel music he heard in various churches. He began his professional singing career in 1954, when he hooked up with Sam Phillips, the owner of Sun Records. Two years later, thanks to hits such as 'Heartbreak Hotel' and 'Blue Suede Shoes', he was the most popular and controversial singer in America. Elvis caused unprecedented hysteria wherever he played. In 1958 he went into the army, and when he came out of uniform in 1960 he embarked upon a career that was markedly mainstream. He appeared in 33 films and many landmark TV shows, and sold more than a billion records. He met everyone from The Beatles to President Nixon, and he remained a superstar all his life. He died at Graceland, his Memphis mansion, on 16 August 1977.

The birth of

THE BEATLES

DATE 27 December 1960, Litherland Town Hall, Liverpool

From the moment Paul McCartney stepped up to the mike in his black leather jacket and screamed the opening line to Little Richard's 'Long Tall Sally', Liverpool belonged to The Beatles. It was two days after Christmas 1960, and the band was playing an engagement at the Litherland Town Hall in a suburb of Liverpool. They had not played their home town for several months now, so no one had any idea of just how potent The Beatles had become. When McCartney opened his voice, the truth was revealed.

On hearing McCartney's clarion call, the large crowd of teenage boys and girls surged forwards. Everyone looking on gasped in amazement. No one rushed bands in those days. People danced and looked at each other. They didn't pay any attention to the band supplying the music, nor did they lose their minds over a version of 'Long Tall Sally' and run towards the band in ecstasy.

But they did that night in Litherland, and so the first local manifestation of Beatlemania was born. Dave Forshaw, a promoter who happened to be present at the gig, was convinced a major fight had broken out. 'I'd never seen any band look like this before,' Forshaw recalled. 'I thought: "What are they? Who are they?"'

They were The Beatles, and with hindsight the reaction to their set raises a different question. Why were they the first band to be rushed? There were numerous other rock'n'roll bands in Liverpool at that time, so what made The Beatles so special, so very different from all the others? What did they have that no other band in the country possessed?

NO ONE RUSHED BANDS IN THOSE DAYS. PEOPLE DANCED AND LOOKED AT EACH OTHER. THEY DIDN'T PAY ATTENTION TO THE BAND SUPPLYING THE MUSIC OR LOSE THEIR MINDS OVER A VERSION OF 'LONG TALL SALLY'

The answer to that question lay in the German port town of Hamburg. In August 1960 the band had travelled to Hamburg to play at a place called the Indra Club. The trip was arranged by their agent/manager, Allan Williams, and the line-up of the band was John Lennon, Paul McCartney, George Harrison, Stuart Sutcliffe and Pete Best.

THERE WAS NO LET-UP FROM THE PUNISHING SCHEDULE. NOT THAT THE BEATLES MINDED: **THEY WERE YOUNG, FULL OF ENERGY AND VIGOUR.** THEY LOVED PLAYING LIVE – AND THAT DRIVE AND ENTHUSIASM SOON BEGAN ATTRACTING A CROWD

The Indra Club was to be found in St Pauli, a part of town well known for vice. Prostitutes sat in the windows of houses, and a lot of gangsters could be found in the area. When the band arrived on 17 August, they were shown to their living quarters – a storeroom in a small cinema named the Bambi Kino. Their room was next to the toilets.

The Indra itself was a sparsely attended transvestite cabaret club. Its owner, Bruno Koschmider, was hoping that some live music would bring in the crowds, and the work schedule he imposed on the band was highly demanding. The band would typically perform for up to six hours a night, with half-hour breaks thrown in.

Given the length of their usual set, the band now had to figure out a way to extend their repertoire by several hours. Twenty-minute versions of songs such as Ray Charles's 'What'd I Say' became the norm for them. One night the band managed to eke that song out for more than 90 minutes.

Koschmider encouraged the band to engage with the audience and would often walk to the front of the stage and shout 'Macht Schau' at them (literally, 'Make a show') if he felt they were not pulling their weight. The members of the band would respond with a series of mad dances – especially Lennon, who one night took to the stage wearing his underpants and a toilet seat around his neck.

There was no let-up from Bruno Koschmider's punishing schedule. Not that The Beatles minded: they were young, full of energy and vigour, and they had been placed in the dead centre of a circle of vice. They loved playing live – and that drive and enthusiasm, coupled with their growing set of rock'n'roll covers, soon began attracting a sizeable crowd. However, there were several complaints about the noise, and so Koschmider was forced to relocate the band to another of his clubs, this one named the Kaiserkeller.

The young Beatles pose at a Hamburg funfair in October 1961. The photographer is Astrid Kirchherr, who dated their bass player, Stu Sutcliffe, and would help change the group's image.

The stage at the Kaiserkeller was an old wooden floor balanced on beer crates. Whilst the band played, happy customers would send up trays of drinks for the boys. There was a lot of drinking, and most nights became party nights.

The band made three very important German friends at the Kaiserkeller: Astrid Kirchherr, Jürgen Vollmer and Klaus Voormann. These new acquaintances were very much into the French existential style and philosophy. Their distinctive hairstyles – common amongst them and their like-minded contemporaries – would later be adopted by the band. Sutcliffe started dating the beautiful Astrid, and her photographs of the band, taken in a funfair near the club, have since assumed a highly iconic status. The band were also drawn by the leather that their three friends wore, and acquired similar clothes.

By playing every night the band improved tremendously, and with this improvement came greater ambition. Hamburg's biggest club was called The Top Ten, and it was there that The Beatles now yearned to play. Eventually, after discreet overtures to that club's management, they left the Kaiserkeller. By way of a parting gesture, McCartney and Best burnt a condom in their 'bedroom'. A jealous Koschmider reported the pair to the police for arson, and the band were swiftly deported back to Liverpool.

LIVERPOOL HAD NOT HEARD ANYTHING LIKE IT. THE BAND TURNED THEIR AMPS ALL THE WAY UP AND HIT THE STAGE IN A VENGEFUL MOOD

Dejected by this turn of events, the band didn't communicate for about two weeks. Then came a call from Bob Wooler, a Liverpool DJ. The Searchers were unable to play their gig at the Litherland Town Hall on 27 December. Could The Beatles deputize? The band thought: of course we will. The line-up now was John, Paul, George, Pete Best on drums and a bass player called Chas Newby deputizing for Stu Sutcliffe, who had remained in Hamburg with Astrid. They joined The Deltones and The Del Renas on the bill.

The promoter advertised The Beatles as 'direct from Hamburg', so everyone who came to the dance that night expected to be entertained by a German band. They soon discovered otherwise. The Beatles' brand of rock'n'roll, honed to perfection in Hamburg, was full of attack and energy and confidence. This, coupled with their stand-out leather jackets and very cool all-black look, turned the heads of the audience – literally. Liverpool had not heard anything like it. The band turned their amps all the way up and hit the stage in a vengeful mood. At the end of the set the audience clapped wildly and gave the band an enthusiastic send-off.

As John Lennon was later to say of this landmark show: 'Suddenly we were a wow. Mind you, 70 per cent of the audience thought we were a German wow, but we didn't care about that. Even in Liverpool, people didn't know we were from Liverpool. They thought we were from Hamburg. They said, "Christ, they speak good English!" Which we did, of course, being English.

'It was that evening that we really came out of our shell and let go,' Lennon added. 'We stood there being cheered for the first time. This was when we began to think that we were good. Up to Hamburg we'd thought we were OK, but not good enough. It was only back in Liverpool that we realized the difference and saw what had happened to us while everyone else was playing Cliff Richard shit.' Lennon – angry young man that he was – despised the bland, sanitized rock'n'roll that Cliff

Richard typified, and that was making the UK charts at the time.

Drummer Pete Best later commented on that same gig: 'Litherland was an explosion in the fortunes of The Beatles. We were playing for dancing in a hall that could accommodate some 1,500

'WE WERE A WOW. MIND YOU, 70 PER CENT OF THE AUDIENCE THOUGHT WE WERE A GERMAN WOW, BUT WE DIDN'T CARE. EVEN IN LIVERPOOL PEOPLE DIDN'T KNOW WE WERE FROM LIVERPOOL'

on the dance floor at one time. But they stopped dancing when we played and surged forwards in a crowd to be nearer to us, to watch every moment, and above all to scream. People didn't go to a dance to scream: this was news.'

Indeed it was. Four years later The Beatles were established as the biggest band in the world.

The Beatles were formed in 1958. They signed to EMI Records in 1962, by which time their line-up consisted of John Lennon (rhythm guitar), Paul McCartney (bass), George Harrison (lead guitar) and Ringo Starr (drums). Their first single 'Love Me Do' reached the top 20. Not one of their singles or albums failed to chart, and almost every record went to number one. By the end of 1964 they were a worldwide sensation. Their irresistible music, combined with their appealing image, triggered a huge response – and not just from teenagers. In 1966, as a result of the chaos that ensued wherever they went, the band decided to stop touring and concentrate on making records. In four years the band produced such notable albums as *Sergeant Pepper's Lonely Hearts Club Band*, *The Beatles (The White Album)* and *Abbey Road*. The death of their manager Brian Epstein in 1967 led eventually to the band's demise as Lennon, Harrison and Starr took against Paul McCartney over the choice of manager. In 1970 The Beatles split up, but more than 40 years on they remain one of the world's most popular bands.

BERRY GORDY'S

first number one at Motown

DATE 11 September 1961, Detroit

In July 1988 he finally ended the dream and sold all his interests in Motown, the company he had fathered, the label he had placed in the history books by dint of his vision, his discipline, his unwavering commitment. On the day he did that, on the day he sold his past life and work, Berry Gordy faced the press. 'In selling Motown, do you feel you are a failure?' a journalist asked him. Gordy looked at him in absolute amazement. 'I am part of a deal worth $371 million. What do you think?'

Motown was a force of nature, and so was Berry Gordy. He had to be; it was harder for a camel to pass through the eye of a needle than for a black man to succeed in a white America. But Gordy did it. He played their game and trumped the lot of them. In doing so, he single-handedly inspired a generation of black music entrepreneurs. Without Berry, no Jay-Z, no Def Jam...

Gordy was one of eight children. His father, Berry Gordy II, instilled in his son tough morals and ethics. Gordy left school early, tried to become a professional boxer. The kid was good, but not good enough. He won eight fights, lost two, drew one. Then the army called. Berry completed his two-year stint, then married 19-year-old Thelma Louise Coleman. He went to work at his father's print shop to support his wife and new child.

But at night the music of Detroit called him. Berry spent much time in jazz clubs, and such was his passion for the music that he set up a record shop, the 3-D Record Mart.

HE NOW KNEW RULE NUMBER ONE: TO MAKE MONEY IN THE MUSIC BUSINESS, SERIOUS MONEY, YOU HAVE TO BE THE BOSS

Berry was smart – but he was in the wrong place right now. Detroit's black citizens made their living in the automobile factories that the town was famous for. On their nights off, tired workers didn't want jazz playing with their heads. They wanted music they didn't have to think about but could dance to, drink the night away to. They wanted the likes of John Lee Hooker.

GORDY'S AMBITION WAS HUGE, AND HE KNEW THAT TO REALIZE YOUR AMBITIONS **YOU HAVE TO DEAL WITH THE WORLD AS IT IS,** NOT AS YOU WOULD LIKE IT TO BE

The jazz shop lasted two years. Only one thing for it now. Berry signed up at the Lincoln Mercury plant. He hated his job, but he found a form of salvation in his active mind. Standing on the production line, Berry began to dream up melodies and riffs, choruses and lyrics. Money was the motivation. He had seen an advert that said songwriters could net $25 a song.

His break came at a local club called The Flame. The word reached him that a local manager, Al Greene, was looking for material for a singer named Jackie Wilson. Gordy knew that name: he had fought Wilson in his boxing days. Gordy found him one day, and the pair began writing together. One of the songs they dreamt up was called 'Reet Petite'. Two hits followed:

'That's Why (I Love You So)' and 'I'll Be Satisfied'. Wilson was now Detroit's biggest star, and Gordy a big cog in his machine.

Despite his success, Gordy's cut was minimal. He now knew rule number one: to make money in the music business, serious money, you have to be the boss. In 1957 Berry Gordy encountered Smokey Robinson at an audition held by Jackie Wilson's manager. Although Smokey was rejected, Gordy liked what he heard. 'Your songs are good,' he told the young singer-songwriter. 'I've got hundreds of them,' Robinson replied, and in that moment Motown Records was born.

The two men sat down and worked their way through Robinson's songbook. They renamed his band The Miracles. By 1959 the men were ready for some action. Whilst Smokey kept writing, Gordy set up Jobete Publishing (named after his daughters Joy, Betty and Terry) along with his record labels: Motown (a contraction of Detroit's nickname Motortown) and Tamla (named after a Debbie Reynolds film *Tammy*). Gordy's plan was to control every aspect of an artist's career, from publishing to issuing records. Later, he would hire people to school his artists in manners and etiquette. In return he would give his artists fame and success. For working-class Detroit kids, scratching their butts, scratching a living, it seemed a good deal.

In the summer of 1959 The Miracles' 'Way Over There' became Tamla's first release. It sold 60,000 copies – a remarkable number for an obscure label. His second breakthrough came early in 1961 when The Miracles' 'Shop Around' hit number one in the R&B chart, two in the national chart. In September 1961 his group The Marvelettes went to number one with 'Please Mr Postman' – and Motown had its first chart-topping hit.

A striking thing about this tune is how white it is, although everyone on the record was black. The vocals recall any number of girl groups of the time, the beat is light and the instrumentation highly contained. This was far away from the raucous R&B of the 50s. But Gordy's ambition was huge, and he knew that to realize your ambitions you have to deal with the world as it is, not as you would like it to be. Gordy also knew that Sun Records' Sam Phillips was right when he said white performers singing black music would clean up. Gordy turned that around. He made black performers sing white, and cleaned up. Motown played the odds, never looked to upset anyone, not until Norman Whitfield and Marvin Gaye and Stevie Wonder came along and said: enough is enough.

With 'Please Mr Postman' the first down-payment was made on that final $371 million. And soon, local black businessmen were setting up music companies by the dozen. Some succeeded whilst others went to the wall. Either way, Berry Gordy was the inspiration – and Motown was the dream fulfilled.

BERRY GORDY
1929–

Berry Gordy Jnr was born on 28 November 1929 in Detroit, Michigan. His family was tightknit and very religious. In the 11th grade Berry dropped out of school, determined to become a professional boxer. In 1950 he was drafted into the US Army. He fought in the Korean War, and moved back to Detroit three years later. Whilst working in a car factory, he began composing songs that he later sold to Jackie Wilson. In 1957 he met Smokey Robinson and started Motown records. Over the next three decades the label would issue a series of significant and huge-selling singles such as 'Dancing in the Street', 'Reach Out I'll Be There' and 'I Heard It Through the Grapevine', as well as landmark albums that included Marvin Gaye's *What's Going On*, Stevie Wonder's *Songs in the Key of Life* and the speeches of Dr Martin Luther King. In 1972 Gordy moved Motown to Los Angeles in search of even greater success. He signed many significant acts, including The Jackson Five. In 1988 he sold the company for millions of dollars, published his autobiography *To Be Loved* and settled down to a quiet life in Los Angeles.

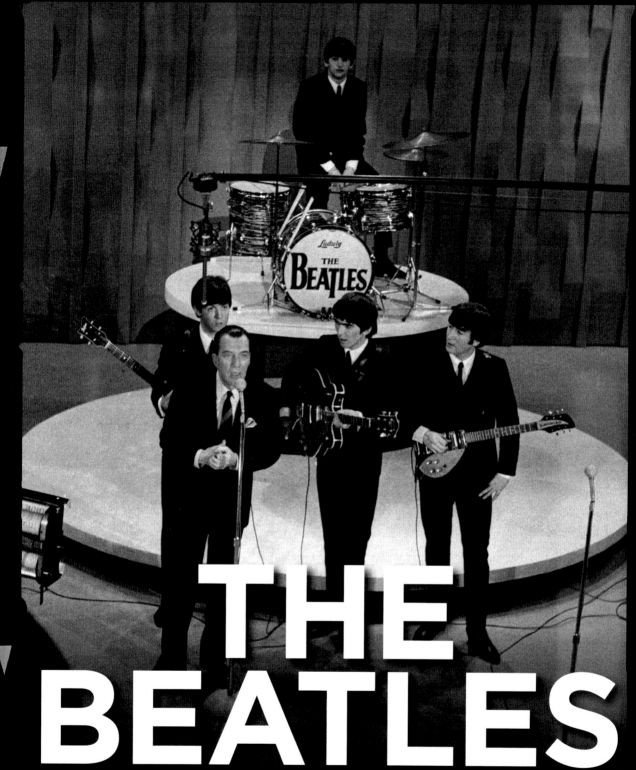

THE BEATLES

appear on The Ed Sullivan Show

DATE 9 February 1964, New York

The Beatles flew out to America for the first time in February 1964. Such was the deep aura of magic and invincibility that had attached itself to the band that the producer Phil Spector, always an anxious flyer, switched a plane ticket so as to be on their flight. He believed that no plane carrying those four gods could ever crash. And he was right.

The Beatles landed safely in America on 7 February, and the events of that first trip turned out to be nothing short of extraordinary. Within two days, in that vast continent that they had admired so much from afar, they had attracted the biggest television audience ever recorded. Seventy-three million Americans tuned in on a cold night to watch this new sensation sing a song on *The Ed Sullivan Show*. Famously, it was reported that the number of crimes committed in New York went down that night. Even criminals were fascinated by the Beatles.

How did this amazing thing happen? How did a band conquer the biggest market in the world without having even visited it? How did a band whose singles had been rejected and ignored for months suddenly become the biggest thing in America? Luck and astute planning is the answer.

The day after The Beatles gave a historic Royal Command performance on 4 November 1963 their manager Brian Epstein flew to America. He was heading west to begin paving the way for this unique moment in pop history. But he had a fight on his hands. Capitol Records, the American branch of EMI, had refused to release the band's first two singles, 'Love Me Do' and 'Please Please Me'. None of the other big guns who had been offered the songs seemed interested either.

HOW DID THIS AMAZING THING HAPPEN? HOW DID THE BEATLES CONQUER THE BIGGEST MARKET IN THE WORLD WITHOUT HAVING EVEN VISITED IT?

EMI placed 'Please Please Me' and 'From Me to You' with an independent Chicago-based record label called Vee-Jay, which was the home of Frankie Valli and The Four Seasons. The next single, 'She

Loves You', found a home on the Swan label, in Philadelphia.

If Epstein was to break the band Stateside, he needed to have a major record company behind him. Epstein's strategy for getting one on board was to secure the band a slot on a major national TV show. This would be his trump card, and in that respect he had luck on his side. Ed Sullivan – one of the biggest names in American television and a man who had a reputation as a starmaker – had a representative in London. This UK-based scout kept Sullivan aware of all major developments in the entertainment world – developments such as Beatlemania. Epstein knew of this, and a meeting was arranged with the producer of *The Ed Sullivan Show*, a man named Bob Precht, who also happened to be Sullivan's son-in-law. All this was in place before Brian set off for New York.

Truth be told, Precht was unprepared for the meeting. He thought the Beatles were some kind of novelty act and said as much to Epstein. Naturally, the manager reared up at this and made a very strong case for the band. The result was that Epstein came out of that meeting with the promise of a headlining slot on not one, not two, but three shows, to be broadcast on consecutive Sunday nights, 9, 16 and 23 February.

Capitol Records now agreed to a January release for 'I Want to Hold Your Hand'. The potential of *The Ed Sullivan Show* to boost sales was something they could

not ignore. Capitol also put aside the very large sum of $50,000 for a concerted marketing campaign.

Brian Epstein went home happy. Meanwhile, other parts of the American media got wind of Beatlemania. Three separate US TV crews landed in Britain and shot the band at their show at the Winter Gardens Theatre in Bournemouth on 16 November 1963.

FOUR THOUSAND FANS DESCENDED ON NEW YORK'S JFK AIRPORT. THE BEATLES HAD NEVER SET FOOT IN THE COUNTRY, BUT AMERICA, LIKE BRITAIN BEFORE IT, WAS FASCINATED AND CAPTIVATED

One of those films, when it was subsequently aired on American TV, caught the attention of a young girl named Marsha Albert. Marsha wrote a letter to her local DJ, Carroll James, requesting that he play some of The Beatles' music on his show. James was intrigued. He hunted down an import copy of 'I Want to Hold Your Hand', and when he came to play the song, he allowed Marsha to introduce it. At its conclusion, James

Chat show host Ed Sullivan talks to George Harrison just prior to the group's historic performance on his show. More than 70 million people watched The Beatles that night in February 1964, and by the morning Beatlemania was well and truly established in America.

asked the audience what they thought of the record. The switchboard lit up like a Christmas tree. So James played the song again the next hour, and got the same enthusiastic reaction. After that, he took to playing 'I Want to Hold Your Hand' every night, garnering the same huge response each time the record was aired.

Now Capitol Records sensed that something was in the air, and the company moved the release of the record back to late December. They were right to do so since American radio had picked up the single and was playing it to death. By the start of the new year it had already sold more than a million copies. Within a few days New York was smothered with stickers announcing that 'The Beatles Are Coming' – a jocular nod to the American revolutionary war-cry 'The British are coming'.

Meanwhile, radio was adding to the growing sense of excitement. On the day that the Beatles were due to arrive in America, the big New York radio station WMCA tracked their progress all the way from London Heathrow to the Big Apple. 'It is now 10.30 Beatle time, and the mop-tops are just a hundred miles from landing...'

PILES OF LETTERS AND TELEGRAMS WERE HEAPED ON THE TABLE. ONE WAS MARKED URGENT. MCCARTNEY OPENED IT. 'IT'S FROM ELVIS,' HE ANNOUNCED. 'WHO IS ELVIS?' DRAWLED LENNON

Four thousand fans descended on JFK, the largest congregation of Americans ever to have gathered at an airport to greet a visitor. The Beatles (apart from George Harrison) had never set foot in the country, but America, like Britain before it, was fascinated and captivated.

After the band disembarked, their first task was to give a press conference inside the airport itself. American journalists were renowned for their cynicism and world-weariness but The Beatles won them over with their cheeky wit and repartee. 'What do you think of Beethoven?' asked a journalist. 'We love him, especially his poems,' Ringo retorted. The room dissolved into laughter. After years of inane press conferences, in which performers issued the most vapid of replies, The Beatles were the proverbial breath of fresh air.

The Beatles were now driven to the Plaza Hotel, where hundreds of fans had gathered, mainly screaming girls, and then on to the Playboy Club. The next day, the fans still outside their hotel, they undertook a day of interviews, telling the same stories again and again, answering the same questions again and again.

On the Sunday – blessed relief – they would at last get the chance to stop talking and start playing. The Beatles arrived at the studios of *The Ed Sullivan Show*, located at 1697 Broadway, in the afternoon. In the week leading up the show the producers received 50,000 requests for 700 tickets. In their dressing room, piles of letters and telegrams were already heaped on the table. One envelope was marked URGENT in red letters. McCartney opened it. 'It's from Elvis,' he excitedly announced. 'Who is Elvis?' drawled Lennon.

The band played two sets that day, one in the afternoon (for broadcast the following week) and one live that evening. They opened their afternoon set with The

Isley Brothers' song 'Twist and Shout', a respectful nod to the musical source that they so eagerly drank from. (In New York, they spent a lot of their time ringing radio stations and asking to hear R&B favourites of their own such as The Ronettes, The Marvelettes and Marvin Gaye.) Then it was into 'Please Please Me' and 'I Want to Hold Your Hand'.

A CAPTION APPEARED UNDER JOHN LENNON THAT READ, 'SORRY, GIRLS, HE'S MARRIED'. THAT INFORMATION HAD THE POWER TO KILL THE FANTASIES OF MILLIONS OF YOUNG GIRLS

For the evening show, the live performance that would place them at the heart of American national life, they opened with 'All My Loving' and then launched into 'She Loves You'. Paul and John shook their mop-top hair like never before to whip up the young audience. Towards the end of the song a caption appeared under Lennon that read 'Sorry, girls, he's married'. This could have been a major disaster: that information had the power to kill the fantasies of millions of young girls. But the momentum of the whole occasion swept over the incident, rendering it harmless.

The Beatles wore their dark suits, and every time they shook their heads or gathered round a microphone the audience screamed and the walls shuddered. Paul did his cute trick of looking directly into the camera with soulful Bambi eyes. Lennon timed his knowing smiles to the camera with perfection. That was it for their first live televised set in America, but they returned later to close the show 'I Saw Her Standing There' and 'I Want to Hold Your Hand'.

Later that night it was announced that 58 per cent of American homes with televisions had tuned into the show. Yet the US newspapers chose to crucify The Beatles. *The New York Times*, *Newsweek*, the *Herald Tribune* – all of them turned their thumbs down, all of them carried the same cruel message to the boys from Liverpool, England: you look terrible, you play terrible, your songs are weak, and you ain't going to last – that's for sure.

Publicly, The Beatles smiled. Privately, they fumed at the bad reviews. But did Young America take one bit of notice of the hardbitten hacks? Did they hell. Beatlemania had just hit the United States, and after *The Ed Sullivan Show* it was completely unstoppable.

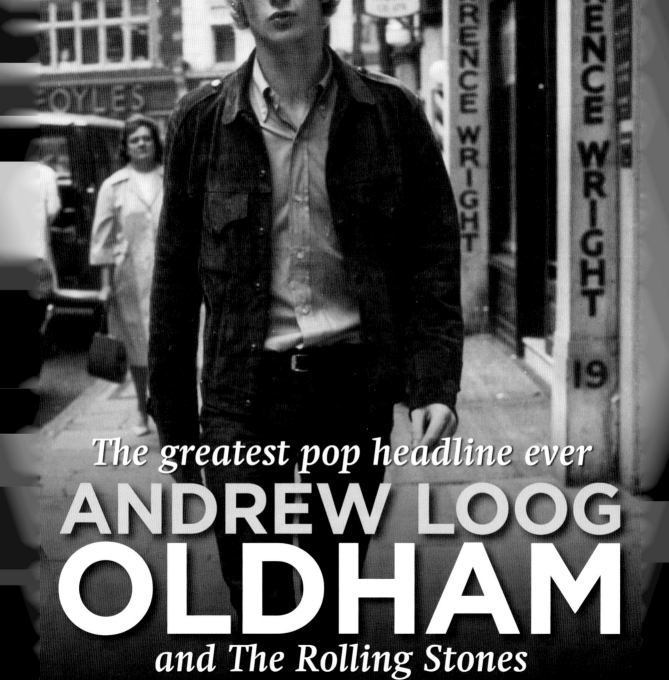

The greatest pop headline ever

ANDREW LOOG
OLDHAM

and The Rolling Stones

DATE 17 March 1964, England

Pop throws up two types of manager. There are the bullies, those not beyond using physical and mental violence to get their own way. Then there are the sharp cookies: the movers, the shakers, the hustlers. Andrew Loog Oldham belonged to the latter category. And then he topped it. No one understood pop like Oldham. He knew everything about it, how the fans thought, how the musicians worked and how the press operated. It made him one of the most formidable forces in the history of 60s pop. No wonder he was employed by both The Beatles and The Rolling Stones.

Andrew Loog Oldham began his working life as an assistant in a clothes shop – but not any old clothes shop. When he left school he got a job at Mary Quant's clothes shop, Bazaar, on the King's Road in Chelsea. Quant later had little memory of him,

> **HE RANG UP MELODY MAKER AND GAVE THEM THE HEADLINE: 'WOULD YOU LET YOUR DAUGHTER MARRY A ROLLING STONE?' THE REST OF THE PRESS CAUGHT ON INSTANTLY**

although she did recall that one day he failed to show up for work – then a month later American *Vogue* called to say that they had a young English kid standing in their office, claiming he was responsible for designing most of Mary Quant's clothes…

On his return to London, Oldham sought his mirror-image and found it in a hustler named Pete Meaden. He was The Who's first manager, the man who had made mods of them. Together Oldham and Meaden opened a PR firm and took on various bands.

Oldham was now living out his celluloid dream. He was a man driven by many things – not least two films: *Expresso Bongo* and, more importantly, *The Sweet Smell of Success*, starring Burt Lancaster and Tony

Curtis. Oldham swooned at the lifestyle shown in this 1957 classic, the unflinching nature of the film, the New York glamour suffused with seediness. Oldham had other heroes as well, chief amongst them the record producer Phil Spector. When Spector came to London in 1962, Oldham was soon by his side, sucking the American dry for valuable information.

Early in 1963 Oldham took one of his bands to appear on a TV show named *Thank Your Lucky Stars*. It was there that he saw The Beatles divest themselves of their TV virginity. Oldham made a beeline for their manager Brian Epstein, and he wheedled a job out of him, there and then, on the spot.

Oldham had no problem attracting the press to his cause: The Beatles were all over the papers. But a month or so later fate intervened with something new. Whilst taking a drink with Peter Jones, editor of a music paper called *Record Mirror*, Oldham was told about a rough-and-tumble blues band tearing it up every week at the Station Hotel in Richmond. The next Friday night Oldham was there, watching The Rolling Stones and falling madly in love. 'I knew what I was looking at,' Oldham recalled later. 'It was sex, and I was 48 hours ahead of the pack.'

Oldham called Epstein, asked if he wanted in. Epstein said no, so Oldham resigned and became The Rolling Stones' manager. In just one month he had turned himself from Epstein's employee to his biggest rival. Oldham relished the challenge. Whilst Epstein prided himself on never having to pull off a publicity stunt, Oldham thrived on them. Stunts were his motor, his petrol, his drive.

His first move was to rid the band of Ian Stewart, the piano player. Too old, too ugly, he told them. The Stones were sex, young sex. They didn't need a father figure in their ranks.

NEXT FRIDAY NIGHT OLDHAM WAS THERE, WATCHING THE ROLLING STONES AND FALLING MADLY IN LOVE. 'I KNEW WHAT I WAS LOOKING AT,' OLDHAM RECALLED. 'IT WAS SEX, AND I WAS 48 HOURS AHEAD OF THE PACK'

Then he went to war with The Beatles. His first move was to position the Stones as the alternative to the Fab Four. Epstein had turned those pill-popping Liverpudlians into a respectable outfit with clean faces and sharp suits. Everyone loved the Fabs. Oldham made sure that everyone except the young hated the Stones. Before the band's first appearance on *Juke Box Jury*, he told them not to take the show seriously, to make jokes, look like they didn't care.

Result? Acres of outrage in all the papers. You can't buy that kind of publicity.

Then, the masterstroke. In early March he rang up the music magazine *Melody Maker* and gave them the headline that would captivate a nation: 'Would You Let Your Daughter Marry a Rolling Stone?' As he envisaged, the rest of the press caught on instantly, and for months the subject was brought up in every interview the band undertook.

To ensure that they lived up to the notoriety he had delivered unto them, Oldham encouraged the band's wilder and wilder behaviour. In 1965 whilst travelling through London's East Ham, the band pulled up at a garage. Bass player Bill Wyman asked the attendant if he could use the toilet. His request was refused, so the band clambered out of the car and urinated against the garage wall. 'We piss anywhere, man,' Jagger told the attendant. Loutish, arrogant, condescending, the Stones were now one of Britain's biggest draws. Oldham had done his job spectacularly.

Oldham's mistake was to develop a parallel image. He began to indulge in all kinds of rock'n'roll behaviour that at first amused the band, then annoyed them. He had forgotten one of pop's golden rules: never overshadow your artist. In 1966 it was agreed that he should walk away, and this he did to start up his own label, Immediate Records. Typically, his first release, 'Hang On Sloopy' by The McCoys, went straight to number one.

ANDREW LOOG OLDHAM 1944–

Andrew Loog Oldham was born on 29 January in 1944 in London. His father was a United States Army Air Force lieutenant who was killed before Andrew was born. He attended various schools but was forever drawn to London's Soho and the first stirrings of teenage culture that were taking place at clubs such as The 2i's. He became a PR man, most notably for producer Joe Meek and The Beatles. In April 1963 he discovered The Rolling Stones and became their manager. For three years he guided the band to the top of the charts. He negotiated groundbreaking contracts that allowed the band to keep control of their tapes, and he got Lennon and McCartney to pen the band's first hit, 'I Wanna Be Your Man'. In 1966 he walked away to start Immediate Records. With artists including Small Faces and Chris Farlowe, Immediate scored many chart entries and lasted about five years. After it collapsed, Loog Oldham married Colombian model Esther Farfan and moved to her country. He has published two autobiographies, *Stoned* and *Stoned 2*, and works as a DJ in America.

The tragic shooting of
SAM
COOKE

DATE 11 December 1964, The Hacienda Motel, Los Angeles

At the time of his death, early in the morning of 11 December 1964, America's finest soul man was naked except for an overcoat and a shoe. There was a bullet in his chest, and he was slumped against the wall in the office of a motel. The receptionist, Bertha Franklin, sat at her desk, waiting for the police to arrive. Like the uniformed officers who were about to swarm into the building, she did not yet have any idea who she had just killed.

Sam Cooke had arrived at the motel in the early hours of the morning accompanied by a young girl who was clearly not his wife. 'You will have to sign in as Mr and Mrs,' Bertha had said, glancing meaningfully at the young girl. The man had done as he was asked.

He had met Lisa Boyer at a club early that night. She was pretty and sexy and cute, and Sam Cooke wanted to bed her. Badly. He got talking to her, and the next thing they knew they were in his car – looking for a motel.

Later, Lisa would tell the world she didn't want to go to any motel with Cooke, but he insisted they get a room. 'You are so pretty,' he kept telling her. Once they were in the room, Lisa claimed, Sam pushed her on to the bed and removed her sweater. Fearing rape, the 22-year-old waited for her chance. When Cooke went to the bathroom, Lisa grabbed a handful of his clothes and made a dash for the nearest phone box where she called the police. An enraged Cooke went looking for her.

At the time Bertha Franklin was in her office talking to her boss on the phone. Cooke knocked on her closed door. Bertha put the phone down and opened the door. She told the singer she had not seen the

LISA BOYER WAS PRETTY AND SEXY AND CUTE. SAM COOKE GOT TALKING TO HER, AND THE NEXT THING THEY KNEW THEY WERE IN HIS CAR, LOOKING FOR A MOTEL

Sam Cooke fools around with yet another sweet melody. The suave musician with the voice of an angel was also a shrewd businessman trying to break down racial barriers in 50s America.

girl. Cooke went away, and Bertha went back to her conversation. Minutes later, Cooke returned. When he knocked again Franklin refused to open the door. So Cooke broke it down, and rushed in. He was convinced Lisa was in there somewhere. He went straight to the two rooms adjoining the office and then came back. He grabbed Franklin by the wrists, demanding to know where she had hidden Boyer.

Franklin pushed him back, and they both fell to the floor. Franklin testified that Cooke would not leave her alone, that she started biting him in an attempt to get him off. Finally, she managed to raise herself up and make a dash for the TV. There, on top of

it, lay a gun. Bertha Franklin grabbed that gun, swivelled and, as Sam Cooke moved towards her, she shot him in the chest. 'You shot me,' he exclaimed in wonderment, and staggered towards her. As he did so, Bertha reached for a stick and hit Cooke on the head with it. The stick broke, and Cooke slumped to the floor.

Bertha grabbed the phone. Her boss was still on the line. She told him to call the police. She put the phone down and sat alone, staring at the dead body. Not long after, the police arrived. The scenario was nothing new to them. In this town, men were regularly killed in fights. Why should this incident be any different?

The investigation was perfunctory. The police took statements, and then removed the body to the local medical examiners. Alcohol was discovered in the man's bloodstream, but no narcotics. Then the police contacted the man's family; his wife broke down in tears. By mid-afternoon the body lay in a funeral home on South Central Avenue.

It was then that the police realized this was not the ordinary murder of an ordinary man. Radio stations began playing the same songs over and over again – 'You Send Me', 'Only Sixteen', 'Twisting the Night Away', 'Bring It On Home to Me', 'A Change Is Gonna Come'. Young men and women gathered at the scene of the shooting to lay flowers. At the funeral home, a long line of people formed, stretching further and further back, to view the body of their slain hero.

The funeral itself was attended by a sea of well-wishers. Sam Cooke was dead, and Black America mourned terribly. Why? Because they had just lost one of their true leaders, a symbol of absolute hope in a racially divided country. Cooke was a highly talented singer-songwriter, and he was a man on a mission. He wanted to reach both black and white, to create a music that would cross the divide and bring together both sets of people in a time of great division.

His songs were catchy, hewn from pop and soul and gospel elements. His singing was pure and clean, like spring water, and many of his songs featured sweet strings so as to lighten the sound. His records rarely had the earthiness of an Otis Redding track or the sly sexiness of Al Green. But they had brightness and a cleverness about them that was irresistible, and they were made beautiful by his wondrous voice. Sam Cooke had everything a musician could want. And then some.

SHE PUT THE PHONE DOWN AND SAT ALONE, STARING AT THE DEAD BODY OF SAM COOKE

Yet Cooke's ambitions did not stop at creating great records. Cooke was a true pioneer, one of the first modern black performers to create his own record label and publishing company. Like Berry Gordy, he was a man bent on steering his own career, and in so doing lay down a path for others to follow. At a time when blacks were truly considered third-class citizens, Cooke was determined to succeed.

This individual spirit was apparent in Sam Cooke from an early age, from when he started singing gospel music in fact, started getting noticed for his dynamic voice and good looks. By his teenage years, Sam was a member of a gospel band called The Teen Highways Gospel. And although he was admonished by his church that any music outside of gospel belonged to the devil, Sam could not help being drawn to the wonderful harmonies of bands such as The Ink Spots.

Sam's reputation as a gospel singer made him something of a star within this closed world, a reputation boosted by his good looks. The Queen of Soul herself, Aretha Franklin, recalls having to deal with devilish thoughts as she watched Sam perform in church. The top gospel band at this time was called The Soul Stirrers, fronted by a wonderful singer named R.H. Harris. When Harris retired, Sam Cooke was chosen to replace him. It was like being asked to follow Caruso.

Cooke knew it would be foolish to emulate Harris's style. Instead, he relied on his own voice, and in so doing he sent the churches wild. Sam was confident enough to start writing original material for the band, some of which was released on the Specialty label. Even then, his band members recall, he was talking about finding a way to a much larger audience. It seemed to Sam that gospel music was full of catchy tunes, driving beats and top harmonies – that it was not so different from R&B, soul or even pop. And he was right. Consider the number of songs 'inspired' by the gospel canon. Hear The Soul Stirrers sing 'Stand By Me Father'. Now listen to Ben E. King's immortal song, 'Stand By Me'. Brother and sister, right?

In 1956, following his father's advice that the Lord had given him a voice to make people happy, Sam dipped his toes into the waters of commercial music, the so-called devil's music. He released a song called 'Lovable' under the name Dale Cooke. The result was instantaneous: The Soul Stirrers fired him.

FOLLOWING HIS FATHER'S ADVICE THAT THE LORD HAD GIVEN HIM A VOICE TO MAKE PEOPLE HAPPY, SAM DIPPED HIS TOES IN THE WATERS OF THE DEVIL'S MUSIC

A year later, in 1957, Cooke signed to a non-religious label and released a song that he had written, 'You Send Me'. It sold two million copies. Hit after hit followed. His songs were innocent, playful. They dripped with innocence but also carried a real sense of class and sophistication. And they did what Sam Cooke hoped they would, they reached a very wide audience.

Sam was now an icon and a role model, and he was conscious of the trials and tribulations of his people. One of the last songs he wrote 'A Change Is Gonna Come', is rightfully perceived as one of the greatest songs to have emerged from the civil rights struggle. It is a song that links Cooke with the work that protest singers such as Bob Dylan and Phil Ochs were then producing. But the song is not classifiable. It is not soul, not pop, not rock. It is just a great song that transcends categories, and that was how Sam Cooke wanted it.

Then he met Lisa Boyer, and the dream ended. Whatever the reason for his tragic passing, one thing remained true: rarely has a man's death stood in such a strong contrast to his art. The cheap motel, the flighty girl, the drunken violent behaviour – few could believe that such things could lead to the death of the man whose spirit had felt so clear, so entrancing. How could a man with such a heart fall in this terrible manner? It did not seem possible.

In the months after the shooting of Sam Cooke, the conspiracy theorists were handed potent ammunition. First, Lisa Boyer was arrested on a prostitution rap, which raised a lot of eyebrows. Then Sam Cooke's widow remarried. No shame in that, except that her new husband was Cooke's closest friend, the singer and songwriter Bobby Womack.

Some people strongly suspected that America's authorities could not tolerate such a successful black symbol in their midst, and had created the circumstances for Cooke to perish.

Whatever the truth about his death, Cooke's music plays on, and his soul still shines. He was the link between Nat King Cole and Stax and Motown. It is whispered that on the day Cooke died God covered his eyes with his hand, so that He could not see the devil smiling back at Him.

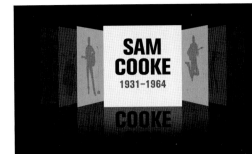

Sam Cooke was born Samuel Cook on 22 January 1931, in Clarksdale, Mississippi. He grew up in a large God-fearing family and began singing gospel at an early age. He made his name as a vocalist in a band called The Highway QCs, before being asked to join gospel's finest band, The Soul Stirrers. Despite disapproval from within the church, Cooke was determined to make his music appeal to a much wider audience, so he began recording secular music for non-religious record labels. This led to his banishment from the gospel world, but early hits such as 'You Send Me' proved that Cooke's intuition was absolutely correct. Future hits such as 'Bring It On Home to Me' and 'Chain Gang' established Cooke as a consummate performer and amazing vocalist. He used his success to start up his own label and publishing company. At the time of his death in a Los Angeles motel he was looking to build a massive musical empire. His passing was deeply mourned not only by Black America but also by those who strongly believed in equality for all, and in the power of music to heal great divisions.

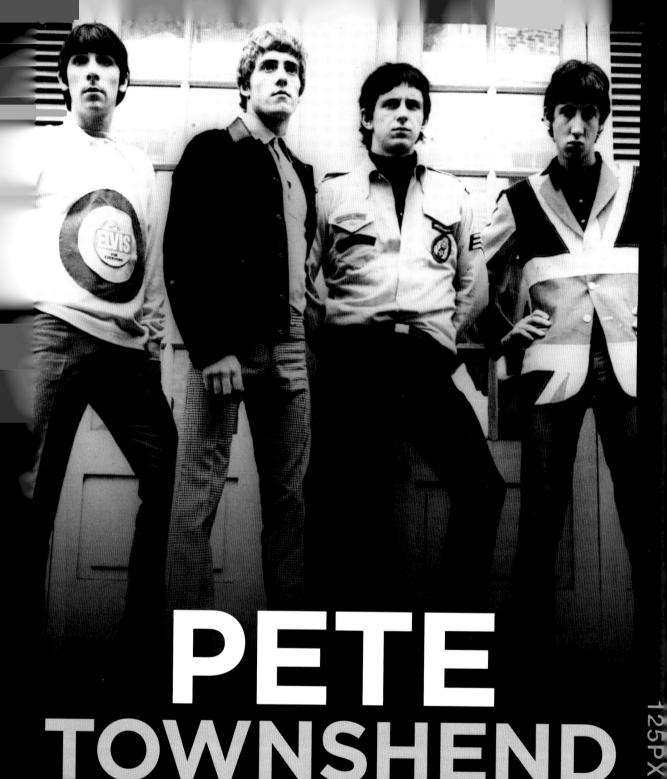

PETE
TOWNSHEND
writes 'My Generation'

125PX

DATE June 1965, Belgravia, London

It is the song that defines The Who, a song with a classic opening guitar riff that will be forever associated with Pete Townshend, the band's songwriter, and with the decade from which it sprang. 'My Generation' was written in 1965, and almost half a century later its ability to pulverize the listener into submission remains completely undiminished. 'My Generation' is one of the key anthems of the 60s and of youth in general. And it might never have been written but for the royal family.

In the 60s the young took over every art form. They seized the power in film, theatre, books, fashion, television and music. 'My Generation' caught that mood perfectly. It is a song about young defiance, about lashing out at the squares, those who put the young down without rhyme or reason. 'My Generation' is two fingers stuck up at the adult world, and that is why its eternal power and its appeal to every generation since is assured.

The song was written, depending on which Townshend interview you read, either on a train or else in the man's Belgravia flat. He had moved into this flat in June 1965. The Who had formed a year previously, and by January 1965 were in the charts with a single 'I Can't Explain'. The band had deliberately set out to win over Britain's huge mod community. Their dress was bright and neat and eye-catching,

and their songs were succinct distillations of the trials and tribulations of being an adolescent male.

'I Can't Explain' was one such song, a brilliant take on the inarticulacy of the young. The follow-up was 'Anyway Anyhow Anywhere'. It also charted – but Townshend knew they needed something very special if they were to become the leaders that they suspected they could be.

'MY GENERATION' IS TWO FINGERS STUCK UP AT THE ADULT WORLD, AND THAT IS WHY ITS APPEAL TO EVERY GENERATION SINCE IS ASSURED

'If ever there was a time when The Who might have split,' Townshend later noted, 'it would have been in the days of "My Generation". We had an image of no time for nobody and mod arrogance, in a period when we were actually a very ordinary group. We hadn't really done anything good, but we knew we were capable, so over a period we got it together.'

'MY GENERATION' WAS BORN, A THREE-MINUTE SALVO OF VIOLENCE AND FURY AIMED AT THE HEART OF THE BRITISH ESTABLISHMENT

Such was the belief that new manager Kit Lambert had in the young Townshend's songwriting abilities, he gave the young musician recording equipment worth more than £1,000 – a huge sum in those days. The idea was that Townshend would sit in his flash Belgravia flat and fulfil his potential as a songwriter. To help him, Lambert would come round and encourage his protégé to write.

One day Townshend's car, a 1935 Packard Hearse, was towed away. This was supposedly on the order of the Queen Mother who apparently disliked having to look at it as she swept past on her way to nearby Buckingham Palace. Townshend already felt highly uncomfortable living in Belgravia. These were not his people. He had been born in west London's Chiswick, attended art college, and adored raw R&B music. He had nothing in common with the rich of Belgravia. For his property to be so disdainfully treated infuriated him, and so 'My Generation' was born, a three-minute salvo of violence and fury aimed at the heart of the British Establishment.

Fittingly, the recording sessions for the single were filled with tension and violence, the band coming close to blows on several occasions. This was not unexpected. The band was always fragile, always liable to erupt into violence. Townshend and Keith Moon carried a self-destructive gene that manifested itself in regular drink and drug sessions – which annoyed Roger Daltrey no end. 'You're all junkies,' he would scream at them. Bass player John Entwistle never seemed to give a damn about anything.

The song was sung by Daltrey in a stuttering manner. Down the years both Townshend and Kit Lambert have claimed this idea as their own. Certainly, the effect Daltrey sought – to imitate the speech of a mod so wired on speed he can hardly talk – ch-ch-ch-chimed with the band's audience, who sent it hurtling up to number two in the charts. The success was deserved, the song claimed many firsts: the first single to feature a bass solo; the first to end in a bucketful of feedback and chaos; the first subversive anthem in the UK.

At the time, Townshend loved the attention and success and recognition and money that 'My Generation' brought, but as the years went by the line about hoping to die before he got old would come back to haunt him. By the time he got old, or at least middle-aged, he was part of a mainstream rock act, famous for its rock-opera concept albums *Tommy* and *Quadrophenia*, in third place behind The Beatles and the Stones. Townshend, meanwhile, accepted the role of elder statesman of rock, and spent hours with interviewers offering his thoughts on music, religion, life in general. That's all well and good, but it's a far cry from the song that said everything in 199 seconds.

FITTINGLY, THE RECORDING SESSIONS FOR THE SINGLE WERE FILLED WITH TENSION AND VIOLENCE, THE BAND COMING CLOSE TO BLOWS

'My Generation' has rightly been inducted into the Grammy Hall of Fame as one of the 500 songs that shaped rock'n'roll. It is a template that every angry band since has followed. The song sums up a crucial part of the 60s, but it is also timeless in every generation. And that is some achievement.

The Who came together in 1964. Their original line-up consisted of Pete Townshend (guitar), John Entwistle (bass), Roger Daltrey (vocals) and Keith Moon (drums). Known as a premier mod band, by 1969 they had numerous top-ten singles behind them as well as a number of classic albums, including *My Generation* and *The Who Sell Out*. They had a reputation for riotous live shows, in which the band would often smash up their guitars and equipment, and they found worldwide acclaim in 1969 with their concept album *Tommy*. They were often wryly cited as the world's third-greatest rock band, but albums such as *Live at Leeds*, *Who's Next* and *Quadrophenia* maintained their success and artistic credibility. In 1978 Keith Moon died from an overdose of pills designed to wean him off his alcohol dependency. His place was taken by ex-Small Faces drummer Kenney Jones, and was later held by Ringo Starr's son, Zak. John Entwistle died in Las Vegas in 2002, a day before the band's American tour was due to start. His death was attributed to heart attack brought about by cocaine use.

BOB
DYLAN
goes electric

DATE 25 July 1965, The Newport Folk Festival, Rhode Island

I n 1965 Bob Dylan One was desperate to become Bob Dylan Two. There was only one problem. His fans didn't want Bob Dylan Two. That was because Dylan was their leader, the torch lighting the way, the young prodigy who had already penned three classic songs in 'Blowin' in the Wind', 'A Hard Rain's A-Gonna Fall' and 'The Times They Are A-Changin''. His incisive lyrics were both political and philosophical – set to a hard-driving acoustic guitar and harmonica style, they told the world how his audience felt, thought, imagined.

With his scruffy clothes and earnest expression, Dylan looked the part and he played the part. Only Dylan didn't want the part any more. He was bored with it. 'It's such a drag to be told how wonderful you are when you don't think so yourself,' he told an interviewer.

Truth was, other influences had entered his life, and he could not resist them. He loved The Beatles ('Outrageous what they are doing with chords') and he was really excited by the idea of electric blues. The Animals' version of 'House of the Rising Sun' was a regular fave, and so was the album *So Many Roads* by John Hammond Jnr. (Coincidentally, the backing vocals on that album were supplied by a band named Levon and the Hawks, who would later be transformed into The Band and work with Dylan extensively.)

Throughout 1964, recording sessions were marked by excursions into both acoustic and electric territory, as Bob Dylan Two sought to shape the sound that he could hear raging in his head. Drugs played their part: Dylan dropped LSD in 1964 after experimenting with amphetamines and marijuana. His reading was equally free-form, taking in the wild poetry of Allen

DYLAN'S LIFE WAS NOW FILLED WITH INANE PRESS CONFERENCES, FANS, WELL-WISHERS, GIRLS, DRUGS, SOUNDCHECKS, EARNEST AUDIENCES

Ginsberg and the decadent French verse of Arthur Rimbaud as well as the novels of Jack Kerouac. The books and the drugs and the man's own fertile imagination helped to produce a new lyrical style, something of a more personal kind that nevertheless bore touches of the surreal and the fantastic. It was a style never before experienced in popular music, and it was one of the main factors in elevating Dylan to the top of the musical tree.

HIS RECORD COMPANY BAULKED AT RELEASING 'LIKE A ROLLING STONE'. SIX MINUTES LONG? WORDS THAT ARE NOT JUNE AND MOON? YOU'RE KIDDING US, RIGHT?

In May 1965 Dylan toured Britain, and returned home in a frazzled state. His life was now filled with inane press conferences, screaming fans, hotels packed with well-wishers, girls, drugs, many girls, many drugs, travel, soundchecks, earnest demanding audiences. Thoughts of quitting the job now flitted across his mind, but then a new song – 'Like a Rolling Stone' – came to him. He grabbed it and he moulded it, and it changed everything. The stone of the title was a milestone in pop singles, an exhilarating love song whose explosive sound mirrored the excitement of Dylan's lyrics – lyrics that were both cruel and compassionate.

Moreover, 'Like a Rolling Stone' tore up the rule book by lasting more than six minutes. No pop single was six minutes long. Normal releases came in at three and half minutes – tops. And 'Rolling Stone' debuted a very new style and sound, one built around Dylan's melodic guitar, his sneering vocal and Al Kooper's haunting, wistful organ lines. It was a sound Dylan would later describe as 'wild as mercury'.

Naturally CBS, his record company baulked at releasing it. Six minutes long? Words that are not June and moon? You're kidding us, right? But one enterprising employee knew the score. He took an acetate of the song to a hip New York club and passed it to the DJ, who played it. When it finished, the audience screamed for it again and again until the acetate wore out.

The record company bowed to pressure. 'Like a Rolling Stone' is now considered one of the most important singles in rock music. Five days after it was released, Dylan arrived at the Newport Folk Festival to meet his old audience. He was dressed for confrontation in a polka-dot shirt, Cuban-heeled boots, a suit, with his eyes hidden by sunglasses. This was far removed from the uniform of checked shirt and raggedy jeans that had been handed down from folkie to son.

Bob Dylan performing electric music at the Newport Folk Festival on 25 July 1965. His decision to offend the folk purists that night is still being analysed by keen Dylanologists.

Dylan's first engagement was a songwriters' workshop on the Saturday afternoon. Hundreds came to see their messiah. Such was the crush inside the tent that Dylan only managed to play one song before hastily returning backstage.

It was here that he bumped into The Paul Butterfield Blues Band, and asked them to back him. Some say it was annoyance at an organizer's put-down of the electric blues style that pushed him into making the move; others that with 'Rolling Stone' blaring out of the radio Dylan had already decided to play electric. Only Dylan knows. What is clear is that pianist Barry Goldberg and organist Al Kooper were also invited to join Dylan on stage. They agreed, and that evening retreated to a nearby mansion to begin rehearsals. By all accounts it was a tortuous night. The Paul Butterfield Blues Band were disciplined musicians, and found Dylan's approach to his music anathema. They learnt three songs, then called it a day at dawn.

The next night Dylan strode on stage with his backing band and launched into an electric version of 'Maggie's Farm'. When he sang that he wasn't going to work on Maggie's Farm no more, the implication could not have been clearer. He was wearing a black leather jacket, black trousers, corkscrew hair and sunglasses.

TO HIS AUDIENCE, DYLAN'S ELECTRIC STYLE WAS AN UNWELCOME TSUNAMI OF SOUND. THEY REACTED WITH BOOS AND CATCALLS. OR DID THEY?

On hearing Dylan's opening salvo the festival's organizers, Pete Seeger and Alan Lomax, freaked out. They summoned producer Joe Boyd backstage and told him to go to the mixing desk and get the volume turned down. Boyd made his way there, only to be given the finger by Dylan's engineer. Seeger then started to look for an axe to cut the electricity leads. He now claims he had no problem with Dylan's new music, just with the fact that the sound was distorted.

These were not the only signs of panic and disapproval. To his audience, Dylan's electric style was an unwelcome tsunami of sound. They reacted with boos and jeers and catcalls. Or did they? It is possible to find people who will tell you the audience didn't boo; that was just the press guys down the front. Others say no, it wasn't the hacks, it was the other performers watching from sidelines. Others say: rubbish, it was the audience that booed – no doubt about it.

All we know is this – people at Newport were reacting because, right before their eyes, Bob Dylan One was disappearing fast. With the sound of boos still ringing in his ears, Dylan launched into 'Like a Rolling Stone', the song that weeks later would sit at number one in the US charts. He finished the set with 'Phantom Engineer', a piece that would later resurface as 'It Takes a Lot to Laugh, It Takes a Train to Cry'. With a curt 'That's it', Dylan and the band left the stage to still more howls of disapproval.

Off stage, Johnny Cash was waiting with an acoustic guitar. He grabbed his friend Dylan, handed the instrument to him, and told him go back out there and play – but without the band. Dylan loved and respected Cash, and he did as he was asked. He took the stage again and played – to the audience's delight – a handful of acoustic songs, finishing on 'Mr Tambourine Man'. It was a pointed choice for a finale. The previous year at Newport, Dylan had played this song only to be met with disapproval. The song's surreal imagery just did not cut it with this crowd. Now it was number one in the charts, courtesy of The Byrds' cover version, and Dylan was making a very astute point. The song finished, he turned on his heels – and then he was gone.

JOHNNY CASH WAS WAITING WITH AN ACOUSTIC GUITAR. HE HANDED THE INSTRUMENT TO DYLAN AND TOLD HIM TO GO BACK OUT THERE AND PLAY – BUT WITHOUT THE BAND. DYLAN CHOSE 'MR TAMBOURINE MAN' AS HIS FINALE

Dylan's performance that night remains one of the most confrontational interactions ever between a performer and his audience. And despite his refusal to react to their disapproval, it took a lot out of the man. At the party after the festival, the singer Maria Muldaur asked him to dance. 'I can't,' replied Dylan. 'My hands are on fire.'

Robert Allen Zimmerman was born on 24 May 1941 in Duluth, Minnesota. In 1961 Dylan he came to New York to visit his musical idol, Woody Guthrie. He played many folk clubs around the Village, and signed to CBS Records. Dylan established himself as one of the world's premier songwriters, but drifted away from folk towards electric rock. In 1967 he was involved in a motorcycle accident that removed him from the public eye. When he returned he was a gentler artist. In 1975, after breaking up with his wife Sarah, he released *Blood on the Tracks*, an album that for many people surpassed his 60s output. He toured with a group of musicians he called the Rolling Thunder Revue and released more critically acclaimed albums. In the late 70s he converted to Christianity. Since then his musical output has varied in quality. But albums such as *Time Out of Mind* and *Modern Times* were both critical and commercial successes, and Dylan continued to tour the world. He has appeared in many films, and in 2004 published the first part of his autobiography, entitled *Chronicles*.

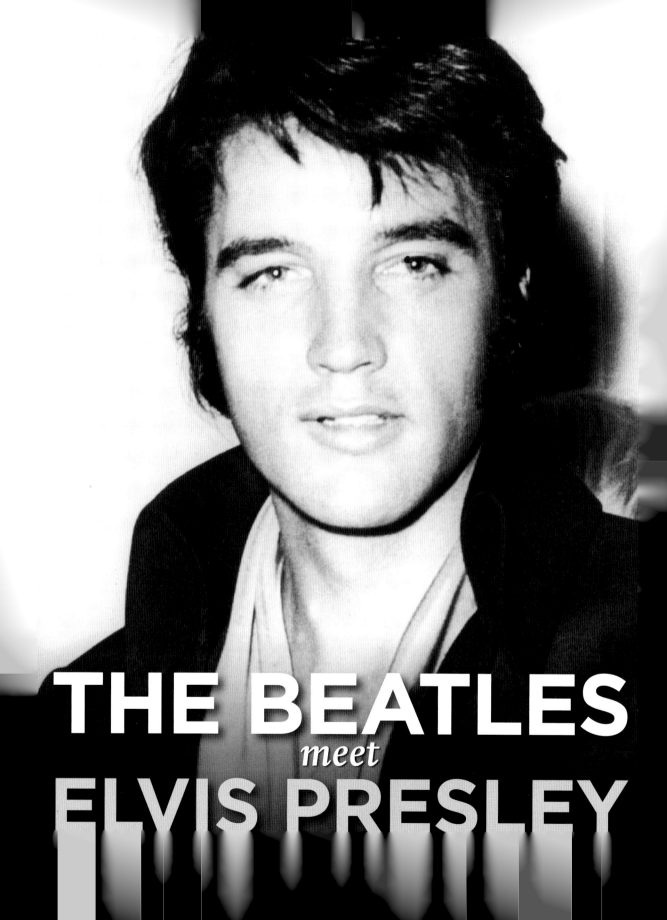

THE BEATLES
meet
ELVIS PRESLEY

There was only one person that The Beatles really wanted to meet in America – Elvis Presley. The rest of them – the Frank Sinatras, the Dean Martins – they didn't really care for. They knew it was only their massive popularity that drew such high-profile entertainers towards them. It had nothing to do with their music; they were miles apart on that score. But Elvis – Elvis was different.

The Beatles had grown up on Elvis, had been such young men when his records exploded out of the radio and changed Britain and America for good. Before Elvis, music was saccharine and soft. After Elvis, it was sexy and vibrant. Elvis was the catalyst, the change for the better, and even if his career had slid ever downwards since the halcyon days of 'That's All Right', 'Blue Suede Shoes' and 'Jailhouse Rock', the fans still held him in the highest esteem. He was Elvis, and that was enough.

The Beatles had tried to hook up with Elvis on that first hysterical tour of the States in 1964, but commitments on both sides had prevented any contact. Or so they said. The truth was, The Beatles wanted to meet Elvis, not the other way round. That gave the Presley camp the upper hand.

A year later, in the summer of 1965, whilst The Beatles were taking a break from their American tour and staying at Zsa Zsa Gabor's house, the meet was arranged. It took three days of planning, three days of back-and-forth between both camps, with secrecy high on the agenda. Not high enough, though. Someone talked. When the Beatles arrived at Elvis's Hollywood

EVENTUALLY, ELVIS ANNOUNCED: 'IF YOU'RE JUST GOING TO SIT THERE AND STARE AT ME, I'M GOING TO BED'

home at 565 Perugia Way, Bel Air, fans were waiting for them. The band drove into the driveway where they were met by Elvis's entourage. Elvis's people, and Elvis's wife Priscilla, were excited to meet the four Liverpool lads, the phenomenon from England. Elvis himself, however, was nonplussed. He was the King, not them.

The band were ushered into the house, where Elvis greeted them in the living room. He was wearing a red shirt, grey trousers. The Beatles said hello, and then silently gasped at the splendour of Elvis's

JOHN LENNON LATER COMMENTED: 'THIS WAS THE GUY WE HAD ALL IDOLIZED FOR YEARS, FROM WAY BACK WHEN WE WERE JUST STARTING OUT IN LIVERPOOL. HE WAS A LEGEND IN HIS OWN LIFETIME, AND IT'S NEVER EASY MEETING A LEGEND IN HIS OWN LIFETIME'

abode. The pool tables, in particular, caught their attention. 'It was like a nightclub,' Lennon later said, and the similarity was reinforced when Elvis's manager, Colonel Tom Parker, revealed a roulette wheel hidden inside a coffee table and asked Brian Epstein if he would like to play.

Elvis placed Paul and John either side of him on the sofa, whilst Ringo and George sat cross-legged on the floor in front of them. A record player played Charlie Rich's 'Mohair Sam'. Suddenly, the Beatles found themselves experiencing an emotion that had not troubled them for years – fan worship. They became tongue-tied. John Lennon later commented: 'This was the guy we had all idolized for years, from way back when we were just starting out in Liverpool. He was a legend in his own lifetime, and it's never easy meeting a legend in his own lifetime.'

Eventually, Elvis announced: 'If you're just going to sit there and stare at me, I'm going to bed.' That eased the tension. Drinks appeared: Scotch and Coke for the boys, 7Up for Elvis. The Beatles offered Elvis a cigarette, but he passed.

As small talk was made, some musical instruments appeared: a bass, some guitars. Elvis went on bass, John, Paul and George took the guitars and Ringo was left to tap out a beat on the side of his chair.

Elvis's choice of bass delighted Paul. 'That was a great thing for me, that he was into the bass,' he said later. 'So there I was, well let me show you a thing or two, El... Suddenly, he was a mate. It was a great conversation piece for me. I could actually talk about the bass, and we just sat around and enjoyed ourselves.'

The Beatles play to 50,000 screaming fans at the Shea Stadium, New York, on 15 August 1965 – one of the biggest concerts ever held. Lennon later said he went mad on stage that night.

They started the jam session with a Cilla Black song 'You're My World' but quickly progressed to Presley's own material – 'That's All Right' and 'Blue Suede Shoes'. Then they hit The Beatles song 'I Feel Fine'. 'Quite promising on the bass, Elvis,' McCartney said.

THIS WAS NOT THE ELVIS THEY HAD FALLEN IN LOVE WITH ALL THOSE YEARS AGO. THIS ELVIS WAS THE KIND OF SAFE MAINSTREAM ENTERTAINER ROCK'N'ROLL HAD SET OUT TO DESTROY. AND IT SHOWED

They played for about an hour, and then lay the instruments aside. Talk turned to their shared experiences. Elvis recalled a show in Vancouver where the fans had nearly tipped the stage over. Lennon, perceptive as ever, pointed out that at least there were four Beatles to look after each other during the madness, the hysteria that was with them most hours of the day. Elvis was totally on his own.

Lennon, unable to curb his mouth, gently chastised Elvis for abandoning his raw rock'n'roll roots to make meaningless movies and records that he obviously cared little about. Elvis curtly responded by saying: 'Well I might just get around to cutting a few sides and knocking you off the top,' and everyone laughed – but a tension had been established.

The conversation moved on to the problem of flying, and then they spoke about cars. Lennon discovered that he and Elvis shared the same model of Rolls-Royce, a black Phantom.

At two o'clock the party ended. Knowing that Elvis was a big Peter Sellers fan, Lennon shouted back in his best Sellers voice as he left the house: 'Tanks for ze music, Elvis – and long live ze King!'

In the course of their talk, the four boys invited Elvis to meet them the next night. Elvis told them he would see what he could do. The next day, word came to The Beatles from the Presley camp: thanks but no thanks. Lennon sat down and wrote Elvis a message: 'If it hadn't been for you I'd be nothing.'

In public the Beatles always kept to the party line: it was a great night, Elvis was fab. Privately, however, they had been disappointed. Elvis was now an all-round entertainer, and a jaded one at that. When Lennon had asked Elvis what his upcoming film was about, Elvis replied: 'I play a country boy with a guitar who meets a few gals along the way and sing a few songs.' Lennon looked at him perplexed until both Elvis and Colonel Tom Parker explained that this was the unchanging Elvis movie formula. They had moved away from it once for a film called *Wild in the Country* and lost money. Never again.

Such acquiescence to showbiz formulas was completely alien to The Beatles. For Lennon and McCartney in particular, it was about vivid imagination, invention, pushing boundaries – these were the things that should be the motors of artistic lives, not cynically exploiting audiences with tried-and-tested formulas. This was not the Elvis they had fallen in love with all those years ago. This Elvis was exactly the kind of safe mainstream entertainer that rock'n'roll had set out to destroy. And it showed. 'It was just like meeting Engelbert Humperdinck,' Lennon privately observed.

IN HIS MEETING WITH NIXON, ELVIS ATTACKED THE BEATLES. THEY WERE DRUG USERS, HE TOLD THE PRESIDENT. MOREOVER, THEY WERE A FOCAL POINT FOR ANTI-AMERICAN ACTIVITY

But there was more to the strange meeting between Elvis and the Beatles than a clash of generations and a streak of disappointment. A darker twist to this encounter emerged many years later when FBI files revealed that on 21 December 1970 Presley hopped onto his private jet and made an unauthorized visit to the American President, Richard Nixon. He had with him a letter for Nixon, which put forward the following plan. The President would make him an FBI agent and in return Elvis would spy for the government. His targets would be drug users, hippies and Black Panthers. He delivered the letter at 6.30 a.m. and then booked into a nearby hotel and waited for a response.

The White House responded with an invitation for him to meet Nixon that very morning. In their conversation, Elvis attacked The Beatles. They were drug users, he told Nixon. Moreover, they were a focal point for anti-American activity. They had come to America, made millions of dollars and then gone home and publicly trashed the country that had fed them. Elvis's stature as a performer would allow him to keep an eye on The Beatles as well as others that he met at concerts, in recording studios and so forth.

Fearing bad publicity if it leaked out that he had refused the help of the King, Nixon played along and handed him an FBI badge. He also made sure he got his photo taken with the clearly deranged singer. Might help with the youth vote.

Happy as a kid at Christmas, Presley returned home. He was now a fully fledged FBI agent, and he would bring those Beatles down. Unfortunately for him, they had broken up eight months previously.

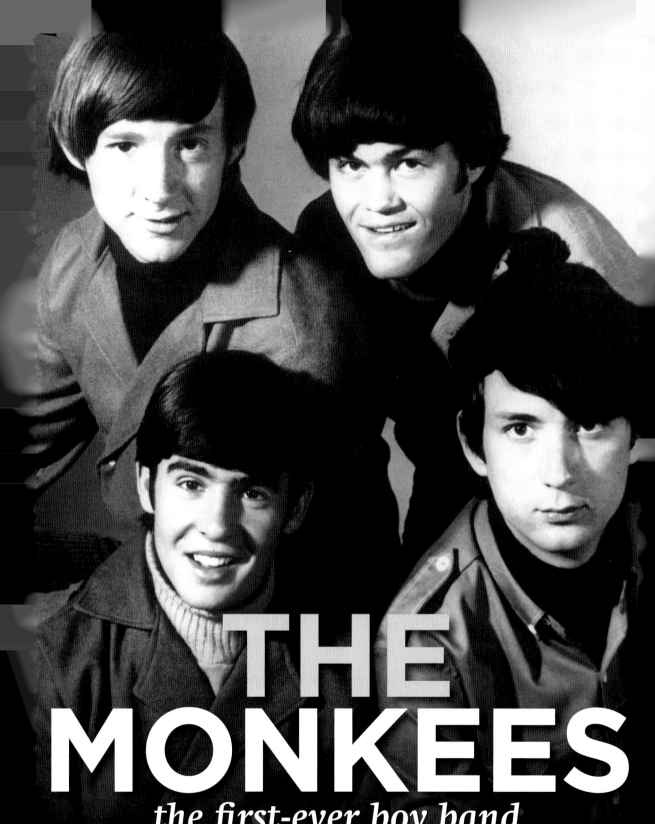

THE
MONKEES
the first-ever boy band

DATE 15 September 1965, Los Angeles

After watching *A Hard Day's Night*, filmmakers Bob Rafelson and Bert Schneider came to a decision. America, they agreed, needed its own Beatles. How could that be achieved? Simple. Assemble a rock'n'roll band that they could control from day one. Make sure that, as with The Beatles, the band has four distinct personalities, then create a TV series around them. Voilà! Big bucks for all – guaranteed.

On 15 September 1965 ads appeared in the Hollywood trade papers announcing auditions for the parts of 'four insane boys'. The four successful applicants all had previous experience in showbusiness. Davy Jones was with the Broadway cast of *Oliver!*; Mike Nesmith was a songwriter whose work had already been recorded by The Paul Butterfield Blues Band and Linda Ronstadt; Mickey Dolenz was in a children's TV show called *Circus Boy*; and Peter Tork was a folk musician.

Rafelson and Schneider decided to call their creation The Monkees. They didn't know it, but they had just invented the boy band, the precursor to Backstreet Boys, New Edition, Take That – all those acts manufactured and controlled by Svengalis. Only the Monkees' storyline would prove far more interesting than the bands they would inspire.

With the band in place, Rafelson and Schneider contacted Don Kirshner, the head of music at Screen Gems, to find suitable songs. He handed the job to two producers, Tommy Boyce and Bobby Hart, who wrote the band's theme, 'Hey Hey We're the Monkees', and their debut single, 'Last Train to Clarksville'. Neil Diamond later wrote them 'I'm a Believer' and 'A Little Bit Me, a Little Bit You'; Gerry Goffin and Carole King contributed 'Pleasant Valley Sunday' and 'Porpoise Song'.

Rafelson and Schneider's ideas for the TV show were fresh and innovative. The main thrust of the story was that the

SCREAMING HORDES OF YOUNG MONKEES FANS TURNED OUT; IN THE FIRST TWO WEEKS, MORE THAN £500,000 WAS TAKEN IN TICKET SALES

Monkees were an unsigned band seeking fame. They lived together in a house where their madcap adventures always began. Naturally, each member had been chosen to fit a stereotype. Dolenz was kooky; Nesmith was serious; Tork was shy; Jones was the boy-next-door.

The stories would be fluid and fast-moving. Each episode would include a sequence showcasing a song. That footage could then be used to promote the song. In this way, the band became the first-ever video group, securing a large audience through the visual medium.

THE BAND HAD BEEN STUNG WHEN IT WAS REPORTED THAT **THEY HAD NOT PLAYED ON THEIR RECORDS.** MANY PAPERS DUBBED THEM THE PRE-FAB FOUR

The first show aired on 12 September 1966, and The Monkees quickly became a worldwide pop sensation. Their album, *The Monkees*, hit number one in the US and the UK charts. In December 1966 the band undertook their first tour. Screaming hordes of young Monkees fans turned out; in the first two weeks, more than £500,000 was taken in ticket sales.

This success led the boys to think that they should be involved in making artistic decisions – an attitude that did not play well with Kirshner, who thought the band musically incompetent. He refused to let them play on their own records, although he did allow Nesmith to produce some of the sessions as long as he promised not to use any band members (Nesmith agreed, then brought in Tork to play guitar).

In January 1967 Kirshner issued a second album, *More of the Monkees,* without consulting the band. Legend has it that the group were not even given a free copy. The following month Kirshner was gone: a glitch in the contract made it possible for the boys to sack him. But the band had been stung when it was reported that they had not played on their records (many papers dubbed them the Pre-Fab Four). They recorded an album of their own, then went on tour, starting in Britain – where they met The Beatles. Lennon told the boys that he never missed an episode of the TV show, and Nesmith got close enough to hang out at Abbey Road (he was there when 'A Day in the Life' was recorded).

The band returned to the States to shoot a second series of the show, but somehow it wasn't working any more. The band agreed to Rafelson and Schneider's suggestion they make a movie. *Head* was to be no cute cinematic experience. This film would be a psychedelic trip that would explore the band's psyches as well as the failure of the music business to take them seriously. *Head* would correct misperceptions of the band, relaunch them and gain them a hipper audience. The script was written by Rafelson, Schneider and a young actor by the name of Jack Nicholson. Nicholson even wrote a song for the film, a pastiche of the band's signature tune.

IN 1967 THE MONKEES HAD SOLD MORE RECORDS THAN THE BEATLES. TWO YEARS LATER THEY COULDN'T GET ARRESTED

The film bombed. Teenagers didn't understand it, and the hippies wouldn't go near it. The marketing was dreadful (at one point the producers wanted to use a picture of the band with the tag line 'The Monkees Give You Head'). Nesmith later said that the film's failure was a deliberate ploy on the part of Rafelson and Schneider, who wanted to be rid of an unprofitable project.

In 1967 the Monkees had sold more records than The Beatles or Elvis Presley. Two years later they couldn't get arrested. Yet a lesson had been learnt. The year the Monkees fell apart, a cartoon-only group called The Archies shot to number one all over the world with a song called 'Sugar Sugar'. The man behind it? Don Kirshner.

SCHNEIDER AND RAFELSON 1960s–

Producer Berton 'Bert' Schneider and director Bob Rafelson would each play a significant part in the history of 70s American cinema. They met in Los Angeles in the early 60s, drawn together by shared political views. Schneider, whose father was once head of Columbia Records, was a rebellious drop-out from Cornell University. So radical were his views that the US Army refused to take him. The success of The Monkees gave Schneider and Rafelson the chance to break into films. They created Raybert Productions and produced the classic film *Easy Rider*, which was a huge success. Their next film *Five Easy Pieces* was also a hit, helping to establish the young Jack Nicholson as a leading Hollywood actor. Rafelson would direct Nicholson in four more films, including *The King of Marvin Gardens* (1972), *The Postman Always Rings Twice* (1981), *Man Trouble* (1992), and *Blood and Wine* (1996). In 1975 Schneider won a Best Documentary Oscar for his work on the film *Hearts and Minds*, which was a searing indictment of America's involvement in the Vietnam war.

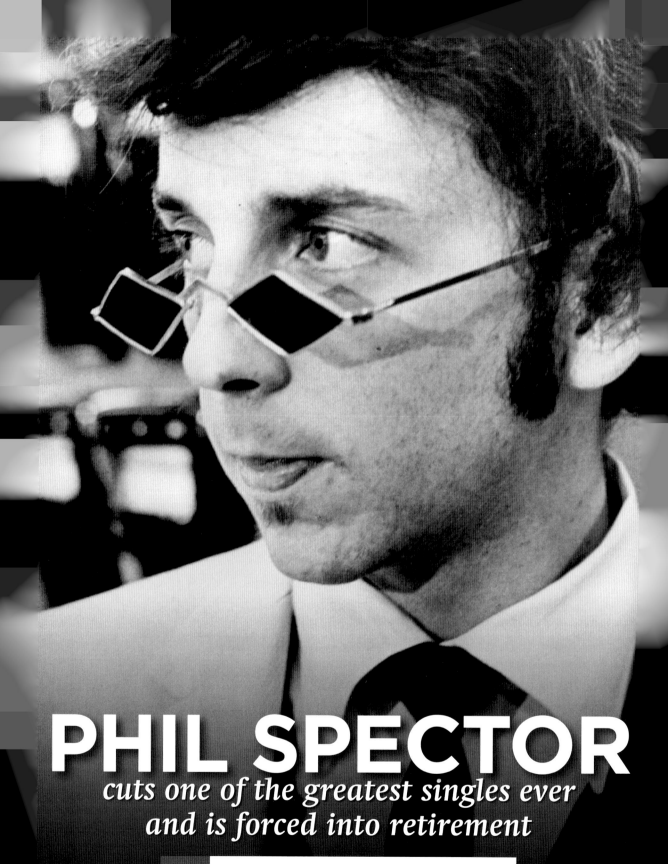

PHIL SPECTOR

*cuts one of the greatest singles ever
and is forced into retirement*

DATE 14 March 1966, Gold Star Studios, Los Angeles

The magic was gone. Everyone knew it, even the man who had made it all possible in the first place. Yes, Phil Spector knew as early as 1965 that he was on the way out. 'I remember we were in the studio with The Ronettes, cutting "Born to Be Together",' recalled longtime Spector man, Jack Nitzsche. 'During the playback Phil stood next to me and said: "It's all over. It's over. It's just not there any more." The enthusiasm was gone. We had done it so many times...'

The thing that Spector and Nitzsche had 'done so many times' was the 'wall of sound', the trademark production style that Spector had created and used to craft some of the best singles ever. The sound required overloading the studio with musicians, using echo chambers to their very limit, placing an R&B singer up front and fashioning a music that bristled with the innocence of the early 60s and the excitement of rock'n'roll. Over three years the formula produced classics such as 'Be My Baby', 'Then He Kissed Me', 'Da Doo Ron Ron' and 'Baby, I Love You'. Spector's sound had ruled the airwaves and made him the first superstar producer.

Spector told the world that he was about creating 'teenage symphonies'. For a glorious spell that is exactly what he did, but now his success had run its course. Philles, Spector's label, was fast losing all its top acts. Already gone were The Crystals and Bob B. Soxx; The Righteous Brothers would disappear in a maze of legal wrangling and bitter disputes. Spector's wife's band, The Ronettes, could hardly get a booking. A different kind of music was now in the ether. Who wanted to dance to Phil Spector when Bob Dylan held the key to the mystery of your life?

Faced with all this, Spector decided to go for broke, play his final trump card. He would create the ultimate Phil Spector single, a record which would stand as the apotheosis of everything he had striven for. In his fevered mind this single would take the wall of sound to its most extreme point, and would be so triumphant in sound and vision, it would instantly return him to his rightful place at the top of the heap.

Then, when he rang ex-wife Annette and asked her meekly: 'Am I as big as The

Phil Spector and Tina and Ike Turner pose for the cameras in a bid to publicize their single 'River Deep – Mountain High'. The record's failure to take off in America sent Spector into a two-year depression. Only the offer of working with The Beatles would bring him out to play again.

Beatles? As Bob Dylan?' her answer would not be so obviously faked but would ring loud and clear and true. 'Yes, Phil,' she would say, 'you are bigger than both of them put together.'

He knew who he wanted to front this grandstand single. Her name was Anna Mae Bullock, better known as Tina Turner. Her singing career began the night she clambered on stage in a St Louis club and asked the leader of the band if she could perform. Ike Turner agreed, and within a year the couple were married and the Ike and Tina Turner Revue was on the road.

Spector was first exposed to Tina Turner's dynamic stage performance when he arranged a concert called The Big TNT Show. He was highly impressed by Turner's vocals ('She reminded me of a female Ben E. King') but also by her ability to work a young white audience into a frenzy. Although excited by Turner, he was scared of her husband Ike. Drink, cocaine use and rumours of wife-beating followed Ike around like a faithful bull mastiff. Spector did not want him anywhere near the studio when they began work. To compensate the rebuffed and suspicious Ike, he promised him a deal with his label Philles at some unspecified date in the future. He also handed him $20,000, which helped to smooth the waters.

With Ike safely out of the way, Spector now contacted a songwriting team that had served him well in the past. Ellie Greenwich and Jeff Barry had written, 'Be My Baby', 'Baby, I Love You', 'Da Doo Ron Ron' and 'Then He Kissed Me'. Spector had fallen out with the pair over a song called 'Chapel of Love' but this animosity meant little to him. When it came to work, he was always prepared to put aside differences.

Spector charmed the couple, and within a month they were hard at work in Los Angeles on a song entitled 'River Deep – Mountain High'. The song consisted of three major riffs that the parties brought to the table. Normally, you would junk one of them for fear of overcrowding, but Spector was confident that his wall of sound coupled with Tina's vocals, would circumvent the problem. Lyrically, all three wanted to write a love song that was quite unlike anything else out there. That was the brief.

'The whole thing about "River Deep" was the way I could feel that strong bass line,' Spector later recalled. 'That's how it started. Then Jeff came up with that opening line. I wanted a tender song about a chick, who loved somebody so much, but a different way of expressing it. So we came up with that rag doll and "I'm going to cuddle you like a puppy."'

The first two recordings sessions for 'River Deep' took place in late February 1967. The venue was Studio A at the Gold Star Studios where Spector had cut so many brilliant singles. He crammed up to two dozen musicians into his favourite recording spot, determined to go further than he had ever done before. He used four guitars, four basses, two percussionists, three keyboard players, a six-piece brass section and a partridge in a pear tree.

When Tina arrived to lay down her vocals, Spector had 20 singers ready to back her up. Unused to such grandiose musical settings, the young singer was left totally confused and could not perform. Tina understood R&B structure but this song had anything but structure. It stopped, it started, it rushed, it broke down, and it came back up again...

WHO WANTED TO DANCE TO PHIL SPECTOR WHEN BOB DYLAN HELD THE KEY TO THE MYSTERY OF YOUR LIFE?

Spector sent her away to rehearse the song for a week. When she returned on the evening of 7 March, Spector had wisely cleared the studio for the night. Tina settled down, and with just Spector and engineer Larry Levine looking on she began her performance. Spector, ever the perfectionist, constantly interrupted her every line: 'That's good, that's good, but try it again,' he would say, pulling her back again and again and again and again. The session dragged on long into the night; the singer was bathed in sweat. Round about midnight, Tina Turner lost it. She ripped off her blouse and, standing in a darkened room, reached down into her very soul to drag out one last amazing vocal *tour de force*.

The session wound down, and Tina Turner left the studio not even sure if her performance that night would be used in any form or fashion. Spector, too, was unsure. It would take a week of intensive mixing and dubbing before he announced that he was satisfied.

And so he should have been. 'River Deep – Mountain High' is one of most immense singles ever created, a record that fashions a huge wave of music that is sent to slam against Tina Turner's vocal and then explode into an epic of outrageous proportions. This was Spector at the zenith of his talents. If his other records had been teenage symphonies then this was a stunning move into opera. He must have been overjoyed at the result, anxious to place it before the people and see them once again kneel to his genius.

On 14 May 1966 the front page of *Billboard* carried a picture of Ike and Tina Turner advertising the single. Two weeks later the single slipped into the *Billboard* Hot 100 at number 99. The next week it went up to 94. Following week 93, week after that 88 and then... it was gone.

America turned its back on this amazing single, and Phil Spector was absolutely devastated. He had put everything he had into this recording, and it had not been enough. For the first time in his life Spector felt the keen pang of rejection and humiliation in the deepest part of his very being. Spector locked himself in his LA mansion for two very long years. His label ran itself down, and he was barely seen in public. In fact, he would not work again until, one day, The Beatles came knocking at his door.

TINA TURNER RIPPED OFF HER BLOUSE AND, STANDING IN A DARKENED ROOM, REACHED DOWN INTO HER VERY SOUL TO DRAG OUT ONE LAST AMAZING VOCAL TOUR DE FORCE

Over the years many reasons have been given for the abject failure of 'River Deep' in America. (In Britain, it quickly went top five.) Spector said it was simple: people didn't like the song, and that was that. Others thought differently. Ike thought it was down to race, that radio stations just could not understand what an R&B singer was doing fronting this incredible slice of Wagnerian pop music.

'The R&B stations wouldn't play it because they thought it was pop,' Turner pointed out, 'and the pop stations wouldn't play it because it was R&B.'

Jeff Barry thought that Spector's reputation in the music business as an arrogant man, disdainful of humans and devoid of all charm, had finally caught up with him. He recalled that Spector had ridiculed a major DJ one night, and the story had spread around the industry. 'So the stations and the industry as a whole when they heard about it... you see they have a very negative attitude all the time, an attitude of "Oh yeah? Let's see what you have come up with here..." They look for any reason, I think.'

Spector's own refusal to go on a promotional tour for the single, to meet and greet influential music-industry figures, also weighed against him. It was also pointed out that the kind of singles that Spector specialized in – innocent, frivolous tales of teen love and loss set to epic music – was now out of fashion. Music was turning serious. The people who said so had a point. The Beatles had turned the focus on to the album, and in doing so they had considerably lessened the importance of the single.

Perhaps a combination of all these factors conspired to bring down a man the writer Tom Wolfe once dubbed 'the tycoon of teen'. That title no longer applied to Spector. 'A man out of time' would have been a far more accurate sobriquet.

Harvey Philip Spector was born on Christmas Day 1940. Nine years later his father committed suicide. At high school, Spector formed a band called The Teddy Bears. The band's second single, 'To Know Him Is to Love Him', took its title from the epitaph on his father's gravestone. In 1961 Spector formed his own record company with Lester Sill – Philles – and forged the style known as 'the wall of sound'. The Ronettes' 1963 single 'Be My Baby' is considered one of Spector's greatest achievements. He married the group's lead singer, Veronica Bennett. In the late 60s Spector was asked to produce the Beatles' final album, *Let It Be*. He subsequently worked with George Harrison and John Lennon on various solo projects. He produced punk band the Ramones in the 70s, but by the 90s was virtually a recluse. On 3 February 2003 an actress named Lana Clarkson was found dead in Spector's Hollywood mansion. After two major trials, Spector was found guilty of the murder and sentenced to 19 years in prison. He will be 88 years old before he is eligible for parole.

KEITH RICHARDS
AND MICK JAGGER
get busted

DATE 12 February 1967, Redlands, West Wittering, Sussex

On the night that the Stones got busted, it is said that the police did not raid Redlands, Keith Richards's country house, until they had proper confirmation that George Harrison and his girlfriend Patti Boyd had indeed left the premises the night before. They were out to bust the country's most notorious band, and arresting a man still seen as one of the loveable mop-tops would just muddy the waters. They would get to The Beatles later.

The police bided their time, waiting for the party to wind down. Present at the gathering in Keith Richards's house were Mick Jagger and his then-girlfriend, the singer Marianne Faithfull, along with various friends and acquaintances including Nicky Kramer, Robert Fraser, Mohammed Jajaj, Michael Cooper and David Schneidermann.

Kramer was a hanger-on, Fraser was an art dealer and Jajaj was his servant. Cooper was a photographer, and David Schneidermann – well, no one was really sure who Schneidermann was, to be honest. Only a few things were known about him: he was American, his nickname was the Acid King and he had in his possession a quantity of White Lightning, which was a new type of LSD. On his arrival in the UK, Schneidermann had contacted the Stones' camp with this information, and it had been decided that Richards's house would be the perfect setting for this new wonder drug to be ingested.

AT FIRST HE THOUGHT HE WAS HALLUCINATING FOR STANDING RIGHT IN FRONT OF HIM SEEMED TO BE A MAN IN A WHITE TRENCH COAT WITH 20 POLICE OFFICERS STANDING BEHIND HIM

The party began on Saturday. Harrison and Boyd, later followed by Beatle associate Tony Bramwell, left that evening. Everyone else stayed the night. At nine on Sunday morning, Schneidermann made everyone a cup of tea containing the drug. Within an hour they were all tripping. By all accounts the drug proved pleasant, and the party spent hours exploring nearby forests in a haze of wonderment. As evening fell, the drug started to wear off and the party returned to the house.

AS THE POLICE SWARMED INTO THE LIVING ROOM, MARIANNE FAITHFULL FLASHED HER BREASTS. SHE WAS TAKEN UPSTAIRS BY A FEMALE OFFICER TO BE SEARCHED

Whilst the others lolled around the room, listening to albums by The Who and Bob Dylan being played at full blast, Marianne Faithfull went off and took a bath. She later reappeared in the sitting room wearing just a fur rug. No one was perturbed by her appearance.

Gradually, the party people became aware of a loud knocking. Despite giggling pleas from Jagger and Faithfull to ignore the noise, Richards went and opened the door. At first he thought he was hallucinating for standing right in front of him seemed to be a man in a white trench coat with 20 police officers standing behind him.

When Chief Inspector Gordon Dineley said: 'Are you the owner and occupier of these premises?' and shoved a search warrant into his hands, Richards's confusion quickly cleared. The police swarmed into the house as Richards rushed back to the room to alert his guests. They found the whole scenario extremely amusing; LSD will do that for you.

As the police swarmed into the living room, Marianne Faithfull stood up and flashed her breasts. She was taken upstairs by a female officer to be searched. Meanwhile the police frisked Robert Fraser and found two boxes of pills on him, speed and heroin. Incredibly, the officer apologized to the upper-class art-gallery owner for searching him.

Another policeman brought a green jacket into the sitting room. It belonged to Mick Jagger. The police officer pulled out a lump of dope from one of the pockets, but – unbelievably for a man on a drugs raid – he thought it was dirt and put it back into the jacket.

Then, from another pocket, he pulled out a small phial containing four pills. 'Are these yours, sir?' he asked the singer. Jagger said that they were, and explained that his doctor had given them to him on prescription. He was lying. The pills belonged to Marianne Faithfull, who had bought them at an Italian airport. (Later, when Faithfull pleaded with her boyfriend to let her take the rap, Jagger gallantly refused, explaining it would kill her career

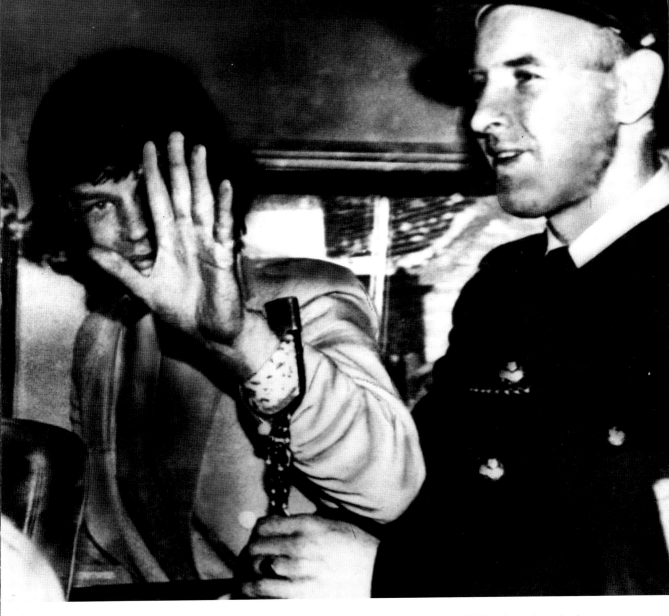

Mick Jagger is remanded in custody as the court case against him, Keith Richards and art dealer Robert Fraser continues. The severity of the sentences handed down to them caused outrage.

stone dead. He then added that she was not to worry because the band 'thrives on publicity like this'.)

Another policeman went over and opened David Schneidermann's briefcase. Everyone held their breath. They all knew that in the case was a plethora of mind-bending drugs, everything from heroin to cannabis and all the stops in between. 'That's film,' said Schneidermann as the police stared at numerous little packets wrapped in aluminium foil. 'Please don't open those, you'll expose it.' 'Certainly, sir,' said the policeman, shutting the case and walking away. The police now left, apparently satisfied with their findings. Mick and Keith were in a state of high relief.

Nothing had been found on them except some prescription pills. The only warning of the storm to follow came from the departing chief inspector who told Richards: 'If tests reveal illegal drugs were used on your premises and not related to any individual you will be held responsible.' The guitarist retorted: 'I get it, pin it all on me.'

After all the policemen had departed, questions began to be asked by the party guests. Why had the police chosen to raid Richards's house at that exact time? How did they know an acid party was being held? Who had told them? Who, in the end, had set the Stones up? Pretty soon, everyone's mind skipped back to event of the previous week.

On 5 February two *News of the World* reporters had hung out with Rolling Stones guitarist Brian Jones in a club, pretending to be huge fans. The next day the front page of the newspaper carried the story of their night out. The musician, they claimed, had used illegal drugs (Mandrax) in a club and asked various girls back to his flat to sample more. There was only one problem. The journalists thought Brian Jones was Mick Jagger and duly called him that throughout the whole article. Obviously one long-haired singer looked pretty much like the next to these guys.

On Monday evening an incensed Jagger appeared on the *The Eamonn Andrews Show* and announced he would be suing the paper. Twenty-four hours later a writ from Jagger's solicitors landed on the editor's desk at the newspaper. They stood to lose thousands for their libel. A week later the police show up Richards's house and bust Jagger. That's a coincidence?

THE POLICE OFFICER PULLED OUT A LUMP OF DOPE FROM A POCKET BUT – UNBELIEVABLY FOR A MAN ON A DRUGS RAID – HE THOUGHT IT WAS DIRT AND PUT IT BACK INTO THE JACKET

A month after the drugs raid the police announced that they were charging Mick Jagger with possession of four amphetamine tablets, Keith Richards with allowing his house to be used for illegal drug-taking, and Robert Fraser with possession of heroin and speed. The Stones' camp was shocked. It was obvious they had been made targets, that someone was out to get them.

The Stones stood for rebellion and liberation. Only recently Mick Jagger had granted an interview to the *New Musical Express* in which he praised New York hippies as well as questioning the war in Vietnam, the persecution of homosexuals and the illegal status of both abortion and drug-taking. Many would have baulked at Jagger's liberal views. Some might have decided to take covert action against him.

On Wednesday 10 May it was reported that police had raided Brian Jones's house in Chelsea and charged him with possession of cocaine, methedrine and cannabis. The bust had obviously been timed to prejudice Mick and Keith's trial. 'They know bloody well they haven't got enough evidence to do us, so they have gone out and nicked Brian,' Jagger fumed. 'Every member of any jury we get will think of drugs and the Stones as being synonymous.'

At their first hearing, Jagger and Richards were freed on bail and ordered to stand trial in June. That trial took place at West Sussex Quarter Sessions and was presided over by Judge Block. Robert Fraser appeared first and pleaded guilty. Block remanded him in jail until sentencing.

Mick Jagger's case was next. He stuck to his story that he had bought the pills in Italy and on his return to England his doctor had okayed their use over the phone. Jagger's general practitioner, Dr Dixon Firth, took the stand and confirmed the singer's story.

The defence argued that the doctor's verbal acceptance constituted his issuing a legal prescription. Judge Block did not think so. Directing the jury he told them to take no notice of this defence, since

'these remarks cannot be regarded as prescription'. The jury had no choice but to deliver a verdict of guilty.

Sentencing was postponed until after Richards's trial. Jagger and Fraser were then driven to Lewes prison to stay the night. The next day Richards's trial began. He was accused of allowing guests to smoke marijuana in his house.

The behaviour of his guests was now placed in the spotlight, and great play was made of the mystery girl who appeared in a fur rug. (At lunchtime boastful police officers told reporters that they had discovered Jagger eating a Mars Bar placed inside Marianne's vagina, thus creating an urban myth that has cruelly followed the singer all her life.)

THE STONES' CAMP WAS SHOCKED. IT WAS OBVIOUS **THEY HAD BEEN MADE TARGETS,** THAT THE ESTABLISHMENT WAS OUT TO GET THEM

Richards's defence was simple. The police had planted the cannabis in his house, so that Mick would be convicted and thus forced to drop his libel action against the *News of the World*. It was a theory later given great credence by one of the policemen's admission that they had raided the house after a tip-off from a national newspaper.

When Judge Block questioned him about Marianne's nudity, Richards replied honestly: 'We are not old men, we're not worried about petty morals.' It was not the kind of thing to endear him to an old man who had his life in his hands. But Keith did not care one iota. He had always been the toughest man in the Stones, capable of taking anything people wanted to throw at him. Including prison.

KEITH HAD ALWAYS BEEN THE TOUGHEST MAN IN THE STONES, CAPABLE OF TAKING ANYTHING PEOPLE WANTED TO THROW AT HIM. INCLUDING PRISON

The day ended and Richards was taken to Wormwood Scrubs where the inmates welcomed him with open arms, showering his cell with valuable tobacco. 'Don't worry, baby,' Richards told his admirers, 'I won't be here long.'

The next day that statement rebounded on him. The jury found him guilty, and Judge Block sentenced Keith to a year's imprisonment and ordered him to pay £1,000 towards the trial's cost. Unbelievably, Robert Fraser – despite being caught with sizeable quantities of speed and heroin – received six months, half of Keith's sentence, whilst Jagger was given three months. A severely shaken Jagger was taken to Brixton prison with Robert Fraser in tow. Richards was returned to Wormwood Scrubs.

As Richards, Jagger and Fraser began their sentence a groundswell of opposition to their treatment began to take shape. The next day's papers expressed huge surprise at the severity of the sentencing. There was now great danger that the Stones were about to become martyrs.

Discreet pressure was applied. At lunchtime the same day, the High Court released Keith and Mick on £20,000 bail. The pair went and celebrated in a bar where the barman gave them free drinks in solidarity. Then that night's *Evening Standard* arrived. In it was as an advert carrying a statement from The Who. Their new single would be versions of two Stones songs, 'Under My Thumb' and 'The Last Time'. The advertisement said that: 'The Who consider Mick Jagger and Keith Richards have been treated as scapegoats... The Who are issuing today the first of a series of Jagger/Richards songs to keep their work before the public until they are free again to record themselves.'

The next day brought the biggest shock of them all. *The Times* newspaper, that bastion of conservatism, published an editorial called 'Who Breaks a Butterfly on a Wheel', written by the then-editor, William Rees-Mogg. Incredibly, the paper came down on the side of the Stones, concluding that the sentences they had received were highly unjust. The following day, all the newspapers, except the *News of the World*, followed suit. Keith's conviction would now be quashed and Jagger given a conditional discharge.

THE TIMES NEWSPAPER, THAT BASTION OF CONSERVATISM, CAME DOWN ON THE SIDE OF THE STONES, CONCLUDING THAT THE SENTENCES WERE HIGHLY UNJUST

Although at the time many believed that the *News of the World* had paid Schneidermann to approach the Stones with drugs and then to tip off the police, it later came to light that an employee of Richards's had spilt the beans. The Redlands incident is significant because this was the day when the Establishment finally declared open war on the counter-culture, the start of a battle that would rage for many years.

A month later the Stones released a new single. It was called 'We Love You'.

The Rolling Stones were formed in 1962 by Brian Jones (guitar). The other members were Mick Jagger (vocals), Keith Richards (guitar), Bill Wyman (bass) and Charlie Watts (drums). At first the band played blues covers, but when Jagger and Richards started writing together they scored chart hits with songs such as 'Time Is On My Side' and 'Ruby Tuesday'. The band really hit its stride with the release of *Beggars Banquet* in 1968. This album included key songs such as 'Sympathy for the Devil' and 'Street Fighting Man'. Subsequent singles such as 'Honky Tonk Women' and 'Brown Sugar', coupled with the band's louche image, saw the title World's Greatest Rock Band bestowed upon them. In the 70s the Stones released what many consider to be their greatest work, *Exile on Main Street*, and in the 80s they issued landmark singles such as 'Miss You' and 'Start Me Up'. As a live attraction, the Stones remain one of the world's biggest bands. As a musical unit they have outlived all of their contemporaries, and are now in their sixth decade of playing together.

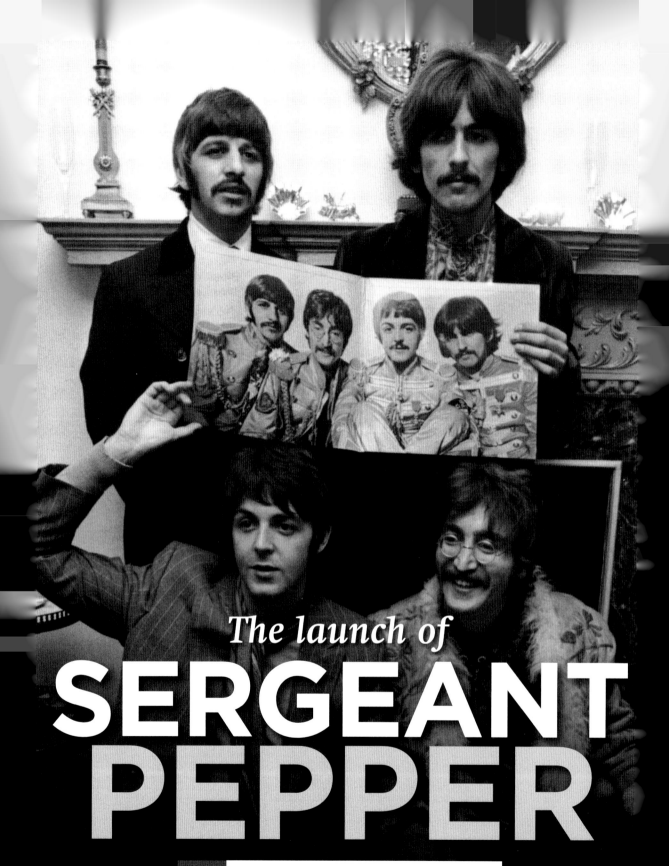

The launch of
SERGEANT
PEPPER

DATE 19 May 1967, Abbey Road Studios, London

On 19 May 1967 a carefully selected group of journalists, DJs and photographers (including a young American by the name of Linda Eastman) made their way to 24 Chapel Street, London. This was the home of Beatles' manager Brian Epstein. Everyone was there to hear an album that would turn the world on its head. Its name was *Sergeant Pepper's Lonely Hearts Club Band*. Also present at the party would be the makers of this extraordinary work – The Beatles.

The press were greeted at the house by Epstein himself. After being served refreshments, the press eagerly awaited the arrival of The Beatles. Finally, they appeared, dressed for the occasion in colourful clothing. John Lennon, in particular, caught the eye. He wore a frilly green-flowered shirt, maroon cord trousers with a sporran – a sporran! – and canary-yellow socks. Physically, he was gaunt, and he seemed to be elsewhere. Ray Coleman, who was present, later wrote: 'John looked haggard, old, ill and hopelessly addicted to drugs. His eyes were glazed, his speech slow and slurred.'

What had happened to the most famous musicians in the world? Quite simply, Beatlemania had happened. Since their debut single, the band had become incredibly famous in nearly every country. They had toured incessantly, produced an incredible run of groundbreaking singles and albums, made two films and given numerous TV and radio appearances. Everywhere they went, pandemonium, chaos. If it wasn't the fans trying to get at them, it was the press. If it wasn't the press, it would be the promoters or the hangers-on. As George Harrison once noted, the only place in the world where

PEPPER FITTED PERFECTLY WITH THE SO-CALLED SUMMER OF LOVE. IT IS AN ALBUM OF SUCH WARM CHARACTER AND INVENTION YOU EASILY FORGIVE ITS WEAKNESSES

Probably the most iconic album sleeve ever. Designed by Peter Blake, this was the first sleeve to feature song lyrics. It has been referenced countless times by bands and magazines.

a Beatle could get any peace and quiet was in the hotel bathroom.

In 1966 the band said: enough. On 29 August, at their show at Candlestick Park, San Francisco, Paul McCartney said to assistant Tony Barrow: 'Make sure you tape this one.' Both men knew something the world did not; that this show would be the last time The Beatles would ever perform live in front of a paying audience.

They could not have been happier. On the flight home George Harrison sat down in his seat and said 'That's it, I'm not a Beatle any more.' And he smiled. From now on, The Beatles would only work in the studio, they would only make records. It was a revolutionary step. No other band had ever attempted such a career switch.

EVEN THOUGH HE WAS REGULARLY DOSING HIMSELF UP ON LSD, THE DRUG HAD NO EFFECT ON LENNON'S HUGE COMPETITIVE STREAK. FAR FROM IT

On arrival in London the band went their separate ways. John to Spain to film a cameo part in the movie *How I Won the War;* George to India to study sitar with Ravi Shankar; Paul to start work on the soundtrack for *The Family Way;* and Ringo on holiday.

The break did them good. In Spain Lennon would write 'Strawberry Fields Forever', one of his greatest songs. He would then return to his home in Weybridge, and start taking huge amounts of LSD. On 9 November, having stayed up for three days on the drug, Lennon travelled to the Indica Gallery in Mason's Yard, London, to see an exhibition entitled 'Unfinished Paintings and Objects'. It was there he first met a Japanese artist named Yoko Ono. The

rest of the time, before work began again, he was more than happy to spend tripping off his head.

When the band came together at the Abbey Road Studios in November, McCartney knew what he wanted the band to do. In the words of Mark Lewisohn, the world's leading Beatles expert, McCartney wanted 'to make the album a piece of art by its content and by its cover. He wanted to say this is the album, and this is what you can do with it'.

'Strawberry Fields Forever' was the first song the band recorded, and it was unlike anything they had ever attempted before. Everything about it – its structure, its overall sound, its oblique lyrics – was fresh and inspirational. It took some 45 hours to bring the recording to perfection. This was a remarkable amount of time to spend on a single song. It demonstrated not only the band's unshakeable desire to get everything right, but also the changes that had occurred since The Beatles first arrived at Abbey Road back in 1962. At that time recording sessions were strictly limited to two hours. The first Beatles album was made in one day.

Pepper would consume five months of their lives and was recorded at the most haphazard of times. A session might be scheduled to start at seven, but, such was their standing now, a Beatle might not arrive until ten or eleven. Like most bands, The Beatles were night people. Their creativity was always more likely to shine when the rest of the world lay sleeping. After 'Strawberry Fields Forever' was completed the band turned their attention to a new McCartney number called 'Penny Lane'. Like 'Strawberry Fields', the song's lyrics referred back to the songwriter's childhood. It was classic McCartney music, a song brimming with melody and invention and drive. EMI was keen to release a new single by the band. To get the company off their backs the band threw them what could arguably be called the greatest pop single ever: 'Strawberry Fields Forever' backed with 'Penny Lane'.

Yet a surprise was in store for the band. Engelbert Humperdinck's 'Release Me' denied the band the number-one spot, thus prompting more media speculation about the band's future. After all, at Christmas The Beach Boys had replaced The Beatles as the world's number one band in a *New Musical Express* poll. Even more insultingly, Cliff Richard was voted best vocalist over Lennon. The band shrugged their shoulders and carried on recording. What was happening at Abbey Road was far more interesting than silly press speculation.

Even though he was regularly dosing himself up on LSD, the drug had no effect on Lennon's huge competitive streak. Far from it. In a short space of time he composed 'Lucy in the Sky with Diamonds', 'Being for the Benefit of Mr Kite' (the lyrics taken from a circus poster Lennon bought whilst filming the promotional film for 'Strawberry Fields' in Knole Park, Kent),

'Good Morning Good Morning', which was inspired by a TV advert for cornflakes, and 'A Day in the Life'. McCartney returned fire with 'Getting Better', 'Fixing a Hole' and the exquisite 'She's Leaving Home'.

He also submitted a song entitled 'Sgt Pepper's Lonely Hearts Club Band', which gave him the idea that would help *Pepper* become The Beatles' most famous album. The concept was that Sergeant Pepper was a fictitious band, played by The Beatles. The album would be a document of one of their shows, performed by The Beatles. It was an idea enthusiastically taken up by his fellow band members.

What was also special about these sessions was the freedom. With no live engagements to fulfil, the band could take as much time as they liked to perfect their songs. Tape loops, echoes, delays, anything that lay to hand, they would try out. On 'Being for the Benefit of Mr Kite', Lennon demanded a fairground sound. On 'When I'm Sixty-Four' McCartney asked that his vocal sounded ten years younger than his years. And so on.

The apotheosis of all this creativity happened when the band put together 'A Day in the Life', one of the few songs on the album that Lennon and McCartney had worked closely on together. Lennon had written most of the song but needed a middle eight. McCartney had been fooling around with some idea about getting out of bed in the morning. By a great coincidence – one typical of the magic surrounding the album – the section fitted perfectly into John's structure. McCartney, who had been eagerly exploring London's avant-garde scene, now thought of an instrumental interval created by an orchestra instructed to start on the lowest note on their instrument and then rise to the highest.

DESPITE THEIR GREAT ARTISTIC ACHIEVEMENTS, THE BAND WERE UNSURE HOW THE WORLD WAS GOING TO TAKE PEPPER. 'WILL THEY BUY IT,' A NERVOUS AND VERY STONED LENNON ASKED RAY COLEMAN

At the recording session on Friday 10 February, 40 musicians arrived, and after settling down were told to put on funny hats, red noses, balloons on their bows, etc. Suitably attired, they recorded five takes, McCartney conducting them, and friends such as Mick Jagger, Marianne Faithfull, Donovan, Mike Nesmith and Brian Jones hanging around. A camera captured this unique scene.

The song was placed at the end of the album, and a crashing piano chord, a collage of noises, including a dog whistle, was added at later dates to end one of the most remarkable albums of all times. *Pepper* perfectly fitted in with the ideas and creativity that were driving forwards the so-called Summer of Love. It is an album devoid of hate, an album of such a warm character and invention you easily forgive its weaknesses.

It was Robert Fraser, a gallery owner and friend of McCartney's, who suggested they ask Peter Blake to design the cover. Blake asked The Beatles to nominate people they wanted to see on the sleeve. Numerous names were submitted. Meanwhile, the band went to London's Berman theatrical outfitters and kitted themselves out in uniforms of striking colours and then had their picture taken.

And now, here they were at Brian Epstein's house, high with a little help from their friends and extremely apprehensive. Despite their great artistic achievements, the band were unsure how the world was going to take *Pepper*. 'Will they buy it?' a nervous and very stoned Lennon asked Ray Coleman. 'I like it, we all feel it's another step up, but will they buy it?'

On 3 June *Sgt Pepper* entered the UK charts and stayed there for 201 weeks. It lived for 175 weeks in the US charts. It has sold 32 million copies and is regularly nominated as the greatest album ever made. But more than that, in that summer of 1967, The Beatles showed everyone the huge possibilities of the album format – to the benefit of us all.

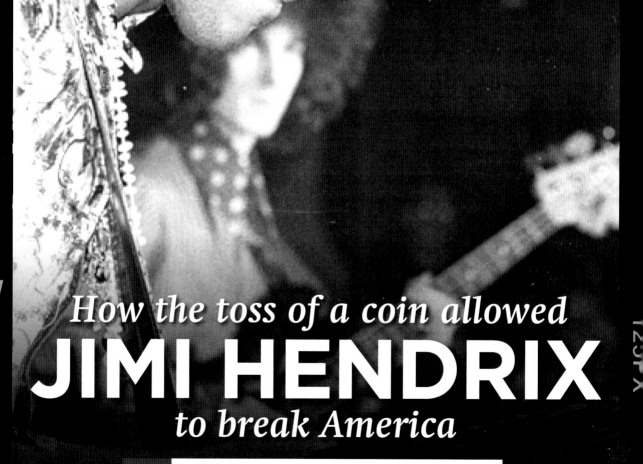

How the toss of a coin allowed
JIMI HENDRIX
to break America

DATE | 18 July 1967, The Monterey Pop Festival, California

I n January 1967 two young entrepreneurs, Ben Shapiro and Alan Pariser, attended the Human Be-In festival in San Francisco's Golden Gate Park. The festival had been organized as a public protest against the banning of the drug LSD. Amongst the acts that played that day were The Grateful Dead, Quicksilver Messenger Service, Jefferson Airplane. Various iconic counterculture figures such as Allen Ginsberg appeared, and Timothy Leary is said to have brought along 100,000 tabs of LSD and handed them out for free.

This was the day when the hippies announced their presence in the world, a day when thousands upon thousands of young people came out to tune in, turn on and drop out, and Shapiro and Pariser were mightily impressed. Realizing the potential of this new movement, they set about organizing a similar event for the July of that year. The location they chose was the Monterey fairground site, which was located between San Francisco and Los Angeles. They needed about $50,000 to cover expenses. They secured it from various record companies, who realized that a festival such as Monterey would allow them the chance to cherrypick the cream of the rock fraternity.

With the money secured, Shapiro and Pariser approached The Mamas and the Papas and offered the band's leader,

John Phillips, $5,000 to appear at their event. The band turned down the money. The whole thing seemed too organized, 'too Colonel Parker'. Instead they made a suggestion. Why not put on a festival organized by the musicians themselves?

Shapiro and Pariser were sharp, knew that this idea would attract a large crowd. They set up a board of governors to put the festival together. On that board were Brian Wilson, Paul McCartney, Mick Jagger and Smokey Robinson. It was Paul McCartney who insisted the festival book an act called The Jimi Hendrix Experience.

Although he was unknown in his own country, all London's rock cognoscenti knew of Hendrix and were in awe of his technical ability, his deep imagination and his powerful live shows. When the spirit took him, Hendrix smashed his guitars and speakers, such was the intensity he drove himself to. At first, many believed he was simply copying Pete Townshend, who was by now well known for his guitar-smashing antics. 'Hendrix was the first man to walk all over my territory,' Townshend once said. 'I felt incredibly intimidated by that.'

ALTHOUGH HE HELD HIM IN THE HIGHEST MUSICAL ESTEEM, **TOWNSHEND WAS WARY OF HENDRIX**. THAT IS WHY HE WANTED TO GET ON STAGE BEFORE HIM

Hendrix was added to the bill, a real chance for him to show his prospective audience what he was made of. By Thursday 15 June the rest of the bands had been confirmed. They included The Association, Eric Burdon and the Animals, Simon and Garfunkel, Canned Heat, The Byrds, Laura Nyro, Jefferson Airplane and Buffalo Springfield. A good smattering of R&B acts had also been invited, including Lou Rawls, Booker T. and the MGs, and Otis Redding – whose performance would gain that great singer a new audience. 'I got myself the love people,' he said afterwards. Five short months later he was killed in a plane crash.

On Friday the incoming trickle of hippies turned into a torrent. Some 30,000 people entered the grounds, although only 7,500 could be admitted into the main arena. The attendance rose to 90,000 over the weekend, yet there was little trouble. The police adopted a softly-softly approach, often ignoring the crowd's drug use.

The crowd for their part acted with restraint. Many seemed happy just to hang out with each other and forget about the music. They wanted to show the world that their much-scorned peace-and-love philosophy was highly practical, and could work in any given situation.

To keep everyone happy, the organizers had arranged entertainment outside the main arena. This included the chance to play a synthesizer or to play music on a specially constructed stage. Everybody had a good time. Brian Jones wandered around the festival in bright-coloured clothing, and there were numerous sightings of Paul McCartney, prompting rumours that The Beatles were about to appear live.

By Sunday everyone present knew that they were attending a very special event. As the filmmaker D.A. Pennebaker roamed around with his crew capturing the event for posterity, as managers and record companies thrashed out big deals backstage, as thousands of hippies blissed out in the sunshine, it seemed that a new world was about to be born.

But backstage, any idea of spiritual harmony was being dissipated by a growing

Already massive in Britain, Hendrix returned to America in June 1967 to perform at Monterey, where his outlandish stage antics and brilliant guitar playing would make him a star in his own country.

argument between Jimi Hendrix and Pete Townshend. Each act wanted to play before the other. Months before, The Who had followed Jimi on stage at the Saville Theatre, London. Hendrix had finished his set by trashing his equipment, so when The Who followed suit at their set's conclusion, the crowd was nonplussed. One act destroying equipment and instruments will thrill an audience; two acts and the impact is lessened. Although he held him in the highest musical esteem, Townshend was wary of Hendrix. That is why he wanted to get on stage before him.

Hendrix knew what he had done to The Who in London, and he didn't want the same medicine applied to him, especially at such an important show. But Townshend would not budge. He too had his eye on the vast American market. With only one hit single ('Happy Jack') to The Who's name in the US, Monterey was their chance to make a huge impact.

The issue was finally resolved when John Phillips intervened and suggested they toss a coin. Both acts stopped, thought about it, and then agreed to the proposal. Phillips tossed, and Pete chose correctly.

Hendrix would be the last act on stage that night. Hendrix reacted to this news by strapping on his guitar and playing, according to Townshend: 'some amazing guitar, just standing on a chair in the dressing room underneath the stage. Janis Joplin was there, Mama Cass, Brian Jones, Eric [Clapton] and me and a few other people... And then he got off the chair and turned round to me and said: "If I'm going to follow you, I'm going to pull out all the stops." Then he walked away.'

The Who took to the stage in a determined mood, delivering a blistering set that ended with Townshend smashing up his guitar and Daltrey knocking over the microphones, as well as smoke bombs exploding all over the stage.

The Grateful Dead followed, and their delicate music calmed matters down somewhat. Then Rolling Stone Brian Jones walked on stage and announced: 'I'd like to introduce a very good friend, a fellow countryman of yours... he's the most exciting performer I have ever heard – The Jimi Hendrix Experience.'

Jimi hit the stage and tore into 'Killing Floor'. He swept his arm over the guitar, jamming it against the speaker for feedback, and tongue-wagging his instrument lasciviously. Then it was into 'Foxy Lady' before meting out an R&B-cooked version of Dylan's 'Like a Rolling Stone'. Monterey roared out its approval: he is a Dylan fan; he is one of us! Then it was 'Rock Me Baby', 'Hey Joe', 'Can

You See Me' and 'The Wind Cries Mary', one of Jimi's greatest-ever ballads.

At the song's conclusion Hendrix addressed the crowd: 'It was so groovy to come back here this way and, you know, really get a chance to really play... I can sit here all night and say thank you, thank you, thank you, but I just can't do that... So, I'm gonna sacrifice something...' The band hit 'Wild Thing', and Hendrix went to town. He played the guitar behind his back, between his legs, on his knees. He ran his tongue up and down the strings. He rammed his guitar's neck into the amplifiers and then

JIMI GRABBED THE GUITAR'S NECK AND PROCEEDED TO SMASH IT ON THE FLOOR. HE THEN FLUNG OUT BITS TO THE CROWD BEFORE STALKING OFF STAGE TO MASSIVE APPLAUSE

he threw the instrument onto the floor. And then the coup de grace, an act suggested by PR man Keith Altham: Hendrix walked to the back of the stage and returned with a can of lighter fuel. He sprayed the fuel all over his guitar and then he lit a match. The guitar shot up in flames. Jimi grabbed its neck and proceeded to smash his guitar on the stage floor. He then flung out bits of the guitar to the ecstatic crowd, before stalking off the stage to massive applause.

Hendrix had not just set his guitar alight, he had set Monterey alight. And he had broken America. The next day he and his band flew to San Francisco for a six-night engagement at Bill Graham's Fillmore West, where they were supporting Jefferson Airplane. After just one show the Airplane pulled out. There was just no way they could follow Jimi.

Townshend caught the plane back to London the next day. In his pocket he found a pill of STP, a hallucinogen 20 times more powerful than acid. Keith Moon produced another, and the pair spent the flight tripping out of their brains. Soon Pete Townshend was in the grip of a nightmare. 'I have had bad trips on LSD many times before,' he later said, 'but nothing like this one. At one point I was so disgusted with what I was and what I was thinking and my body and the way that I felt, I actually came out of my body. I was looking down at myself in the seat, and in the end I realized I must go back otherwise I was gonna die... I never touched acid again after that, because the shock of that bad trip was so stunning and so awful, I didn't even smoke a cigarette again for four years.'

Townshend would find himself an Indian guru, Meher Baba, and embark on a spiritual course that led him to write his rock opera, *Tommy*. This in turn gave him the American success Hendrix had grabbed by calling the toss of a coin incorrectly.

James Marshall Hendrix was born on 27 November 1942 in Seattle, Washington. He was the oldest of five children. His parents divorced when he was nine, and his mother Lucille died two years later as a result of alcoholism. At the age of 15 Jimi acquired his first guitar. In 1961, after stealing two cars, he was enlisted into the army. When he came out, he spent the next few years playing with various bands, including The Isley Brothers. All the time he was developing his unique style, which would include playing guitar with his teeth. In 1966 he was spotted in New York by Chas Chandler, former bassist with The Animals. Chandler brought Hendrix to London, where he became an instant hit with singles such as 'Hey Joe' and 'Purple Haze'. He returned to America and, thanks to a scintillating performance at the Monterey Pop Festival, became very well known and a huge icon of the hippie culture. His landmark albums include *Are You Experienced* and *Axis: Bold as Love*. He died on 18 September 1970 in London, when he asphyxiated on his own vomit. He was 27 years old.

OTIS REDDING

records 'Dock of the Bay'

DATE 7 December 1967, Stax Studio, Memphis

Somehow, this young neighbourhood kid had been able to wander into the session. He wore jeans, a cloth cap and sneakers, and he quietly positioned himself behind a cluster of microphones. Those who did notice him figured he belonged to someone else, and so he was never questioned, not by the singer, nor the band, nor the producer. They just got on with recording the song that would become a standard, a key moment in the history of Stax Records, a song that would forever attach itself to its creator and singer, Otis Redding.

That milestone of song was '(Sittin' On) The Dock of the Bay', which Otis Redding had written with guitarist Steve Cropper. Although it was recorded on 7 December 1967, the genesis of the song went back to June of that year. That was the month when Otis Redding, soul's premier vocalist and the King of Stax Records, experienced two major epiphanies.

The first eye-opening moment was hearing The Beatles album *Sergeant Pepper's Lonely Hearts Club Band*. Like the rest of the world in that first summer of love, Otis fell in love with *Sergeant Pepper*. He played it endlessly, soaking in its every nuance. By absorbing a music that was way outside the arena he operated in, Otis felt his own musical instincts stirring and it excited him. He started thinking to himself: What if there was a soul *Sergeant Pepper*...?

Redding's second epiphany occurred on the evening of Saturday 17 June, when he walked on stage at the Monterey Pop Festival and delivered a set that would enter into folklore. He played five songs that night: 'Shake', 'Respect', 'I've Been Loving You Too Long', 'Satisfaction' and 'Try a Little Tenderness' – and he shook the place up. 'This is the love crowd, right?

OTIS FELT HIS OWN MUSICAL INSTINCTS STIRRING, AND IT EXCITED HIM. **HE STARTED THINKING TO HIMSELF: WHAT IF THERE WAS A SOUL SERGEANT PEPPER?**

We all love each other, right? Am I right?' Otis shouted to the crowd. The crowd shouted back: 'Yeah!' And Otis shouted back at them: 'Let me hear you say yeah!' and the crowd again shouted: 'Yeah!' In that moment, he had them; he was theirs, and they were his. And the reviews were sensational. Critic and future Bruce Springsteen manager Jon Landau wrote, 'Otis Redding's performances constitute, as a whole, the highest level of expression rock'n'roll has ever attained.'

Redding embarked upon a storming West Coast tour, using a houseboat in Sausalito as his base. He shared this space with his road manager, Speedo. It was there that 'Dock of the Bay' first saw light. He played its first movements to Speedo, got him to tap out various rhythms as he struggled with its form and presentation on acoustic guitar. Speedo had heard nothing like it from Otis. 'Dock' was slow and meandering and written with a musical structure he didn't recognize. 'He was changing with the times is what was happening. And I was looking at the times change, but I wasn't that far with it yet,' Speedo admitted.

Otis went home and played the song to his wife Zelma. She didn't get it either. In November he went to the studio with dozens of new songs and ideas, but 'Dock of the Bay' was the song he wanted to record first. The great writer Stanley Booth saw it all. He was there the night they recorded, and he saw Otis sitting there by the desk with his cracked guitar, playing the song over and over, adding lyrics, changing words. He saw Booker T., that great keyboard player, arrive with the bass player Duck Dunn. They took up their instruments, started experimenting with ideas and sounds. Drummer Al Jackson sat down behind his kit. He said: 'One, two, three,' and they hit the groove. As the music played, the horn section arrived. Cropper and Redding took them aside and started singing the lines to them.

THE CROWD SHOUTED BACK: 'YEAH!' AND OTIS SHOUTED BACK AT THEM: 'LET ME HEAR YOU SAY YEAH!' AND THE CROWD AGAIN SHOUTED: 'YEAH!'

As they rehearsed, the boy in the sneakers and the cap crept in. Maybe he had been browsing in the Stax record shop at the front of the building, had seen these great musicians sauntering in and decided to follow, see what was occurring. Maybe a sound had wafted into his ear, and he had followed that sound down the corridor and into the studio. Who knows? He was there, and he was watching as the band began rehearsing, until the time was ready and the recording tapes were switched on.

In a few takes, 'Dock of the Bay' was committed to immortality. They gathered by the mixing desk and played back the song. When it finished, Otis turned to Cropper and said: 'That's it.' Cropper knew he was right, and he nodded in full agreement. 'That's a mother,' said Booker, and that was when the kid in the sneakers piped up. 'I like that,' he said, 'that's good singing. I'd like to be a singer myself.'

That little boy never saw Otis again. Two days after the session Otis got on a plane with his band and flew to Cleveland to record a television show. That night they performed at club called Leo's. The next day it was to Madison for another show. The weather was terrible, but Otis never liked to let his audience down. He insisted they make the gig. At 3.28 that afternoon, his plane crashed into the icy waters of Lake Monona. There was just one survivor. It wasn't Otis.

Stax Records went into mourning, but 'Dock of the Bay' was released as a single in January 1968 and shot to number one on the R&B charts. It topped the charts for four weeks, thus fulfilling Otis's vision of crossover success. The song went on to win two Grammy Awards, Best R&B Song and Best Male R&B Vocal Performance.

And somewhere Otis Redding was watching all this and telling the people all around him 'See, I was right. I knew that song would give me my first number one.' And then he smiled, walked back into the light – and was gone forever.

Otis Redding was born on 9 September 1941 in Dawson, Georgia. The family moved to nearby Macon when he was five years old. He began singing at an early age, winning several talent contests. He also joined several groups, notably Johnny Jenkins and the Pinetoppers, with whom he recorded some material. At the end of one recording session he was allowed to cut a version of his song 'These Arms of Mine'. The song became a regional hit, and brought him to the attention of Stax with whom he now signed; he would be inextricably linked with the label for the rest of his life. His emotive voice and performances quickly brought him the title the King of Soul whilst his strong performance at the rock-orientated Monterey Pop Festival in 1967 introduced him to a much wider audience. His album *Otis Blue* is considered to be a milestone in 60s R&B music. In December 1967 Otis Redding was killed in a plane crash. His single 'Dock of the Bay' was released posthumously the following month, and gave him his first number-one hit record.

The offer behind

VAN
MORRISON'S

classic album Astral Weeks

DATE January 1968, New York

He has in his jacket pocket an envelope that contains $20,000, and he is headed to the third floor of a deserted New York building. Fear is playing upon his nerves like a demented jazz pianist. His name is Joe Smith, and he is vice-president of Warner Brothers Records. The reason he has the money on his person is that he wants to sign an artist named Van Morrison to his label. To make that happen, he must pay what he assumes to be Mafia gangsters.

'I was told to come alone,' Smith recounts in Johnny Rogan's biography of Van Morrison. 'I had twenty $1,000 bills in an envelope when I got up to this tiny room, and there were two unpleasant guys there who were not common to the record company world. We looked at each other, the contract was signed and witnessed and the money counted out. My concern was that as soon as I turned for the door, I was going to be hit on the back of the head and wind up with no $20,000 and no contract.'

Thankfully, no such scenario took place. Smith walked slowly out of the room and then ran down the stairs and out of that building as fast he could. Morrison could now leave Bang Records and record one of the greatest albums in popular music, thanks to Smith's actions. That record was called *Astral Weeks*.

Bang Records was run by a character named Bert Berns. The son of Russian-Jewish immigrants, Berns was a songwriter whose works included 'Twist and Shout' and 'Cry to Me'. He was also in business with gangsters. His partner was Tommy Emboli, acting head of the powerful Genovese family.

> MY CONCERN WAS THAT AS SOON AS I TURNED FOR THE DOOR, I WAS GOING TO BE HIT ON THE BACK OF THE HEAD AND WIND UP WITH NO $20,000 AND NO CONTRACT

Berns had signed Morrison in 1967. The two men had previously worked together in Morrison's band Them (Berns had written and produced Them's 1966 hit, 'Here Comes the Night'). Although the two men repeatedly clashed, their fraught relationship would produce such classic singles as 'Gloria' and 'Brown Eyed Girl'. Unfortunately, Berns suffered a huge heart attack on 30 December 1967 and died at the age of 38.

GANGSTERS DIRECTLY THREATENING MUSICIANS WAS NO NEW THING; IT HAD BEEN HAPPENING FOR A LONG TIME

By then Morrison wanted out of Bang anyway. Any goodwill he had for the label had disappeared, and with Berns's passing he saw his chance to move on. One of Berns's associates had different ideas. His name was Carmine 'Wassell' Denoia. He was big, bad-tempered and a great believer in loyalty. When he found out about Morrison's intention to leave Bang, his temper broke. He rushed to Morrison's New York hotel, where the singer was holed up with a girlfriend, Janet Planet. Carmine started angrily banging on the door, shouting: 'You're finished in the music business, Morrison.'

Gangsters threatening musicians was no new thing; it had been happening for a long time. The famous Al Capone ran a number of jazz clubs in Chicago. If he wanted something from a musician he just asked – then he threatened. Bing Crosby, Frank Sinatra, Dean Martin and many others had contact with mob figures.

In the rock'n'roll era, too, there were still those looking, in Mafia parlance, to wet their beaks. One was Morris Levy of Roulette Records. He was nicknamed The Godfather, a nod to his supposed ties with the mob. Levy went into music publishing when he acquired the rights to the song 'Lullaby of Birdland'. His fortunes rose, as did his ties with various gangsters.

In 1969 The Beatles released their *Abbey Road* album. The opening song on the album, John Lennon's 'Come Together' was eerily close to a Chuck Berry song called 'You Can't Catch Me', and Levy owned the rights. He sued Lennon straight away. Lennon made him a counter-offer: drop the charges, and I will record three of your songs on my album of rock'n'roll covers. Levy agreed, but when Lennon seemed to be stalling, Levy stole the master tape and released the album as mail order only under the name *Roots*. Lennon didn't complain, and Levy made another fortune.

In 1988 Levy was exposed on TV as a mob conspirator and sentenced to ten years in jail for his part in extorting money from a man named John Lamonte. He died whilst waiting for his appeal to come to court. He was immortalized in HBO's awardwinning TV series *The Sopranos*, as the character Herman 'Hesh' Rabkin.

As for Van Morrison, he would also be immortalized, but through his music. After Carmine had departed, Van and Janet did the most sensible thing possible – they quit New York. They went to Cambridge, Massachusetts, and settled there. Morrison picked up with various local bands, including one led by J. Geils frontman Peter Wolf. Morrison began composing what would be his first great album. *Astral Weeks* carries little suggestion of city life in its form. Instead, it is a stunning set of songs that have been hewn from the rocks of blues and jazz and folk, and brought together in remarkable synthesis.

CARMINE STARTED BANGING ON THE DOOR, SHOUTING OUT: 'YOU'RE FINISHED IN THE MUSIC BUSINESS, MORRISON'

Van Morrison never spoke of his run-in with gangsters. But he did write a song about his experience. It was called 'Big Time Operators'. The song was released 20 years after the incident at the hotel. Had it really taken him that long to face up to what had gone down? One really wouldn't be surprised if that was the case.

George Ivan Morrison was born in Belfast on 31 August 1945. His mother was a singer and his father a shipyard electrician. His father also owned a huge record collection, and Morrison grew up listening to artists such as Jelly Roll Morton, Solomon Burke, Ray Charles and Leadbelly. He was given a guitar when he was 11, and as a teenager he performed in local bands before joining the band Them, which scored hits with 'Baby Please Don't Go' and 'Here Comes the Night'. Bert Berns, the producer of their second album, persuaded Morrison to record a solo album for his Bang label. 'Brown Eyed Girl' emerged from this period, but Morrison was unhappy with Bang's treatment of him. He moved to Warner Brothers where, as a solo artist, he recorded many landmark albums including *Astral Weeks*, *Moondance* and *It's Too Late to Stop Now*, often considered one of the greatest live albums ever. Van Morrison has continued writing and recording and issuing fine albums such as *The Common One* and *Avalon Sunset*. He remains a major figure in today's musical landscape.

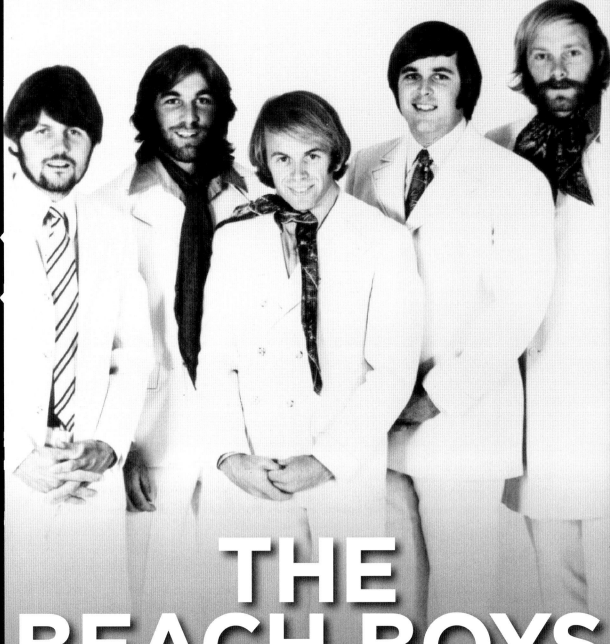

THE BEACH BOYS

nearly sign Charles Manson to their record label

DATE April 1968, Hollywood

125PX

Two attractive teenage girls stand on a Malibu road, hitchhiking. Their names are Ella Jo Bailey and Patricia Krenwinkel. It is April 1968, a lovely spring day in Malibu. Suddenly, a red Ferrari pulls up. The girls run to the car. Behind the wheel is a very handsome 24-year-old man. The girls like the look of him. They get in the car, and in doing so set in motion one of the darkest chapters in pop history.

The driver of the Ferrari reveals that he is a drummer with a band they might have heard of – The Beach Boys? The girls shriek in recognition, and Dennis Wilson smiles happily. Although known as a bit of a stud, Dennis drops the girls off at their intended location and bids them goodbye. A few days later – unbelievably – the same scenario is played out again. The girls are out hitchhiking and suddenly there is the red Ferrari. This time, Dennis takes the girls back to his beautiful rented mansion on Sunset Boulevard in Beverley Hills.

After a tour of his sumptuous house, Wilson and the girls strip off, and the three of them spend the afternoon making love to one another in Dennis's bedroom. When early evening arrives, Dennis tells them he has to go. He is due in the studio that evening for work on a new Beach Boys album. The girls thank him and then return home to the commune (basically, a large bus), which they share with many other young girls and a young man whose name is Charlie Manson. They call themselves The Family, and Charlie is their father.

That evening over supper, Charlie asks the girls where they have been that day. Excitedly, the girls tell him all of their adventures. They hold back on nothing. In

'ARE YOU GOING TO HURT ME?' WILSON BLURTS OUT. CHARLIE MANSON SMILES BEATIFICALLY. **'DO I LOOK AS THOUGH I AM GOING TO HURT YOU?'** HE SOFTLY ASKS. THEN HE KNEELS DOWN AND HE KISSES WILSON'S SHOES

The Beach Boys – without Brian Wilson – sing 'Do It Again' on the UK's *Top of the Pops*, 30 November 1968. Back home, wondering if the group would sign him, sat Charles Manson.

this commune there are no boundaries. Charlie tells the girls he has met Wilson twice before. Once at a dope house in San Francisco, once at Elvis Presley's mansion. (Neither story has ever been confirmed.)

Charlie now says: Why don't we go back to Wilson's house and meet the man? Everyone thinks this is great idea, so the whole commune get into their rickety black bus, and they drive to Wilson's house. The house is empty when they arrive, so they break in and make themselves at home.

Meanwhile, Dennis Wilson is hard at work in a studio on a new Brian Wilson song entitled 'Busy Doin' Nothin'' (in which the eccentric Beach Boys' leader gives details of how to reach his house – but that, as they say, is a whole other story).

At three o'clock in the morning, after boasting to the band about his double conquest that afternoon, Dennis says his goodbyes and drives home. As he parks in his driveway, he sees the large black bus. He also notices that some of the house lights are on. And as he steps out of his car, he can hear Beatles music blasting through his stereo system. Growing more anxious by the moment, Wilson decides it would be wise to head towards the back of the house, and enter through the kitchen door.

As he reaches the kitchen door a small wiry man steps out onto the patio. 'Are you going to hurt me?' Wilson blurts out. Charlie Manson smiles beatifically. 'Do I look as though I am going to hurt you?' he softly asks. Then he kneels down and he kisses Wilson's shoes.

Totally disarmed by the man's behaviour, Wilson allows Manson to guide him into his own house. In the sitting room Dennis recognizes Patricia and Ella Jo, but he knows none of the other girls who are sitting around drinking his whisky, eyeing him up provocatively. Manson takes the Beach Boy upstairs to his bedroom and begins talking to him in a soothing and gentle manner.

Soon the two men are rapping like old friends. Charlie suggests maybe Dennis would like to partake of some chemicals and maybe a girl or two? He has just knowingly and deliberately pushed two of Wilson's most prominent buttons: drugs and girls. Wilson never could resist either of them, and Charlie is acutely aware of that fact. By accepting them both, Wilson has made a silent pact with Charlie.

For the summer of 1968 the Charles Manson Family take over Dennis Wilson's house. And they do what they like. They take Dennis's jewellery and clothes and money, and pay him back in sex and drugs. Manson, however, has bigger plans where Dennis is concerned. He knows that The Beach Boys have just begun their own Brother Records label, and he, Charlie, wants to be their first signing.

CHARLIE SUGGESTS MAYBE DENNIS WOULD LIKE TO PARTAKE OF SOME CHEMICALS AND MAYBE A GIRL OR TWO? HE HAS PUSHED TWO OF WILSON'S MOST PROMINENT BUTTONS: DRUGS AND GIRLS. WILSON NEVER COULD RESIST EITHER

One night Manson gives Wilson an LSD tab and starts playing him various songs he has written. Soon, Dennis becomes convinced of Manson's burgeoning talents. He starts urging his fellow band members to meet this extraordinary songwriter. He even mentions Manson in a 1968 interview with *Rave* magazine. You might think that Manson is duping Dennis. Far from it. Wilson isn't the only one to be impressed by Charlie's musical talent. Neil Young is also knocked out by the man's songs.

After an afternoon spent with Charlie at Wilson's house, Young phones Mo Ostin, head of Warner Brothers Records, and recommends that he signs Manson.

Meetings with Charlie and the rest of The Beach Boys – Brian and Carl Wilson, Al Jardine and Mike Love – now take place. Doris Day's son, record producer Terry Melcher, also meets Charlie. Melcher is a face on the LA music scene. He has sung on The Beach Boys' masterpiece *Pet Sounds,* and he has produced, amongst others, Paul Revere and the Raiders, The Byrds, Glen Campbell and The Mamas and the Papas.

THE BEACH BOYS RECORDED CLOSE TO 100 HOURS' WORTH OF CHARLIE'S MUSIC. IT IS ALSO ALLEGED THAT MANY OF THE SESSIONS TURNED INTO FULL-BLOWN ORGIES, FUELLED BY CHEMICALS OF ALL KINDS

Manson is taken by Melcher, especially when he discovers that he is loosely employed as a music scout for The Beatles' Apple label. Unknown to Melcher, Charlie is obsessed with The Beatles.

As these meetings wind on, Wilson becomes further involved with the Manson Family way of life. He happily gives the group money, pays for all their bills and starts echoing Manson's philosophies on the laws of life. 'The smile you send out will return to you,' he tells a British journalist.

Word spreads amongst the hippie fraternity in LA that Dennis Wilson's place is an open house where you can party to your heart's content. All is on offer. Streams of people now descend upon his property. Chaos ensues. A close associate of Wilson's tells him to move out and stop all this madness. Wilson finally sees sense and asks Manson and his people to move on. Manson, unwilling to do anything that might jeopardize his chance of a recording contract, takes his leave. He and his Family head to a farm owned by one George Spahn. Despite the distance between them, Manson keeps up regular contact with Wilson. In fact, on some occasions Wilson ferries members of The Family in his huge Rolls-Royce to garbage tips, where they scavenge for supermarket food with the millionaire Beach Boy drummer sitting in his huge car, looking on. Incongruous does not even come close.

Wilson also parties with Manson at the Spahn ranch, all the time making vague promises about recording contracts. Then he shoots off on a European tour. With the Beach Boy out of town, Manson homes in on Wilson's close friend, Gregg Jakobson. Using his usual mix of charm and charisma, Manson greatly impresses Jakobson, who is taken by the man's physical energy. He dutifully arranges a recording session where Charlie records 14 of his songs.

When The Beach Boys return from Europe, Manson keeps up his campaign, showing up at Brian Wilson's house with his drugs and girls, and over a period of time managing to record another batch of songs. The Beach Boys' manager, Nick Grillo, later told *Rolling Stone* magazine that they recorded close to 100 hours' worth of Charlie's music. It is also alleged that many of the sessions turned into full-blown orgies, fuelled by chemical substances of all kinds.

By all accounts, Manson's talent for producing great songs is highly questionable, although one song, 'Cease to Exist', makes a big impression on Dennis. At the next Beach Boys recording session, Wilson puts forward Manson's song to record. He changes the title to 'Never Learn Not to Love', and he also replaces many of Manson's lyrics with his own.

Buoyed by this partial success, Manson pushes harder and harder for his own deal. There is a stumbling block, though: Terry Melcher. He does not rate the man's songs and certainly has no appetite for the craziness that seems to accompany Manson like a faithful handmaiden.

Manson begins hustling Melcher, who avoids him at every turn. Finally, it is relayed back to Manson that Melcher will be dropping by that very night to hear his material. Charlie is ecstatic. Charlie prepares the ranch. Charlie should not have bothered. Melcher never shows up, driving Charlie into a fury.

Melcher has other problems, though. His stepfather has just died leaving behind a host of financial problems. Melcher's mother, Doris Day, is distraught. Melcher decides that it would be a good idea if he and his girlfriend, Candice Bergen, move back into his mother's house to care for her in this distressing time.

HE READS THE SONG AS A WARNING OF AN IMPENDING APOCALYPTIC RACE WAR IN WHICH WHITE SUPREMACY WOULD FINALLY TRIUMPH

Their rented property now goes out on offer. The address is 10050 Cielo Drive. It is quickly snapped up by a film director named Roman Polanski and his wife, an actress named Sharon Tate. A year later, four members of Manson's Family would come to this very location and commit one of the most gruesome mass murders in living memory.

In the meantime, Manson keeps badgering Wilson for progress in reference to his contract. The fact that the band have failed to pay Manson any royalties for his song now gives Manson the upper hand. Finally, in March 1969, Wilson puts Manson in a studio. There are no girls hanging around this time, but guitarist Bobby Beausoleil is there to help out. Again, the tapes do not catch anyone's imagination in a meaningful manner. At this point Gregg Jakobson, still convinced that Manson can be a huge star, suggests that the recording studio is the wrong location to capture the man's talent. The process would be much better served if they were to tape Manson in his home environment, sitting round a fire backed up by his Family members on George Spahn's ranch.

Initially sceptical, Terry Melcher finally agrees to visit Manson at Spahn's ranch. 'Manson played the guitar,' he later recalls, 'and all the girls sung parts and harmonies and background stuff, and it was quite an interesting thing. They talked about how they all shared this and that, and it was one big happy family…'

Yet Manson's vision is far removed from such a cosy description. In 1968 The Beatles released their new album simply entitled *The Beatles* (but known the world over as the *White Album*). In his drug-addled mind Manson truly believes that the album contains 13 songs addressed solely to him, all containing hidden messages that he – and only he – can access. One of these songs is 'Helter Skelter', Paul McCartney's manic song with its scatter-shot images of coming up and down. Manson sees the song differently. He reads it as a warning of an impending apocalyptic race war in which white supremacy will finally triumph. He calls on the Book of Revelation in the Bible, which foresees the end of the world, and in his mind he creates a crazy distorted vision in which McCartney's song is the soundtrack to the war that is about to explode.

MANSON HATES THE LOVE-AND-PEACE VIBE. HE INSISTS THE FILM OF HIS COMMUNE BE INTERCUT WITH FOOTAGE FROM HITLER'S THIRD REICH

Oblivious to all this, Jakobson now persuades Melcher that the best way forward is to start documenting Manson and his Family, to portray this commune as a kind of blueprint for living. Manson loves the idea of being filmed and photographed, although he baulks at any suggestion that his set-up in any way mirrors other hippie communes. Manson actively hates the love-and-peace vibe. He tells Melcher and Jakobson of his 'Helter Skelter' vision, and then insists that the film be intercut with footage of Hitler's Third Reich.

Disturbed by Manson's rantings, both men promise to get back to him at the earliest opportunity and make a swift retreat. Again the men begin to avoid Manson at all times, unaware that terrible events are about to take place around Manson and his Family.

For the past few years Manson has been telling his followers that he would soon lead them into a brave new world. Now those very same followers are starting to get impatient. When exactly is this revolution going to happen?

Manson senses the dissent in the ranks, and he knows that he cannot allow it to fester. He moves quickly. In August 1969 he tells four of his followers that Helter Skelter has arrived, and that they should go to Terry Melcher's old address and kill everyone in that house. This is the night that the notorious 'Sharon Tate murders' take place...

In the years since Manson's arrest and imprisonment, Wilson, Melcher and Jakobson have refused to talk about their involvement with one of America's most notorious criminals. Not that Manson was at all worried. His dream of being a rock star was reignited many years later when Guns N' Roses and Marilyn Manson covered his material on their albums.

Sitting in his jail cell, Manson could not have been happier. As the author Simon Wells notes: 'That was what it was all about in the end. Manson didn't want a revolution; he didn't want to change the world. He was like everyone. He just wanted what most of his generation wanted; he wanted to be a rock star.'

The Beach Boys were formed in 1961 in Hawthorne, California, by the Wilson brothers, Brian, Carl and Dennis. They were joined by their cousin Mike Love and friend Al Jardine. They were managed by the Wilsons' father, Murry. It was Dennis, the only surfer in the band, who suggested the band write about the local surfing scene. The band's first single 'Surfin'' was released in late 1961 and became a local hit. The Beach Boys signed to Capitol Records and began producing a string of memorable classics, including 'California Girls' and 'Good Vibrations'. Their album *Pet Sounds* is regarded as one of the greatest ever made. The strain of writing and recording it, coupled with his drug intake, induced a breakdown in Brian Wilson. The band strolled on fitfully without him, creating critically acclaimed albums such as *Holland*. Dennis and Carl Wilson have passed away and the band has since split into various line-ups. Brian Wilson pursues a solo career. The band holds the record for the most American top-40 hits (36), with 56 top-100 hits.

JAMES BROWN

stops a riot single-handedly

DATE 5 April 1968, Boston

When Martin Luther King, that man of peace, was murdered, violence erupted across America. In dozens of cities African-Americans went on the rampage. Despite a dusk-to-dawn curfew, they took to the streets and looted and pillaged. They burnt down shops and properties and anything else that caught their angry attention. And then they fought street battles with the army and the police.

Dr King was killed by a single bullet whilst standing on the balcony of his hotel in Memphis, and Black America erupted. One of the millions who felt King's death deeply was James Brown. He was resting at home after completing a short trip to Africa when he heard the news. He later stated that America had just lost its best friend, only most Americans did not realize it

Once he gained his composure, the first thing Brown did was to phone the radio stations that he owned in Knoxville and Baltimore and go on air, urging his listeners to stay indoors, to stay calm and to honour Martin Luther King's legacy of non-violence by refraining from rioting. He then taped several messages that reiterated this plea and ordered his radio managers to play them at regular intervals throughout the day and night. 'I believe they had some effect,' he later said in his biography, 'because those two cities had less trouble than most.'

Brown had great standing in the black community. He was a musical giant, a pioneer at the same level as his white contemporaries. His 1965 singles 'I Got You (I Feel Good)' and 'Papa's Got a Brand New Bag' heralded the start of a fresh new music that would become known as funk.

HE LATER STATED THAT AMERICA HAD JUST LOST ITS BEST FRIEND, ONLY MOST AMERICANS DID NOT REALIZE IT

Politically Brown cut something of a lone figure. He believed in the American dream. He wanted success as much for himself as he wanted it for others. His message was: look, if I can do it, so can you. This stance made him unpopular in some quarters, although they still danced like dervishes to his wonderful music.

Brown loved and respected King, but he did not always agree with his philosophies. The two men once spent a night arguing about the best way forward. Brown left that meeting with huge regard for King. They were both on the same page, just reading different lines. Brown knew King's murder would hit his audience, his communities, terribly. He understood the anger that would be generated. On the other hand he firmly believed violent demonstrations would not achieve a thing, People would get killed, black and white, and that was wrong. His mission now was to try to keep the peace.

On the day after King's death, Brown went to Boston for a scheduled gig. The town was tense, alert. The National Guard was on stand-by. On arrival, Brown was told that Boston mayor Kevin White had considered cancelling the show. A black councilman named Thomas Atkins had argued that such a move might trigger protests, but the mayor was not convinced. A different idea was put forward: broadcast Brown's show live on TV. That way, people would stay indoors in front of their televisions instead of taking to the streets. The mayor thought this a good idea. The show could go ahead, but only if it was screened live.

That placed Brown in an awkward situation. He had just recorded a TV special. Part of the contract clearly stated that he could not perform on TV before the special was broadcast. Meanwhile, when Brown arrived for his soundcheck he saw his fans at the box office demanding refunds. If the show was to be broadcast live, why pay money for it? Brown now lost his cool, pointing out that he was losing money and would be playing to an empty auditorium. A compromise was reached. If Brown's people could renegotiate his TV contract, the mayor would cover his losses. Calls were made and deals were struck.

BROWN LATER ADMITTED THAT DURING THE SHOW HE CRIED, THAT TEARS ROLLED DOWN HIS CHEEKS AS HE THOUGHT OF MARTIN LUTHER KING AND HIS ACHIEVEMENTS

The mayor himself introduced Brown that night. Brown's own first words were words of peace: 'Let's not do anything to dishonour Dr King,' he announced. 'Stay home. You kids especially. I want you to think about what you are doing. Think about what Dr King stood for.' Between each song Brown urged the people not to tear apart what little they had. 'I'm still a soul brother,' he said, 'and you people have made it possible for me to be a first-class man. I used to shine shoes in front of radio stations. Now I own radio stations. You know what that is? It's Black Power.'

Brown later admitted that during the show he cried, that tears rolled down his cheeks as he thought of Martin Luther King and his achievements. Outside, the streets remained empty as Boston tuned in. Such was the show's impact that it was repeated on TV directly after its conclusion.

Brown was asked by other cities to come and play. He chose Washington. He thought it a symbolic gesture, a black man invited to the home of the White House. When he arrived, he could not believe his eyes. Sections of the city had been burnt to the ground in the riots. Twelve thousand armed troops were patrolling the streets.

In the afternoon he went on TV and told America: 'The real answer to race problems in this country is education, not burning and killing. Be ready. Be qualified. Be something. Be somebody. Martin was our hero. We have an obligation to try to fulfil his dream of true brotherhood. You can't do that with violence.'

The following month Brown accepted an invitation from President Johnson to return to Washington and dine at the White House. One of the first things the president said to Brown when they met was: 'Won't they call you an Uncle Tom for doing this?' 'No,' Brown replied. 'Why not?' 'Because I'm not one,' said James Brown, Soul Brother Number One.

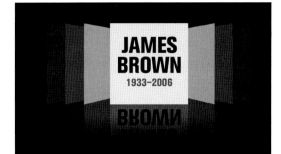

James Brown was born on 3 May 1933. He was raised in extreme poverty, first by his father and then by an aunt who ran a brothel. He dropped out of school, and at 16 was serving time for attempted armed robbery. In reform school Brown met Bobby Byrd, and on his release he joined Byrd's band, The Avons (later The Flames). Brown scored his first hit in 1956 with his composition 'Please, Please, Please'. In 1963, against the wishes of his record company, he financed his own album *Live At the Apollo*; it stayed in the charts for 14 months, peaking at number two. With hits such as 'Papa's Got a Brand New Bag', Brown single-handedly invented funk music. In the 70s he maintained this momentum with songs such as 'Get Up (I Feel Like Being a) Sex Machine'. His raw funk influenced numerous bands. Brown was caught offguard by the advent of disco, but in the 80s much of his music was co-opted by rap artists. Brown toured the world throughout the 90s and the Noughties, to huge acclaim. He died on Christmas Day 2006, a true musical legend.

The gig that broke
LED
ZEPPELIN
in America

DATE 26 January 1969, The Boston Tea Party Club, Boston

I t is Christmas Day 1968, Los Angeles, the Chateau Marmont Hotel where sin breathes and entices. And Robert Plant is worried, so very worried. It is hard to believe, but the man who would transform himself into the ultimate 70s rock god, a swaggering, howling, preening love man, is jetlagged, homesick and in a state of absolute trepidation about the American tour that awaits him.

Touring America is the ultimate test for the most seasoned of bands. Led Zeppelin, the band Plant fronts, have been together for – what? – three months. They have played just a handful of shows in the UK – headlined the Wood Green Fishmongers Hall amongst other venues – and now they are in America to play arenas and auditoriums and famous venues such as Whiskey A Go Go and Fillmore West, and they have never played America before. Can he deliver, Plant wonders to himself? Is he up to the task before him? Or is he about to be found out?

It does not help that he knows the leader of the band, Jimmy Page, harbours doubts about his ability to grab audiences and shake them up so hard they never come down. Page has said nothing, but Plant senses his reservations.

As he sits there in silent desperation, how could the 20-year-old singer know that his fears are absolutely groundless, that this will be the tour to break Led Zeppelin in America? Moreover, how is he to know that the band is soon to play the kind of gig that musicians can only dream about, a gig where the audience will literally stop them leaving the stage, a gig where they are forced to play their debut album twice, and in the end, throw their hands up in the air and say to the crowd, we have no more material!

TOURING AMERICA IS THE ULTIMATE TEST FOR THE MOST SEASONED OF BANDS. LED ZEPPELIN HAVE BEEN TOGETHER FOR THREE MONTHS AND PLAYED JUST A HANDFUL OF SHOWS IN THE UK

Plant knows none of this. All he knows is that events seem to be moving too fast, and that is because of the guy sat opposite him, the quietly confident guitarist, Jimmy Page. Led Zeppelin is Page's band. No doubt about that. It is Page who put the band together, Page who had the musical vision that would be the making of them.

Plant also knows he was not Page's first choice. That was cult artist Terry Reid. When Reid refused, Page approached Chris Farlowe, who also said no. But Reid had recommended Robert Plant. Page loved Plant's voice but felt his inexperience could be a stumbling block. Despite that reservation, he took on Plant, who in turn urged Page to check out a drummer called John Bonham. He was a real find, like a better version of Keith Moon. They were joined by bassist John Paul Jones, who had worked with Page on a Jeff Beck track two years previously.

In August 1968 Led Zeppelin (Keith Moon gave them the name) get together in a Soho basement. Within an hour of playing together it is clear something very special is taking shape. Page's idea is spot on: a blues-based approach allied to a classic rock'n'roll sensibility. Page's guitar is all-encompassing, switching effortlessly from cracking guitar riffs to rhythm to stunning lead. The heaviest rhythm section in the country pushes him deeper and deeper, and Plant's voice not only naturally fits into this cauldron but proves itself able to become an instrument in itself.

Page calls his friend Peter Grant right after the rehearsal and wildly enthuses about the music they are making. Grant quits his managerial partnership with Mickie Most and takes the band on. The first thing he does is to send them on tour to Scandinavia. By the end of the month they are in the studio, cutting their first album. Page and Grant pay for the sessions and pay the band's wages. It is a gamble, but neither man is worried. They know, they just know, it's going to come off.

THE HEAVIEST RHYTHM SECTION IN THE COUNTRY PUSHES HIM DEEPER AND DEEPER, AND PLANT'S VOICE BECOMES AN INSTRUMENT IN ITSELF

In November Grant tucks the album under his arm and flies to New York for a meeting with Atlantic Records. He touts the band as the new Cream, knowing that Cream have been a huge earner for the label. It's a cute line. The men at Atlantic laugh, then listen, then offer Grant a mouthwatering $222,000 and a five-year contract with the band granted complete artistic control over their music.

Grant goes home in triumph. He and Page take back what they have already

An early shot of Robert Plant developing his stage presence in America, 1970. Soon the band would be selling out huge arenas, travelling by private plane and causing hysteria wherever they land.

splashed out and then more. Meanwhile, Plant, Bonham and Jones are given £3,000 each, a true fortune for the times.

Grant now receives some interesting news. Jeff Beck has just ruled out a US tour that was due to begin in mid December. Grant knows the promoter, so he calls him up, pulls in a favour. The promoter listens, nods his head, and Led Zeppelin are suddenly set to make their US debut. They fly out just before Christmas, on 23 December, start on 26 December. They will be supporting the likes of Vanilla Fudge and Iron Butterfly and Country Joe and the Fish. They will spend Christmas in America, on their own. Grant forbids

the band to take their lovers on tour with them. Bass player John Paul Jones typically takes no notice of the edict. On the flight over to LA he casually informs the rest of the band he is hooking up with his wife Mo and the singer Madeline Bell for Christmas in New Jersey. He will see them at their first gig in Denver.

Accompanying the remaining band members to LA is Richard Cole, the newly appointed road manager. His nickname is Ricardo. He will spend the next few years diving headfirst into a pool of chaos, excess, violence and destruction. Bonham will be his main accomplice, and Led Zeppelin will gain a reputation for debauchery in clubs, hotels, bedrooms, apartments, wherever, whatever, didn't matter.

But right now, here in Los Angeles, that is all a dream away. For Plant is frightened to death, unable to sleep, unable to concentrate on anything except the nerves surging through his body.

On 26 December the band board a plane to Denver, then make their way to the Auditorium Arena. They are there to support Vanilla Fudge, who have built up a massive reputation as a red-hot live act. People say they have usurped Cream, The Who, Hendrix…

Zeppelin are appearing after a group called Zephyr, and when they walk out on stage they are amazed to find themselves on a revolving platform. Hell, thinks Plant as he tries to get his balance, as if I need any more hassles…

They begin their set, and it is strange at first and kind of weird – especially for Plant who sees a different set of faces in front of him every time he opens his eyes, Despite this, the strength of their music and their musical ability begins to assert itself. They play their own songs, they play covers. They play for an hour, and by the end of the set the crowd are highly appreciative. The band think: you know what, that was great.

On now to Seattle, Vancouver and then the Whiskey and the Fillmore where they are able to crush the audience, leave them screaming for more. Now on to Detroit, then Baltimore, gaining confidence and strength the whole time, feeling the power of their abilities shine through.

And then to a club called The Boston Tea Party, where they are scheduled to play four nights. The place holds 400 people, and with Grant having given American radio their debut album, which is now in heavy rotation, the club quickly sells out. Rock's new generation is about to impose itself for the first time.

THE CROWD SCREAM FOR THE BAND'S RETURN. AND **SCREAM AND BEG AND CAJOLE** AND SCREAM AND SCREAM

Led Zeppelin come out on stage and are welcomed as heroes. Buoyed by the reception, the band rip into their opening number. When they leave the stage an hour and a half later, the crowd is so frenzied, so ecstatic, they force the band to return to the stage and play their album again. They also add in some blues covers, the main source of their magic.

They take 12 standing ovations before quitting. But the crowd won't let them go. It is incredible, the band are absolutely worn out, but the audience is delirious and demanding even more music. The band tumble back on stage and start playing rock'n'roll covers, 'Good Golly Miss Molly' and 'Long Tall Sally'. Goodness gracious, what great balls of fire. They eventually quit the stage.

They figure that is enough. Is it hell. The crowd scream for the band's return. And scream and beg and cajole and scream and scream. By the fourth hour – that's right, the fourth hour – the band are playing whatever comes to mind. You name it, they play it. The Beatles, The Rolling Stones, The Who, The This, The That. Finally the lights go up, and the band, drenched in sweat and joy, stand and bow and wave, and the audience reluctantly goes home.

Word spreads of this incredible night, and at the same time their debut album enters the US top 100 and starts rising and rising and rising. *The Boston Phoenix* reports: 'I expect the Led Zeppelin to be flying high for some time… Their raw power is compelling and hypnotic while their complexity makes repeated exposure a pleasure.'

When the band return to the US in April of that year they are one of the most popular bands in America. Everything they have dreamt of is theirs for the taking. Christmas 1968 is a time in their history to look back at ruefully, and to laugh about and to realize that it is days like these that are always the best thing about that exhilarating journey to the top.

LED ZEPPELIN
1968–1980

Led Zeppelin was formed by Jimmy Page, who had just left The Yardbirds. He brought in Robert Plant on vocals, John Paul Jones on bass, John Bonham on drums. The band played their first show in July 1968, and just one year later had two bestselling albums: *Led Zeppelin* and *Led Zeppelin II*. The band is often credited with inventing heavy metal, a claim that they vigorously deny, but Led Zeppelin were the biggest band of the 70s. All of their studio albums went top ten in the US, six of them hitting the number one spot. Refusing to issue singles (in the UK at least) the band built their reputation with album tracks such as 'Stairway to Heaven', 'Rock and Roll' and 'Kashmir', all of which attracted millions of fans. The band members were also notorious for outrageous behaviour – trashing hotels as they traversed the world in their private jet. In 1980 John Bonham passed away, a death caused in part by his abuse of alcohol. The remaining members, in memory of their drummer, ended the band. They re-formed in 2007 for a one-off show at London's O2 Arena.

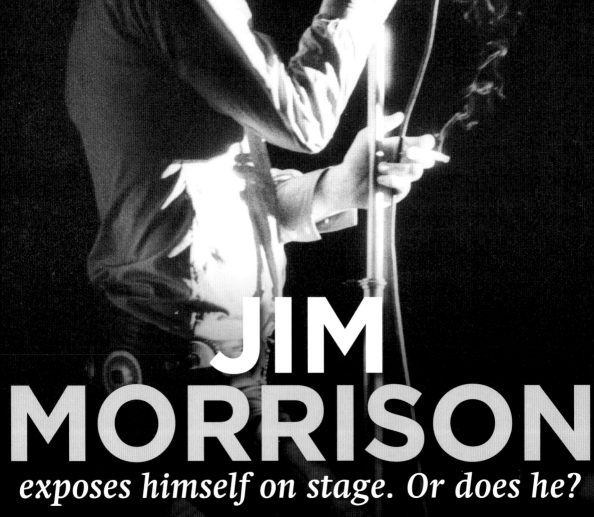

JIM MORRISON

exposes himself on stage. Or does he?

DATE 1 March 1969, The Dinner Key Auditorium, Miami

He was drunk most of the time now, and he was not a good drunk. Never had been. He was a pest when intoxicated. He wrestled with band members, came on to other people's wives, generally made a great nuisance of himself. And now the band that Jim Morrison fronted, the band that had broken through with such style in 1967, was nearing its end. Everyone knew it. Morrison was not helping matters by spending most of his time out of his head. It had been a strange journey for all concerned, a trip that began at the UCLA Film School in Los Angeles and took a downward turn when Morrison exposed himself on stage in Miami. Or did he? That is the question.

Jim Morrison and Ray Manzarek were fellow students at the UCLA Film School. One night Jim 'sang' his poem 'Moonlight Drive' along to a piece of Ray's music. Soon there was a band, the young film buffs joined by guitarist Robbie Krieger and drummer John Densmore. They called themselves The Doors.

With their flamenco-blues guitar, classical-tinged keyboards and jazzy drumming combined with Morrison's beat poetry, the band hit upon a sinister sound which challenged the image of Los Angeles that had been sold to the world. The Los Angeles of The Doors was not one of bikini girls and surfboards and riding the waves to the sound of The Beach Boys. Their LA was cheap hotels, and hookers, and drug addiction, the life of the devil in the city of angels. This was not the America of happy suburbia, but the America about

HE WRESTLED WITH BAND MEMBERS, CAME ON TO OTHER PEOPLE'S WIVES, GENERALLY MADE A GREAT NUISANCE OF HIMSELF

to be engulfed by race riots, political assassination and near civil war.

The band landed a deal with Elektra Records, and hit it big with their second single 'Light My Fire'. So far, so good. But Morrison was a handful. During the recording of the debut album he hosed the studio with a fire extinguisher, later claiming he was on acid. The band's producer, Paul A. Rothchild, thought that sounded like a feeble excuse. Right from the start he thought that Morrison's problem was LSD. Off it, he was manageable; on it, he turned into a dangerous and unpredictable character.

LA WAS CHEAP HOTELS, AND HOOKERS, AND DRUG ADDICTION, THE LIFE OF THE DEVIL IN THE CITY OF ANGELS

With success, Morrison changed his image, poured himself into leather jacket and trousers and created a Lizard King persona. He saw himself as a figurehead for the young, filled with doom and dread but willing to satisfy all. Many girls came to him, and he revelled in his power. He thought he was a genuine poet.

After the success of the first two albums, The Doors found themselves boxed into a corner. New bands had emerged; a bluesier sound had come into vogue. The

Doors were being left behind. As the band's star began to fade, so Morrison became even more obnoxious, provoking fights, antagonizing his band. In 1969 they flew to Miami to play a show at the Dinner Key Auditorium. The venue held 6,000 people; 10,000 crowded in. Morrison took to the stage drunk. The band opened with 'Back Door Man'. Morrison sang a few lines, then he went into a drunken rap. 'You're all a bunch of fucking idiots,' he told the crowd. 'You let people tell you what you are going to do. Let people push you around. You love it, don't ya?'

On he went, on and on. The band kept going into songs, and Morrison would tell them to stop. He would harangue the audience, and they howled their abuse back at him. A fan jumped on stage and drenched Morrison in champagne. Far from being annoyed, the singer motioned for everyone to join him. He formed a circle with the fans. A policeman now ran on and threw everyone back off the stage – including Morrison, who led the fans in a dance. Eventually he was pulled from the crowd and returned to the dressing room.

The next day the band flew to Jamaica for a holiday. It was there that they heard that Morrison was to be charged with indecent exposure and using obscene language. The authorities alleged that Morrison had exposed himself and then simulated masturbation in front of the audience. Confusion reigned. Had he really exposed himself? No one had witnessed it, but that was not to say Morrison was not capable of such a stunt.

Morrison surrendered himself to the authorities, and in August the trial began. Photographer David Levine said he had gone to shoot the gig and remembered being disappointed that Morrison had grown a beard, hiding his good looks. He claimed that at no point did Morrison expose himself. Not so, cried Theodore Jendry, a police officer. 'He pulled out his business and started whirling it.' The jury found Morrison guilty of indecent exposure and profanity. He was given a $50,000 fine and six months in jail. On appeal, the jail sentence was removed.

There was a backlash against the band. Miami radio stations stopped playing the records, and promoters refused to book the band in case the singer was tempted to repeat his lewd act.

Morrison moved to Paris to start a new life as a poet. Just few months later, he was found dead in his bathtub, the victim of a massive heart seizure. He was 27 years old. In 2010 Morrison was posthumously pardoned by the State of Florida. The surviving Doors reacted angrily. 'Nobody would like to have that charge hanging over their head, even if they are dead,' said Robbie Krieger. 'Especially since it never happened.'

James Douglas Morrison was born on 8 December 1943 in Florida. His father was a naval officer, and Morrison was the first of three children. In 1964 Morrison moved to Los Angeles to study film at UCLA. He met keyboard player Ray Manzarek during this period, and together they formed The Doors. After a series of highly charged shows in the LA area, the band was signed to Elektra Records and hit the jackpot with their classic single 'Light My Fire'. Other major hits included 'Hello, I Love You' and 'Touch Me'. By 1967 the band was one of the biggest acts in America, and Morrison had developed a rock-star persona that many referred to as the Lizard King. His penchant for drugs, girls and booze now increased, and as the band's popularity began to slip so Morrison fell deeper into alcohol abuse. By the end of 1970 the band concluded that Morrison's problems made it impossible for him to perform live. In 1971 he moved to Paris, but was found dead in his bath on 3 July of that year. He is buried in Père Lachaise cemetery. His grave has become a place of pilgrimage.

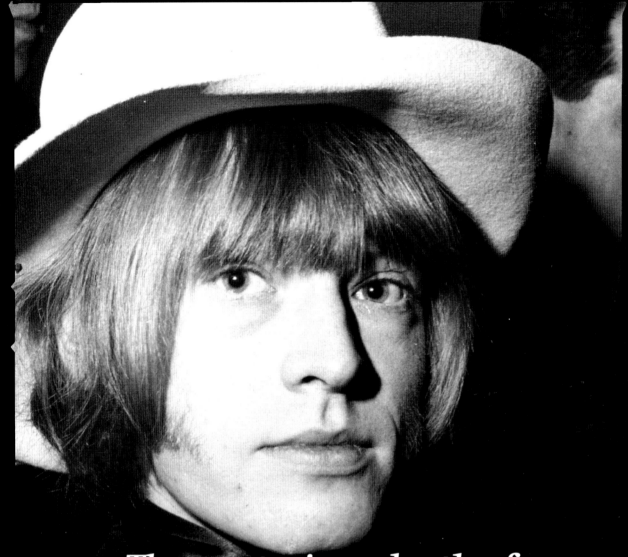

The mysterious death of
BRIAN JONES

DATE 2 July 1969, Cotchford Farm, East Sussex

Too many questions remain; too much mystery still surrounds his death. Only one fact is certain. On the night of 2 July 1969, Brian Jones's body was discovered at the bottom of the swimming pool at his house, Cotchford Farm in East Sussex. Efforts to resuscitate him proved fruitless. Brian Jones, the flamboyant, outrageous Rolling Stones guitarist, was dead. He was 27 years old.

The night that Brian Jones died, three other people were present at Cotchford Farm. They were Frank Thorogood, a builder; Janet Lawson, a nurse; and Anna Wohlin, Jones's Swedish girlfriend.

Many hold Thorogood responsible for Jones's death. He and the guitarist had argued badly that week. Others think that the Stones themselves have to take some blame for Jones's demise. A month previously they had asked him to leave the band he had started. Some believe that the band that Jones wanted to put together, featuring himself and John Lennon, would have dented the Stones' popularity. They also claim that Jones held the copyright on the name The Rolling Stones, and that was a major headache for his ex-bandmates.

Still others believe that Jones was the victim of an Establishment conspiracy to rid the world of a man who dressed like a girl, took drugs like an addict, screwed like a devil. Not a great role model for the young

it was said in the higher levels of society... They might have had a point there.

But Brian Jones was a unique figure in British pop music. He was not a songwriter as such, but a musician whose dress sense was outlandish, eye-catching and stylish. He was also highly fond of drugs, violent to women, manipulative, fragile, argumentative, kind, compassionate, bad-tempered, jealous – but never a bore.

Jones was born in Cheltenham to rich parents. By the time he was 16 his 14-year-old girlfriend was pregnant. Jones

'WHY DIDN'T YOU HELP BRIAN?' WOHLIN SHOUTED AT THE BUILDER. 'WHY DID YOU LEAVE HIM ALONE IN THE POOL?' FRANK SAID NOTHING

moved to London with his 'wife', and fell in love with the blues of Alexis Korner. He formed a band and named it The Rolling Stones after the Muddy Waters song.

In 1963, first Chuck Berry and then Lennon and McCartney gave the Stones their first two hits in 'Come On' and 'I Wanna Be Your Man'. But the Stones really took off when Mick Jagger and Keith Richards started writing their own material. By 1965 they were belting out songs such as 'Satisfaction' and 'Let's Spend the Night Together' to a scandalized country. Soon America was theirs. Brian Jones had everything he could wish for – the girls, the money, the fame. But he was about to lose it all.

BRIAN JONES WAS VIOLENT TO WOMEN, MANIPULATIVE, FRAGILE, KIND, COMPASSIONATE BAD-TEMPERED, JEALOUS – BUT NEVER A BORE

In the summer of 1967, Brian and Keith Richards went on holiday together. With them was Jones's girlfriend, the beautiful Anita Pallenberg, plus a driver. They drove down through Europe to Marrakesh in Keith's car, drinking and smoking and sniffing. One night, a very stoned Jones asked Pallenberg to engage in an orgy with him and a local sex worker. Pallenberg refused; Brian attacked her. She ran to Keith for comfort and protection. The next day Brian went to see a local band. He loved Moroccan music. When he came back to the hotel Anita and Keith had departed. Brian was devastated. He knew then he had just lost the love of his life to one of his closest friends.

On his return to England, Brian began a succession of relationships, one with a Swedish dancer Anna Wohlin. He also bought a house, Cotchford Farm in East Sussex, once the home of A.A. Milne. He called in a builder, Frank Thorogood. Frank was on the Stones' payroll, available at all times. Jones gave him a room above his garage to stay in whilst work on the house began. Thorogood brought in three workmen to help out.

Meanwhile, the Stones headed into Olympic Studios to begin recording a new album. Brian refused to attend the sessions. Keith and Anita's presence was just too upsetting for him. Time and time again a car was sent to Cotchford, and time and time again it returned to the studio empty. Jagger and Richards became increasingly agitated by Jones's non-appearance.

Finally, they made their move. On 7 June 1969, Mick Jagger, Keith Richards and Charlie Watts drove down to Cotchford Farm and held an emergency meeting with Brian. At the conclusion of that meeting, Jones was no longer a member of the band

Aerial shot of the house once owned by the writer A.A. Milne and subsequently bought by Brian Jones. The Rolling Stones guitarist drowned in the pool beside the house in the summer of 1969.

he had started in 1961. But, baby, was he a rich man. The Stones agreed to give him £100,000 plus £20,000 a year for as long as the band stayed together. By all accounts they parted amicably. Wohlin claims Richards gave Brian a wrap of cocaine just before he left. Brian took all of it and was sick most of the night.

Wohlin claims Jones wanted to leave the Stones anyway. She says he often told her he didn't like their music and was now thinking about putting together a new band. John Lennon was on his radar as was Alexis Korner. He had jam sessions with both. According to Wohlin, Jones began cutting down on the drugs and talking openly and positively about the future. Anna testifies that on 29 June, the Sunday before his death, she was on the phone to a friend when Brian suddenly became jealous. He pushed her to the ground. Seconds later a beam that the builders had been working on came crashing down from the ceiling. Inches either way, and Anna would have been dead. The next day a fuming Brian confronted Thorogood and gave him and his crew their marching orders. Jones then called the Stones' office and ordered Thorogood's money be stopped immediately.

The next day Frank travelled to the Stones' office to collect his last wages. He then returned to Cotchford, empty-handed, to confront Jones. As he hated confrontation, Jones apologized and quickly made up with the builder. As a goodwill gesture, he invited Frank to dinner.

Meanwhile, a nurse named Janet Lawson had arrived. Jones assumed she was with Frank; in fact, she was the girlfriend of a driver named Tom Keylock, who worked for the band. After dinner and drinks, Brian invited everyone to the pool. Lawson stayed in the house whilst the other three jumped into the pool.

Wohlin testifies that Brian began taunting Thorogood. He called him middle-aged, unattractive with a low-paid job. But Jones, he had the money, the looks, the house, the fame, the girl. Wohlin told Brian to stop winding the builder up, but Jones continued. Thorogood grabbed Jones and held him under water for a bit. When Brian came up he was laughing loudly.

Wohlin claims that Janet Lawson shouted to her that there was a phone call. Wohlin got out of the pool and told Lawson she would take the call in her bedroom. When she got there and picked up the phone the line was dead.

Wohlin started changing her clothes, and as she did the phone rang again. This time Terry, a friend from Sweden, was on the line with all the latest London gossip. Ten minutes into the conversation Wohlin suddenly heard Janet hysterically shouting and screaming. She rushed downstairs to the kitchen to discover Thorogood with

a towel around his neck trying to light a cigarette with hands that were shaking badly. Pushing past him, Wohlin rushed to the pool, passing a crying Janet who stood by the kitchen door. She could not see Brian anywhere until she looked into the pool. There, at the bottom, Brian Jones lay motionless. Wohlin dived into the water and reached Brian within seconds. She pulled him to the surface of the pool. Holding Brian's head up she swam to the edge and began shouting for Frank to help her. Frank did appear but, according to Wohlin, walked slowly towards her. He finally bent down and helped pull Brian out of the water.

THOROGOOD GRABBED JONES AND HELD HIM UNDER WATER FOR A BIT. WHEN BRIAN CAME UP HE WAS LAUGHING LOUDLY

'Why didn't you help Brian?' Wohlin shouted at the builder. 'Why did you leave him alone in the pool?' Frank said nothing. Janet now came rushing towards them and started giving Jones a heart massage. Finally, she looked up at Wohlin and simply said: 'Anna, it's no use, you've lost him.' An ambulance arrived, and so did the police. Wohlin was taken to her bedroom, and a doctor tried to sedate her. She refused the medicine. By the next morning Anna was convinced that Thorogood had murdered Brian, a conviction strengthened when the pair went to the police station to be interviewed. 'The only thing you need to tell them,' the builder told her as they approached the police station, 'was that Brian had been drinking and that his drowning was an accident. You don't have to tell them anything else. I left Brian to go to the kitchen and light a cigarette, and I don't know any more than you.'

Worn out with grief and lack of sleep, frightened and confused, Wohlin went along with the builder's instructions. She later admitted she buried the truth. She was frightened, she claims, of ending up like Brian. 'Today,' she says, 'I am ashamed for not telling the truth.'

At the inquest the coroner concluded that Brian's death had been misadventure. Yet Brian was a strong swimmer and a seasoned drink and drug taker. Would a few drinks and the one pill found in his system really be enough to disorientate him and send him plummeting to his death? Unlikely.

At The Rolling Stones' free concert in London's Hyde Park, which took place two days later, Mick Jagger read a poem by Shelley in memory of Brian and released thousands of butterflies into the sky. It was a poignant reminder of how Brian Jones had not only lost his girl that summer but had also lost his band – and his life.

BRIAN JONES
1942–1969

Lewis Brian Hopkins Jones was born on 28 February 1942 to a decidedly middle-class family. He was raised in Cheltenham, Gloucestershire. In 1959 he made his then-girlfriend pregnant. She had the baby, which was adopted. Jones moved to London to avoid more scandal, and it was there he formed the band that the world would come to know as The Rolling Stones. Initially, Jones was the leader of the band, but that position was usurped when singer Mick Jagger and guitarist Keith Richards began writing hit songs. Jones's main job then became to provide interesting instrumentation for their records – he was a fine musician. Jones was also a smart dresser and one of the first pop stars to pioneer the androgynous look. As he lost control of the band, so Jones slipped into heavy drug abuse. In 1969 Jones was kicked out of The Rolling Stones. He began plotting a new group that would feature equally famous musicians such as John Lennon, Alexis Korner and Steve Marriott, but passed away before he could bring such a band to fruition.

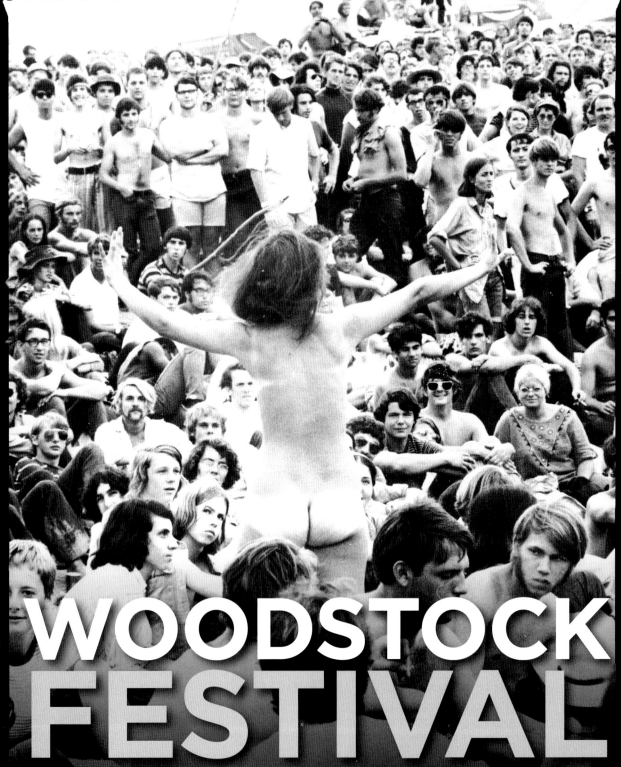

WOODSTOCK FESTIVAL

the defining moment of the 60s

DATE 15–17 August 1969, Bethel, New York

It wasn't meant to happen this way. The main purpose of the festival was monetary, to raise funds to build a highly profitable recording studio in Woodstock, a beautiful location top-heavy with musicians such Dylan and The Band. The real legacy of that plan was the name of the festival, which took place near the town of Bethel, some miles away. The site originally intended for the event was an unlovely industrial park near Wallkill.

It was not meant or planned in any way to be one of the most significant cultural events of the decade, attract half a million people, become a symbol of the decade and bestow the town of Woodstock, New York, with lifelong fame. But then that was the 60s for you. You never knew what was around the corner.

The organizers of Woodstock Festival were four young men: John Roberts, Joel Rosenman, Artie Kornfeld and Mike Lang. Roberts was the heir to a pharmaceutical fortune, and he and his friend Rosenman were looking for a way to invest some of that money and make a profit.

They placed an ad in *The New York Times* that stated: 'Young men with unlimited capital looking for interesting, legitimate investment opportunities and business propositions.' That is how they met Kornfeld and Lang. Through discussions they hit upon the idea of building a studio in Woodstock. The initial money would come from a festival that they planned to stage in August.

The four men settled on Wallkill as the location, and began approaching various bands. Those who turned the men down included Dylan, The Beatles, The Doors, The Byrds, The Moody Blues and Joni Mitchell. It was only when Creedence Clearwater Revival said yes that other bands started to come on board. Tickets

THE YOUNG OF AMERICA SHOWED IT WAS POSSIBLE TO COME TOGETHER AND WORK FOR THE GREATER GOOD. THIS MADE WOODSTOCK THE YARDSTICK BY WHICH ALL FESTIVALS ARE STILL MEASURED

were now printed up, and they were not cheap: $7 for one day, $13 for two, $18 for the weekend.

However, a month and a half before the festival was due to begin, Wallkill council voted against giving the four men permission. The town had no desire to see thousands of dirty long-haired young men and women descend upon them with their loud music and their even louder drugs. Luckily, Max Yasgur, a farmer in nearby Bethel, offered his 600-acre farm to stage the festival. The organizers had to start again, building stages, bringing in food stalls, water, toilet facilities.

On Wednesday 13, two days before the festival was due to start, word leaked

'IF WE JOIN THEM WE CAN TURN THE ADVERSITIES THAT ARE THE **PROBLEMS OF AMERICA** TODAY INTO HOPE FOR A BETTER AND A MORE PEACEFUL FUTURE'

out, and the hippie community moved in. As the organizers rushed around trying to get everything in place, 50,000 people arrived and placed themselves right in front of the main stage. There was no way the organizers could get all of them to pay.

Plus they had already sold a fair amount of tickets in advance.

They had no choice but to declare Woodstock a free festival. On hearing this, one million people tried to get there, and half of them were turned away by the police. That left the organizers to deal with only half a million people.

On Friday night, the folk night, Richie Havens walked on stage, and Woodstock began. That night the huge crowd were entertained by Tim Hardin, Arlo Guthrie and Joan Baez amongst others. On the Saturday more big names delivered stunning performances: Country Joe McDonald, John Sebastian, Santana, Canned Heat, The Incredible String Band, Grateful Dead, Creedence, Janis Joplin, Sly and the Family Stone, The Who and Jefferson Airplane. The latter finished their set at 8.30 on Sunday morning.

The music picked up again at 3.30 that afternoon with Joe Cocker, The Band, Johnny Winter and Crosby Stills Nash and Young. As the day wore on people began to leave. By the time the festival's final performer, Jimi Hendrix, took the stage there were 25,000 people left to hear the dynamic 16-song set.

But what set Woodstock apart was not the music, much of which was exemplary, it was the crowd's behaviour. Despite the aggravation – the quest for water and toilets and food – only three deaths were recorded at Woodstock, one caused by a tractor accident, one a ruptured appendix and one a drug overdose. There were two births and no outbreaks of violence, despite trying conditions that included a lot of rain and mud. The young of America showed it was possible to come together and work for the greater good.

> ## WHEN THE RAIN HITS, SOMEONE TELLS THE CROWD TO TRY NOT TO FALL OVER AS **THERE IS LSD IN THE MUD.** ANOTHER SHOUTS OUT FROM THE STAGE THAT IF THEY ALL THINK REALLY HARD THE RAIN WILL GO AWAY. AND IT DID

It was this realization that gave Woodstock its cachet and made it the yardstick by which all festivals are still measured. Max Yasgur, the farmer, said of the people who were camped on his ground: 'If we join them we can turn the adversities that are the problems of America today into hope for a better and a more peaceful future.'

For the organizers those words might have been beautiful, but they certainly did not cover up the reality – which was that they were now $1 million in debt with some 70 lawsuits filed against them. The fact that they had created what is now considered the greatest rock festival ever was of little comfort.

Their escape came a year later when the film *Woodstock*, which was directed by Michael Wadleigh and edited by Thelma Schoonmaker and Martin Scorsese, became a huge hit. Kornfeld had approached Warner Brothers and asked for money to film the event. Only one executive thought the project worthwhile. Putting his job on the line, Fred Weintraub handed Kornfeld $100,000. The success of the film did much to alleviate the men's financial woes.

As did the release of two Woodstock albums, which used material from all the acts over the three days. Both albums also included memorable stage announcements. When the rain hits, someone tells the crowd to try and not fall over as there is LSD in the mud. Another shouts out from the stage that if they all think really hard the rain will go away.

And it did. On Sunday afternoon, with the crowd chanting. 'Rain, rain, go away,' the clouds suddenly broke, and the sun shone down on the people. It was one of the most magical moments of the 60s, and one of the reasons why this festival is enshrined in history.

Four months later, The Rolling Stones tried to create a Woodstock of their own with the Altamont Festival, and the magic of it all was destroyed.

THE ALTAMONT FESTIVAL

and the end of the 60s

DATE 6 December 1969, California

Eight dollars. Not a lot of money, right? Wrong. Back in 1969 that was an outrageous price for a gig. Most cost three dollars, tops. Eight dollars? That was what it cost to see the Stones on their first American tour in three years. It was the highest price ever for a rock'n'roll concert. The free Altamont Festival at the close of the tour was meant as a kind of peace offering, but when it was over four people were dead, one murdered. That is why for many people Altamont was the festival that signalled the end of idealism, the end of peace and love, the end, in fact, of the 60s.

When the Stones' tour began, their first without Brian Jones in their ranks, venues quickly sold out everywhere. The Stones carried a reputation as the world's greatest rock'n'roll band, and everyone wanted to see that claim vindicated.

Despite this success, the Stones were taken aback by the vitriol hurled at them by the underground press that represented rock culture. Ralph Gleason at *Rolling Stone* was particularly scathing about the band's ticket pricing. He argued that such naked greed was at odds with the culture's idea of itself as a movement of equality, in which music was a liberating force towards building a better world.

To appease the likes of Gleason and the hippies and the right-on freaks, The Stones agreed to organize and play a free festival at the tour's end. The free gig was scheduled for 6 December 1969.

The idea had arisen after informal discussions backstage with Jerry Garcia of the Grateful Dead. The Stones asked Garcia to headline the festival, and Garcia suggested the band use the local Hells Angels as their security. As the Stones had successfully used the British Angels at their Hyde Park Concert that summer, Jagger and Richards thought Garcia's idea had great merit. No police authority figures would be involved at all, and the concert had the potential to be a second Woodstock and therefore appease all the Stones' critics. Perfect.

The original venue for the show was to be the massive Golden Gate Park in San Francisco. However, a football game at

A BUNCH OF STUDENTS HANDED OUT LSD TABS CUT WITH SPEED. THE ANGELS BEGAN GULPING THEM DOWN FOLLOWED BY LARGE AMOUNTS OF BEER AND WINE. **THE CROWD STARTED GETTING PARANOID, AND SO DID THE ANGELS**

the stadium located within that park on the day of the festival ruled that idea out. The venue was then switched to the Sears Point Raceway, but after a dispute over film rights the concert was switched once more, this time to the Altamont Raceway.

The decision on the venue was made just two days before the concert was due to begin and caused a number of problems. There was not enough time to install portable toilets, and very few food stands could be erected. Medical supplies would be in short supply, and there was little drinking water. Worse, because of the geography of Altamont, the stage was situated at the bottom of a slope and could not be positioned at a higher and much safer vantage point.

These issues as well as many others were discussed on the Thursday night in a meeting between the Stones' road manager, Sam Cutler, Rock Scully, the Grateful Dead's manager, and Pete Knell of the San Francisco Hells Angels. Knell opened up by telling the two men that the Angels were outlaws and not into policing events. However, if they were given $500 worth of beer, delivered in buckets of ice, they would ensure that no one from the audience would come on to the stage. This was agreed. Sonny Barger, the most famous Hells Angel in the world, recalls that his brief was to 'sit on the edge of the stage so nobody could climb over me, and I could drink beer until the show was over. And that's what I went there to do.'

The Stones now made public which bands were playing and the order they would appear in. The list named Santana, Jefferson Airplane, Flying Burrito Brothers, Crosby Stills and Nash, the Stones and then the Grateful Dead. On Friday 5 December, the day before the show, people began arriving at Altamont.

At two in the morning of the Saturday Mick Jagger and Keith Richards arrived to take a look at the site. Jagger, dressed in a red velvet cape and cap, was welcomed by the fans. He gave interviews saying how happy he was with the festival and then took a helicopter back to his hotel. Richards stayed on site and got wasted.

At seven in the morning, the Angels allowed the crowd that had been gathering to enter the valley and rush down to the stage. By ten o'clock 100,000 people had arrived. Amongst them were a bunch of Berkeley University students who handed out LSD tabs cut with speed. The Angels were also given the drug, and began gulping it down with large amounts of beer and wine. The crowd started getting paranoid, and so did the Angels.

Santana were the first band on. Halfway through their set a young man tried to get on stage. Several Angels swarmed on to him, punched and kicked him to the ground. Carlos Santana later told reporters that: 'During our set I could see a guy from the stage who had a knife and just wanted to stab somebody. I mean, he really wanted a fight. There were kids being stabbed and heads cracking the whole time.'

Next up on stage, Jefferson Airplane. Months before the band had played support to the Stones and they had stolen the show. At first Jagger didn't want the band anywhere near the festival, but given their standing with the San Francisco counterculture, Jagger acquiesced. But he stipulated that there must be at least three bands between them and the Airplane. Just as the band were about to go into their song 'We Can Be Together', another young man jumped on the stage. Immediately, several Angels started hitting him with pool cues before pushing him back into the crowd. As he staggered around, more Angels jumped off the stage and started beating him again.

Disgusted by these violent scenes, Marty Balin, Airplane's guitarist, jumped off the stage and rushed through to help the hapless fan. He shouted for the Angels to stop hitting that kid, and his reward was a hard punch in the face that sent him sprawling to the ground. As he got up and staggered uncertainly back to the stage, Airplane vocalist Grace Slick got hold of the microphone and shouted: 'Why do we have to fight? Everybody please cool it so we can get on with the fun.'

BUT THE PEACE DIDN'T LAST. MINUTES INTO THE CROSBY STILLS AND NASH SET THE VIOLENCE AGAIN FLARED UP, THE ANGELS WADING INTO THE CROWD BEATING BACK EVERYONE WITH THEIR STICKS AND THEIR FISTS

As she did so, a helicopter came into view. It contained Mick Jagger and Mick Taylor. It landed, and as Jagger exited the machine a man with long hair ran up to him and punched him straight in the face. 'I hate you, I hate you,' he screamed. The badly shaken singer was hustled backstage, where he and the rest of the band began nervously waiting in their trailer. Word kept coming back to them about the chaos and the violence out front.

Some respite came when The Flying Burrito Brothers took to the stage. Their melodic, country-tinged songs seemed to act as balm, and for a while the festival settled down. But the peace didn't last. Minutes into the Crosby Stills and Nash set, the violence flared up, the Angels wading into the crowd beating back everyone with their sticks and their fists. Crosby, Stills and Nash made a quick exit and the wait began for the Stones. Meanwhile, the Grateful Dead announced they didn't like what they were seeing and were going back to San Francisco. The Stones would be the last band on that night.

MEREDITH HUNTER TURNED AND PULLED A GUN OUT OF HIS POCKET. AN ANGEL GRABBED THE GUN FROM HIM, AND ANOTHER KNIFED HIM IN THE BACK A SECOND TIME

One of the Stones' tricks was to make audiences wait for their arrival on stage, so as to build up the tension. Despite pleas from the Angels and the organizers to forget that and take the stage as quickly as possible, Mick Jagger refused. He didn't want to appear until dark, he explained, because of his make-up and clothes. They would look much better in the dark than in the sunshine.

The audience waited, and the violence continued. Many people were tripping out on acid. Some reported that they had seen some of the angels smearing LSD on their cheeks before picking up sticks and wading into the crowd. After an hour and a half the Stones finally made their way to the stage.

They stepped out to find themselves hemmed in on all sides by roadies and Angels. There must have been more than 150 people on that tiny stage. Jagger was wearing an orange-and-black satin cape, and he was right: he looked more demonic in the darkness with the stark lights bearing down on him. The band launched into 'Jumpin' Jack Flash'. As they performed, four Angels spotted someone in the crowd and dived in after him. A fight ensued as the band played hesitantly on.

Sated, the Angels returned to the stage. Jagger pleaded for the people on the stage to move back so he could dance but there was nowhere to move back to. Meanwhile, several individuals rushed the stage only to be beaten back. It was like some sort of sick game, rush and punch.

The band moved into 'Sympathy for the Devil'. A nude girl now made a move towards Jagger. Before she could reach him, five Angels grabbed her, but she gripped an amplifier and refused to budge. The Angels tried to loosen her grip. Jagger saw what

A couple of Hells Angels on the stage at the Altamont Festival where Meredith Hunter would be murdered. The Stones wanted Altamont to be their Woodstock – it turned into hell on earth instead.

was happening and, in that whiny sarcastic voice of his, said: 'Fellas, I'm sure it doesn't take all of you to take care of this.'

The Angels glared at him, infuriated by his put-down. But before they could do anything, Jagger suddenly shouted to Mick Taylor 'Fuck, man... there's somebody out there... there's a cat pointing a gun at us.'

Meredith Hunter was a 17-year-old kid with a black skin and a blonde girlfriend named Patty. On the day of his murder he wore a bright green suit and had ingested a large amount of methamphetamine. When the Stones were due on stage Meredith had gone to the car to get Patty, who was

partying with friends. They came down the hill, Meredith high and determined to get as close to the stage as possible. Eventually he found himself standing next to a young boy called Paul Cox.

Cox later recalled that at the point Meredith arrived he was keeping his eyes on the stage, studiously ignoring a Hells Angel who had been staring at him with violent intent for quite a few minutes. 'He kept looking at me,' Cox said, 'and then suddenly they were hassling this Negro boy next to me...'

The Angel in question now leant down and grabbed Meredith's hair, causing the boy to whoop in pain. The Angel laughed at Hunter's discomfort, and Hunter glared at him. So the Angel leant down, smacked him in the mouth and then leapt down onto the ground in order to beat him further. Hunter tried to run away but was caught by several Angels, one of whom drew out a knife and plunged it into Meredith's back.

Meredith turned and pulled a gun out of his pocket. An Angel grabbed the gun from him and another knifed him in the back a second time.

'THEY KEPT BLOCKING US. THEY KNEW HE WAS GOING TO DIE. **THEY WANTED HIM TO DIE** PROBABLY SO HE COULDN'T TALK. IT TOOK ABOUT 15 MINUTES TO GET HIM BEHIND THE STAGE'

Meredith stumbled to his knees then stood and started limping away as fast as he could. But the Angels caught up with him and pushed him to the ground and started kicking him all over his body and face. When they were done, the Angel who had first hit Meredith stood on his head for a minute and then walked away.

The remaining Angels gathered round the broken boy. 'Don't touch him,' one Angel warned the crowd. 'He's going to die anyway, so let him die.'

The Angels guarded Meredith for several minutes before walking away. Now several people rushed to his aid, one of whom was Paul Cox. They ripped off Meredith's jacket and shirt to expose three large holes in his body: one in his spine, one in his side, the last in his temple. Cox and a doctor named Robert Hiatt then picked up the still-breathing Meredith and started towards the stage to get him urgent medical assistance.

Aware of the commotion, the band ground to a halt. Jagger implored everyone 'to just cool out. Everybody be cool now.' The band started up again, but their playing was uncertain and flaccid. Jagger, who had so wanted to present himself to the world as a rock god of Dionysian proportions, was now rendered a weak, ineffectual boy in a bad Halloween costume.

Someone tried to get on stage to tell Jagger about the knifing, but was thrown back. Jagger stopped the song again. 'Why are we fighting? We don't want to fight at all… we gotta stop right now. You know, if we can't there's no point.'

Some of the audience shouted at Jagger to stop, but Jagger couldn't make out their words. The band started up again as Cox and the doctor tried to get Meredith onto the stage, and from there back to the medical tent. But the Hells Angels wouldn't let them through. 'They kept blocking us,' Cox later recalled. 'They were saying "Go around, go around the other way." They knew he was going to die in a matter of minutes. They wanted him to die probably so he couldn't talk... It took about 15 minutes to get him behind the stage.'

The doctor who finally attended to Hunter was helpless. There was no medical equipment on the site and no helicopter to ferry him out to a hospital. Hunter died within moments of getting help. 'The people in charge of this concert are morally irresponsible,' one doctor was later quoted as saying.

Meanwhile, Jagger was on stage, again pleading for calm, again pleading for the violence to stop. Keith now stepped up to his microphone and lambasted a bunch of Hell Angels who were still fighting. Their response was swift. One of them went up to Keith's mike, looked straight at the guitarist and said: 'Fuck you.'

Finally, everyone settled – in a manner of speaking. The Stones got to perform their 'Brown Sugar', 'Midnight Rambler', 'Gimme Shelter' and 'Honky Tonk Women' before finishing – ironically – with 'Street Fighting Man'. Then they quit the stage and headed for their helicopters, getting out of the hellhole that was Altamont.

The following day one of the performers, David Crosby, gave an interview in which he commented: 'We didn't need the Angels. I'm not downgrading the Angels, because it's not healthy and because they only did what they were expected to do... But the Stones don't know about the Angels. To them an Angel is something in between Peter Fonda and Dennis Hopper. That's not real... But I don't think the Angels were the major mistake. They were just the obvious mistake. I think the major mistake was taking what was essentially a party and turning it into an ego game and a star trip. An ego trip of "look how many of us there are", and a star trip for The Rolling Stones.'

'THE PEOPLE IN CHARGE OF THIS CONCERT ARE **MORALLY IRRESPONSIBLE,**' ONE DOCTOR WAS LATER QUOTED AS SAYING

The Stones refused to comment. They would not visit the States again for three years. In the summer of 1971 Alan Passaro, a Hells Angel, was tried for the murder of Meredith Hunter. Having watched footage of Hunter at Altamont, waving a gun, the jury returned a verdict of not guilty and Passaro walked free. In 2003 the Alameda County Sheriff's Office began a two-year investigation into the possibility of a second Hells Angel having taken part in the stabbing. Finding that Passaro acted alone, the office closed the case for good on 25 May 2005.

STEVIE WONDER
AND MARVIN GAYE
win artistic freedom at Motown

DATE 1971, Detroit

t is early 1967, and Motown is the hottest record label in America. A crack army of musicians, producers and songwriters have created an unstoppable hit-making machine. That year alone, the company is to make $30 million from hits such as 'Bernadette' by the Four Tops, 'Jimmy Mack' by Martha and the Vandellas and 'Ain't No Mountain High Enough' by Marvin Gaye and Tammi Terrell.

On 14 October 1967 tragedy strikes Motown and this changes it forever. Tammi Terrell and Marvin Gaye take to the stage at the Hampden Sydney College in Virginia. They begin singing, and suddenly Terrell collapses into Gaye's arms. He rushes her backstage, and the stricken singer is taken to hospital. She will now undergo eight operations to try to contain the tumour in her brain.

Motown's response is hardly the most understanding. Anxious to maintain the chart momentum that Marvin and Tammi have set in motion, they push her back into the studio at every opportunity. When she is too ill to perform, they bring in a stand-in – Valerie Simpson – to fake Tammi's vocals, most notably on the big UK hit single 'The Onion Song'. Marvin reacts badly to Motown's manoeuvres. He begins refusing to record or perform live. He is disillusioned with the Motown hit machine and its many demands.

His escape route comes from the most unlikely source. One day Renaldo Benson of the Four Tops sees a scuffle between police and protesters over a piece of land called People's Park. It inspires him to create a guitar riff, which he takes to lyricist Al Cleveland. The song they emerge with is called 'What's Going On'.

The other Four Tops refuse the song. It is a protest song, they protest, which is not good for sales. So Benson goes to see Marvin.

MARVIN REACTS BADLY TO MOTOWN'S MANOEUVRES. HE **REFUSES TO RECORD OR PERFORM LIVE.** HE IS DISILLUSIONED WITH THE MOTOWN HIT MACHINE AND ITS MANY DEMANDS

Gaye is still driving Motown mad with his sullen behaviour. In 1967 his masterful version of the song 'I Heard It Through the Grapevine' had shot to number one all over the world. Yet Gaye remains nonplussed by its success, refusing to promote the single or to tour.

GORDY FAMOUSLY DECLARES IT ONE OF THE WORST SONGS HE HAS EVER HEARD. HE SWEARS MOTOWN WILL NEVER SANCTION ITS RELEASE

On 16 March 1970 Tammi Terrell passes away. At the funeral Gaye breaks down in public. He later announces he will never record duets with a female singer again, nor will he perform live. (Within three years he has broken both promises.) Instead, at a Motown family picnic, he announces that he is going to become a professional footballer.

In June 1970 Gaye records 'What's Going On'. Gone is the four-four standard and the percussive drive that made the classic Motown sound. Now there is a mid-tempo groove, a deep bass line, a plaintive saxophone and Marvin's searching lyrics. The vocals have also been double-tracked, an effect that only happened because an engineer pressed the wrong buttons. When the recording is finished, Gaye calls Berry Gordy. He excitedly tells his boss he has cut the best song of his career and wants to record an album of similar material, songs that will tackle the huge social problems America is experiencing both at home and in Vietnam. Gordy is aghast. His reading of Marvin Gaye is simple. The man is a huge sex symbol. Why the hell would he give that up to make protest songs? On hearing the song, Gordy famously declares it one of the worst he has ever heard. He swears Motown will never sanction its release. Marvin shrugs his shoulders and says fine. I will not record a thing until my record is released. The stand-off lasts seven months.

Gordy is spending much of his time in Los Angeles. Back in Detroit, the company know that they need something new from Marvin. The only thing they have in the bank is 'What's Going On', so they bite the bullet and release it. Barney Ales, Motown's vice-president, flies to LA to tell Gordy. By the time he lands, reorders for a further 100,000 singles have been placed. On hearing this Gordy smiles and orders Gaye back into the studio to cut an album that still regularly figures in lists of the greatest albums ever recorded.

At the same time, a young Motown performer called Stevland Judkins, better known to the world as Stevie Wonder, is making a name for himself. He had been a child star, but is now blossoming into a consummate songwriter. He is 21 years old and about to receive $1 million in backdated royalties. On taking his cheque, Wonder springs a surprise. He tells Motown he will not be signing a new contract. Instead, he is off to New York to make an album that he will sell to the highest bidder. In New York Wonder hooks up with Robert Margouleff and Malcolm Cecil from the band Tonto's Expanding Head Band. He is intrigued by their use of a new instrument called the Moog synthesizer, and wants to know everything about it. The pair teach Wonder all they knew about the Moog, and his imagination is set free.

Music comes bursting out of him. 'I think in the first week we recorded close to 35 tunes,' Cecil later recalls, 'and we laid down close to 100 tracks before the album was finished.' The music that Stevie Wonder writes and records in this incredible period places him in a new category, one that puts him on a par with Dylan and The Beatles. His work is also to help tear down the divisions that dog American music.

And there is a happy ending. Stevie Wonder's New York album, the very appropriately titled *Music of My Mind,* is picked up by Motown. The label also agrees to give Wonder the artistic freedom that he so desperately needs. The same concession is made to Marvin Gaye. After winning this hard-earned right, Stevie Wonder and Marvin Gaye go on to create two of the richest and most rewarding bodies of work in music.

Stevland Hardaway Judkins was born six weeks premature on 13 May 1950 in Saginaw, Michigan. His blindness was diagnosed soon after his birth. When he was four, his parents divorced and the family moved to Detroit. He began making music very young, and by the age of 12 was proficient in piano, bass, harmonica and drums. In 1963 he scored his first chart hit with 'Fingertips (Part One)', and by the late 60s was a chart regular with songs such as 'For Once in my Life' and 'My Cherie Amour'. In 1971 Motown handed him $1 million in back-royalties, and Wonder negotiated a contract that gave him complete musical freedom. This allowed him to establish himself as one of the century's leading songwriters with a succession of classic albums that include *Music of My Mind*, *Talking Book*, *Innervisions*, *Songs in the Key of Life*. In the 80s his song 'Happy Birthday' did much to establish Martin Luther King's birthday as a public holiday in the US. Wonder has espoused many social causes, and he is a genuine icon of American music.

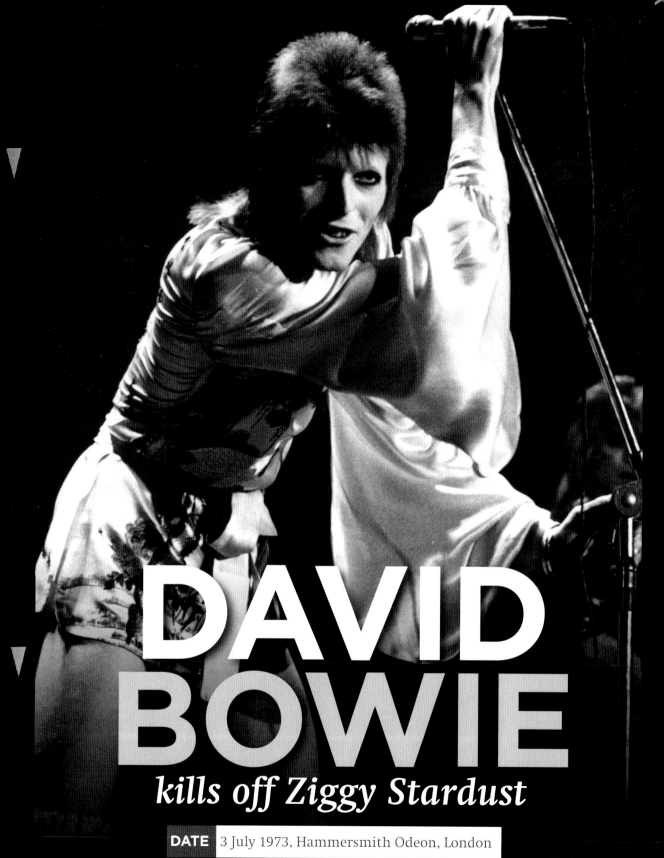

DAVID BOWIE

kills off Ziggy Stardust

DATE 3 July 1973, Hammersmith Odeon, London

O n the night of 3 July 1973, at the Hammersmith Odeon in London, David Bowie steps up to the microphone and addresses his audience. 'This is not only the last date of the tour,' he tells his screaming fans, 'but the last show we will ever do.' And on that score he is correct. Bowie will never again play Ziggy Stardust, the character that catapulted him to fame. That night, Bowie not only kills off his most famous creation. He also puts to the sword the musical genre that Ziggy has come to represent – glam rock.

'If Sergeant Pepper was the culminating statement of the 1960s,' *Creative Loafing* magazine once stated, 'the same can be said of Ziggy in the 1970s.'

Glam rock begins at the start of the decade, lasts about three years. Glam rock is a straight beat and dumb riffs. Its practitioners pour glitter over their hair, apply make-up to their faces and stagger around town in platform boots and gaudy colourful jumpsuits. Glam rock is a nonsense that produces some great singles. For a man who since 1966 has expressed a desire to put some theatricality into rock'n'roll, glam rock is the perfect vehicle.

David Bowie's role in the glam-rock story begins – as all stories do – back in someone's unknowing past. Vince Taylor was a British rock'n'roller who operated in the late 50s and early 60s, played venues

such as The 2i's in Soho, wrote great records such as 'Brand New Cadillac'. He wore a black leather jacket, had greased-back hair and entertained some crazy thoughts. He absolutely believed that there was a link between himself, Jesus and UFOs. On stage one night he declared he was the son of God. His career took a bit of a dip after that pronouncement.

In 1966 Taylor meets a young singer by the name of David Jones. Jones likes Taylor because he parties and he drinks and he has drugs and he does crazy things. Jones recalls sitting on a London pavement watching Taylor point out on a map where the spaceships were about to land.

When David Jones becomes David Bowie, he does not forget about Taylor. Four years later, as he begins putting together the story of the character he named Ziggy

Stardust, Bowie draws on Taylor's life and career. Bowie creates Ziggy Stardust in 1970 in America. For Bowie, a man fascinated by style and image, this is a time of great frustration. All around Bowie is long hair and beads and beards and denim – denim everywhere, on the bands, on their fans. Bowie finds it all so dull.

THEY ARE HIGHLY UNCOMFORTABLE IN THESE CLOTHES UNTIL AFTER THE GIG, WHEN LOADS OF GIRLS RUSH BACKSTAGE TO SLEEP WITH THEM

Yet he knows the ways of pop. He knows that as soon as one thing hits, the opposite will be along to replace it. Prog rock, then punk rock. Bland 70s soul, then hip hop. Bowie will now take music in the opposite direction, towards glamour and outrage. In May 1971 Bowie begins work on the Ziggy project. As he does so, his longtime friend and rival Marc Bolan hits the big time. Bolan's singles 'Hot Love' and 'Ride a White Swan' sell millions. Bolanmania erupts, and Bowie looks on enviously and plans a better strategy.

Bowie now reins in his music, gives it a much harder pop-rock sound than before. His new songs are guitar-driven, succinct and delivered with panache. He knows that the album he has just recorded, *Hunky Dory*, does not have an angle. It is a collection of great songs that are slightly out of time. Bowie turns his attention to forging a more contained sound. Glam rock is now a fact of life, and Bowie must bend to that fact if he wants to survive.

He decides to take the Ziggy concept one step further and actually become the character. This is unprecedented move. To road-test his new direction, Bowie forms a fictitious band called Arnold Corns, fronted by his friend, the fashion designer Freddie Burrett. An Arnold Corns single featuring 'Moonage Daydream' and 'Hang On to Yourself' duly appears and does nada.

In December *Hunky Dory* is released. Bowie's picture on the cover evokes memories of great female Hollywood stars – Bacall, Garbo, Hepburn. The album garners great reviews but fails to sell. This is fortuitous. Without any distractions Bowie is now able to start putting together the Ziggy look.

His co-conspirator is Freddie Burrett, and Burrett's muse is a model named Daniella Parmar. 'Daniella was the first girl I had seen with peroxide-white hair with cartoon images cut and dyed into the back,' Bowie once wrote. 'Blessed with absolute style, she unwittingly changed so much of how female Britain looked – my wife copped her sense of style (and her haircut) 100 per cent...'

Adoring fans hold out their hands to David Bowie. This was the last time he would play his most famous character, Ziggy Stardust, the iconic figure who had launched Bowie into superstardom.

Other influences include the futuristic costumes worn in two Stanley Kubrick films, *2001: A Space Odyssey* and *A Clockwork Orange*. Bowie also takes the calf-high wrestling boot and transforms it into a little tower of shiny vinyl, laced up to the top. The hair style, the bright red top, is borrowed from a picture of a Yamamoto model on the cover of a magazine.

Bowie imagines a series of concerts in which the theatricality will be as important as the music. His main inspiration here is Lindsay Kemp, a mime artist that he has worked with and absolutely reveres. 'I taught him to exaggerate with his body as well as his voice,' Kemp states, 'and the

importance of looking good as well as sounding beautiful.'

Bowie then pulls his masterstroke. He tells *Melody Maker* that he is gay. This admission (he is actually bisexual) sparks massive press interest. At the end of January Bowie unveils the first Ziggy look at a gig in Buckinghamshire. He takes to the stage with bright red hair, bomber jacket, codpiece and red plastic boots. His band wears gold all-in-one Ziggy style suits. They are highly uncomfortable in these clothes until after the gig, when loads of girls rush backstage to sleep with them.

'I'm out all the time to entertain,' Bowie tells the press, 'not just to get up on stage and knock out a few songs. I couldn't live with myself if I did that.'

The shows are received ecstatically, no matter what the crowd size, and Bowie and his band are in fine fettle. They are a great live act that gets better and better night by night. A palpable sense of excitement attaches itself to the Bowie camp. That long-awaited breakthrough is coming into view, and everyone can sense it.

COCAINE AND GROUPIES AND ALCOHOL AND A PUNISHING SCHEDULE, THIS IS BOWIE'S LIFE NOW, AND HE LOVES EVERY MINUTE

In April the first single from the *Ziggy* album, 'Starman', is released. Bowie now pulls a second masterstroke. On a highly popular TV music show, *Top of the Pops*, in front of millions of viewers, he puts his arm around guitarist Mick Ronson's shoulders. The next day in every school in Britain, the kids talk of nothing else. 'Did you see that guy with the strange hair and clothes...' And so the pop process begins.

Interest in Bowie rises considerably. The album *Ziggy Stardust and the Spiders from Mars* is released. It is a concept album, Bowie states in every interview, but like all famous concept albums – think *Sergeant*

Pepper – it is nothing of the sort. Only a handful of the songs on *Ziggy* relate to the story of the tragic magic pop star. But *Ziggy* is certainly an album of its time, an album of many signals, an album of greatness offset by cheap moments, mad moments, inspired moments.

Bowie takes to the road again. At a gig in Oxford, he pulls his third masterstroke. On stage he mimes fellating Mick Ronson's guitar. The place goes crazy. The album rockets into the charts. Bowie now takes the throne.

Success at this level, fans chasing you out of hotels and into dressing rooms and bedrooms, the demands of the media and the promoters and the band and all the others, leads to abuse. Bowie is no different. He later admits: 'It was so much easier for me to live within that character, along with help of some chemical substances at the time, it became easier and easier for me to blur the line between reality and the blessed creature that I had created.'

Cocaine and groupies and alcohol and a punishing schedule, this is Bowie's life now, and he loves every minute. In the way Bolan grabbed 1971 and made it his own, so Bowie takes 1972 and 1973 and refuses to let go. He releases a new single, 'The Jean Genie', in late November, and three months later it is still in the charts. This is the year of 'Blockbuster' by The Sweet and 'Cum On Feel the Noize' by Slade. Glam rock is at its zenith, and Ziggy is the main man. Bowie's new album, *Aladdin Sane*, is released in April 1973. The record has 100,000 advance orders, and Bowie appears on the inside jacket nude and in make-up. Naturally, he sweeps all before him.

He tours once more as Ziggy and somehow finds the time to record an album of cover versions called *Pin Ups*. He then tours America to little response, and squanders a fortune. He returns to the UK and makes the money all over again. He dresses provocatively, his life a manifesto in which no barriers are recognized, be they sexual or otherwise. He plays the pop star to the hilt, acting the spoilt kid for all it is worth and then changing – just like that – into the concerned groovy artist, and all in one day.

For Bowie, the pace proves too fast, too manic. He knows his pop history, knows that for the sake of his career he will have to retreat at some point, like Dylan back in the 60s, to regroup and recover, and then re-emerge in another guise and start the dance all over again.

Which is why on 3 July he kills Ziggy and goes off into the shadows to reinvent himself as something completely different. Glam rock staggers on, but it has lost its leader and starts running out of steam. Within a year it will be gone and forgotten, and the kids will move on to the next thing. And David Bowie will be there waiting for them. Still. For David Bowie there is much more to come – and at least now he can safely say that he has put the ghost of Vince Taylor behind him.

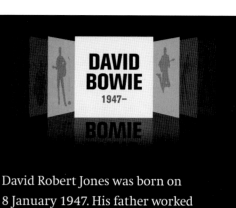

David Robert Jones was born on 8 January 1947. His father worked for the Barnardo's organization and his mother was a cinema usherette. The family lived in south London before moving in 1953 to Bromley in Kent. He attended Bromley Technical School and formed his first band, The Konrads, at age 15. In 1967 he changed his name to Bowie, and in 1969 he hit the charts with his song 'Space Oddity'. A fallow period followed before the *Ziggy Stardust* album catapulted him to fame. Albums such as *Young Americans*, *Station to Station*, *Low* and *Heroes*, established him as the most influential musician of the 70s. Since then singles such as 'Let's Dance' and albums such as *Reality* have sustained his huge appeal. Bowie has appeared in many films and pursued a career as an artist. In 2004 he collapsed on stage and required heart surgery. After that he scaled down his activities. In 2006 he was awarded a Grammy Lifetime Achievement Award. He settled in New York and married the supermodel Iman. He has two children, Duncan (formerly Zowie) and Alexandra.

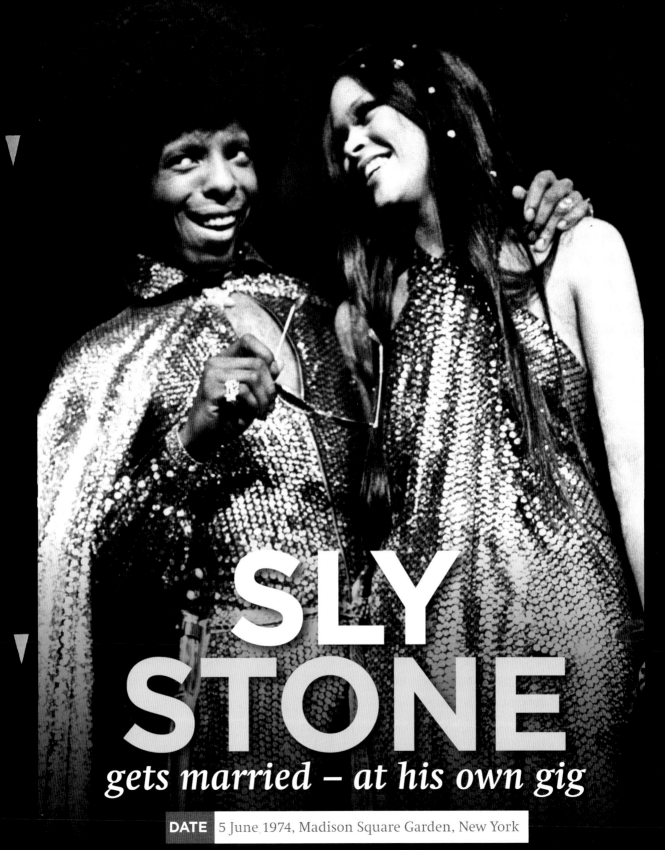

SLY STONE
gets married – at his own gig

DATE 5 June 1974, Madison Square Garden, New York

There were two sisters, Kathleen and April Silva. They were tall and slim, long dark hair falling down their backs, Polynesian, exotic and erotic. It is said that Sly Stone would lie with both girls on his bed, and this arrangement went on for some time. And then one day he chose, and asked Kathleen to marry him. This being Sly, the big bad wolf of funk and soul and pop, he did marry her – but in front of 21,000 fans at Madison Square Garden.

A lot of drugs were around Sly then – cocaine and PCP – and everyone could see the downward path it was taking him on, only no one knew how to get him off it. It was crazy, the stuff he and his brother Freddie were pulling. They would spend their days constantly sniffing cocaine, trying to out-high each other, as somebody put it. Then, on a whim, they would cancel the night's show. Didn't matter where. One time, at Madison Square Garden, the band arrived at the venue, and then Freddie decided not to show. The audience threatened to riot, and the band had to leave hidden in cars that took them out past another huge crowd, the one waiting to get in to see their second show.

Sly fronted it all out, never blinked an eye or apologized. 'Sorry is for sorry people,' he would say. He meant it as well. When eventually – inevitably – the police came to Sly's house and found hundreds of guns and hundreds of pills, Sly was put on trial. Halfway through the proceedings his lawyer went to the toilet only to find his client chopping out lines of cocaine. 'You can't do that,' said the lawyer. 'That is what I pay you for – so I can do this,' Sly replied. 'If you're not the guy that can see to it that I can do this, then I recommend you tell me who the guy is that I should be messing with, because obviously it is not you.'

Yet in the beginning it was all so different. Sly and the Family Stone came together in 1967, and the energy and the colour and sheer bravado they brought was unbelievable. They became one of the all-time great bands, up there with The Beatles and The Isley Brothers.

Sly's music brought together rock and pop and soul in the most exhilarating fashion possible. His band, his art, appealed to American blacks as much as to American hippies. Sly placed R&B in a whole new context by adding rock elements such as guitar riffs and lengthy song structures. The band's sexual and racial line-up and their wild dress sense – all glitter and fringes and crazy clashing colours – reflected this new liberated music.

At Woodstock in 1969 they took to the stage at about four in the morning. Within a quarter of an hour they had thousands of people up on their feet. Yes, that powerful, that good. Didn't matter what audience was in front of Sly and his band, be it all black or all white, they could make any human shake and shimmy.

SLY'S MUSIC BROUGHT TOGETHER ROCK AND POP AND SOUL IN THE MOST EXHILARATING FASHION POSSIBLE

Sly really did ignore all boundaries and taboos, and that is why he was so groundbreaking, why he became a symbol of freedom, and why he was so susceptible to drugs, especially cocaine. In four short years Sly went outwards to inwards, from up to down, from the great exhortations to dance to the music to the brooding dark unpredictable funk of *There's a Riot Going On*, an album that told the world the 60s were over and bad times were coming.

By the time of that album's release Sly was deep into the powders. He was playing the gangster, a man who controlled everyone around him and beat up on his people. He scared his bass player Larry Graham so much Graham truly thought he had ordered a hit on him. And if he had? Well, no eyebrows would have been raised. That is how mean and moody the man had become. 'You can kiss the blackest part of my dark ass,' he once told his manager. The introverted music and irresponsible behaviour did much to damage Sly's standing. People got fed up with paying good money for gigs he never showed up at. His audience began to dwindle.

In 1973, on the phone to his associate Steven Paley, Sly said that he was playing Madison Square Garden, and also that he was getting married to Kathleen Silva. Why don't you combine both events, Paley joked. Sly laughed and then thought...

On 5 June 1974 Sly and Kathleen stood on stage at Madison Square Garden as a preacher said: 'We are gathered here tonight in the sight of God and in this company to join together this man and this woman in holy matrimony...' Beside them 15 models held gold-painted palm leaves. In front of them 21,000 fans roared their approval. If this had been a gimmick to sell out the Garden, then it sure worked,

A party was held afterwards at the Waldorf Astoria. Andy Warhol was amongst the guests, and Steven Paley was Sly's best man. Two writers were given total access to cover the event. One was Maureen Orth. Paley says Sly made a move on her, on his wedding night.

The marriage lasted a year. Kathleen gave him a baby, Sly Jnr, and then the abuse started – abuse of drugs and abuse of trust. In an attempt at reconciliation, Sly and Kathleen flew to Hawaii, her home state, for a break. On their way there she discovered that Sly already had another child, by a member of the band, Cynthia Robinson. She'd had no idea.

They returned to Sly's LA mansion, where he kept his band, his drugs and a vicious pit-bull terrier named Gun. One day, when Kathleen was cleaning the house, she heard a terrible noise. She rushed upstairs to find Gun savaging Sly Jnr who had innocently climbed out of his crib. She knew that pit-bulls never let go of their prey, and so in an inspired move she got on her haunches and began imitating a dog, growling so loudly that Gun dropped the baby and backed away. Kathleen managed to lock the dog in a room. She then grabbed her baby, ran to her car and drove to the neighbours screaming for help. Sly Jnr needed 121 stitches.

Kathleen returned to the house – but only to pick up her possessions. The illusion of her wedding at Madison Square Garden was now gone.

Not long after Sly Stone confessed to a band member 'I think I have done too much shit, too much wrong, and I don't think God will take me back.'

SLY STONE
1944–

Sly Stone was born Sylvester Stewart on 15 March 1944, His family was deeply religious. Whilst attending high school, Sly and his brother Freddie joined bands, one of which was a doo-wop act called The Viscaynes. They released some singles, and Sly also recorded solo under the name Danny Stewart. By 1964 Sly was a disc jockey for San Francisco R&B radio station KSOL, where he included white bands such as The Beatles in his playlists. He also worked as a record producer for Autumn Records, producing for The Beau Brummels and The Mojo Men. One of his productions, Bobby Freeman's 'C'mon and Swim', was a national hit. In 1967 he put together Sly and the Family Stone and over the next five years scored many hits such as 'Dance to the Music', 'Family Affair' and 'If You Want Me to Stay'. Drug abuse and internal dissent did for the band, but Sly kept issuing records of varying quality into the 80s. He then disappeared from view, appearing only occasionally at award ceremonies. In 2008 he went on tour again, but his performances were widely criticized.

SYD BARRETT

and the story of Pink Floyd's 'Wish You Were Here'

DATE 5 June 1975, Abbey Road Studios, London

Up in Studio Three at the Abbey Road Studios, Pink Floyd were in trouble. It was January 1975, and the recording of their ninth album was not going at all well. The ideas were not flowing, the songs were not getting written. There was no urgency and no spark of inspiration for the four musicians gathered there: Roger Waters, Dave Gilmour, Nick Mason and Rick Wright. The band's biggest problem had turned out to be something they could not have anticipated – success. Huge, worldwide, unimaginable success.

Pink Floyd's eighth album, *The Dark Side of the Moon*, had exceeded every expectation. And then some. Released in March 1973, it had started selling and never stopped. Two years on, the album was still prominent in the US charts. It would not drop out of sight for a further 13 years, a staggering statistic. To promote this landmark work the band had toured extensively, and they were exhausted.

In that two years on the road they had managed to work on just three new songs. They blamed this barren period on the commercial consequences of their musical success. 'Suddenly,' observed keyboard player Rick Wright, 'one was aware that Pink Floyd was becoming a product, and that most of our time from then on would be devoted to the business side of the group rather than playing.'

With the world (and not least their record company EMI) urging them to create a follow-up, the band reluctantly returned to Abbey Road in January 1975. The plan was to record the new material they had, and they hoped that the process would provide a springboard for a burst of much-needed creativity. But the band found they were static, moving neither forwards nor backwards. It didn't help that drummer

SYD'S UNRELIABILITY WOULD HAVE BROUGHT THE BAND DOWN. YET WITHOUT SYD BARRETT THERE WOULD HAVE BEEN NO PINK FLOYD

Pink Floyd concerts were known for their incredible visuals and high-quality sounds. Here they are performing in Rotterdam in early 1977. Incredibly, their album *The Dark Side of the Moon*, released in 1973, was still in the charts at this time, remaining there until 1988.

Nick Mason's wife had just left him, and he had no stomach for the sessions ahead. 'I was dead at the drum kit, and it drove everyone crazy,' Mason later admitted.

Roger Waters would describe these initial sessions as 'torturous'. His creativity always came to the fore when he hit upon a concept or overall idea that his songs could then explore to the fullest. No such idea was forthcoming. As the band moved listlessly through every session the impasse they faced seemed unnavigable.

One of the new songs that Waters had ready was called 'Shine On You Crazy Diamond'. It was essentially about the

band's founder, Syd Barrett, the man who had been the band's main songwriter, its creative drive. Syd's use of LSD had rendered him a ghost, a man incapable of speech. Waters had been forced to take over the band and Syd was effectively sacked, since his unreliability would have brought the band down. Yet without Syd there would have been no Pink Floyd. It was a conundrum that had fascinated Waters for years. He would later say: 'It couldn't have happened without him, but on the other hand it couldn't have gone on with him.'

Contemplating Syd's fall from grace, Waters now saw a way out of the fix that the band was in. They had always considered themselves above the machinations of the music business. The selling of albums, the press, the media, all that interfered with the band's sense of themselves as artists creating challenging music. Syd's decline surely symbolized that relationship, the artist smothered by the money-grabbing music business, which cared nothing for art, only for success at any cost. Waters now put forward the idea that his song about Syd would take up side one of the new record. Two other songs, 'Raving and Drooling' and 'You Gotta Be Crazy', would take up side two.

THE ARTIST SMOTHERED BY THE MONEY-GRABBING MUSIC BUSINESS, WHICH CARED NOTHING FOR ART, ONLY FOR SUCCESS AT ANY COST

The band agreed to the plan, but the sessions remained horrible and miserable and fraught with tension. Unable to stand the pressure, Waters called a meeting and urged his band members to unload, to express their dissatisfaction. In doing so, the band realized the trap they were in.

'When you're 15,' Waters later said, 'you dream of a hip bachelor pad, a pretty girlfriend, not getting up until the afternoon, being in a band and having a big hit. Suddenly you have the big hit and your ambitions just evaporate. We were millionaires, and, whatever they say, money changes everything. It put us in a very curious and unpleasant limbo.'

Waters declared he wanted to junk the new material apart from 'Shine On' and start again, this time writing songs that dealt with the relationship between the band and the business world. The only voice of dissent belonged to guitarist David Gilmour. He was madly in love with his soon-to-be wife Ginger, and rigorous self-inspection was the last thing on his mind. But he was outvoted, and the change of direction produced three new songs: 'Welcome to the Machine', 'Wish You Were Here' and 'Have a Cigar'.

On 5 June 1975 Gilmour married Ginger, and a celebration was held at Abbey Road. Before the party began, Waters needed to complete some vocal overdubs on 'Shine On You Crazy Diamond'. The producer Alan Parsons could not make the session so he sent along his assistant, John Leckie. Leckie was standing at the desk when Waters stopped singing and pointed towards Leckie's right.

Leckie turned, and there beside him, holding a plastic bag, wearing a white raincoat, bald and extremely fat, with a toothbrush protruding from one of his coat pockets, was Syd Barrett, the man Waters was singing about at that very moment.

Leckie recognized him straight away. Back in the 60s he had worked with Syd on one of his solo albums. 'Hello,' Leckie said. Syd just grinned. Waters also knew immediately who it was and could not believe the change in Syd's appearance.

THERE BESIDE HIM, WEARING A WHITE RAINCOAT, BALD AND EXTREMELY FAT, WITH A TOOTHBRUSH PROTRUDING FROM HIS POCKET, WAS SYD BARRETT

When Syd Barrett formed the band he was slim, long-haired, wild-eyed and full of creativity. It was he who changed the Floyd from a blues band into a leading exponent of British psychedelic music. Syd gave the band two hits, 'See Emily Play' and 'Arnold Layne', and wrote most of their chart-topping debut album *The Piper at the Gates of Dawn*. His writing methods were unique. 'Arnold Layne' was inspired by a man who stole underwear from washing lines in Cambridgeshire, including one belonging to Roger Waters's mother. 'Apples and Oranges' came about when Syd followed a pretty girl shopping in Richmond and then wrote about her journey that day.

Barrett pushed the band into playing long instrumentals such as 'Interstellar Overdrive', a 16-minute epic that defined the band's early output. Barrett mixed such lengthy improvisations with three-minute pop psychedelia. He was a unique talent, but his use of LSD sapped him terribly.

As his use of the drug increased, so he became ever more withdrawn from the world. His behaviour became erratic. Sometimes he would not even show up for gigs. If he did, he might place Mandrax pills in his hair, and as the lights melted the drug he let the resulting liquid stream down his cheeks. Or he might undertake a TV interview and say nothing. After a while he stopped talking altogether, even to the band. They were forced to give him written notes when they wanted to make any kind of communication.

The band realized that, despite his huge talent, Syd was a liability, a man whose behaviour could finish off the band. The man who had given them fame was threatening to take it all away. They drafted in a new guitarist, Dave Gilmour, and in 1968 Syd left the band. He would record two solo albums (considered masterpieces by the cognoscenti) and then he retired to his mother's house in Cambridge, where he lived until his death in 2006. But at this moment in 1975, here stood Syd in the Abbey Road Studios, listening to 'Shine On You Crazy Diamond'.

Pete Jenner, the band's manager, recalled what happened next. 'I entered the studio. Roger Waters was now sitting on a stool. I sat down next to Roger, who leant over and said: "Do you know who that guy is?" "No," I said. "Isn't he a friend of yours?" "Think," said Roger, "think." I looked, and it suddenly dawned on me. It was Syd! I looked round and Roger had tears in his eyes. It was terribly sad. There was this great, fat, bald, mad person who we used to know and who this song was about sitting there yet quite obviously in another world.'

Jenner went over and introduced himself but the man said very little. Later on they went downstairs to Gilmour's wedding reception, where Syd chatted obliquely to his ex-colleagues, often taking out his toothbrush to rub his teeth before replacing it in his pocket and then smiling enigmatically. He explained his weight gain thus: 'I've got a very large fridge, and it has a lot of pork chops in it.'

And then suddenly he was gone. Off into the night to who knew where? The next day the band flew to Cleveland to start their American tour. All the talk was of Syd, and underneath that talk a sense of guilt was clearly developing. Syd had obviously been very ill when he departed. Should not the band have reached out to him. Were they wrong to have abandoned him in the way they did? Their actions had not been malicious, but born out of exasperation. But now they saw they could have acted far more honourably, and with greater compassion and kindness.

It was a mistake that the rest of the band still feel to this day.

The Pink Floyd were formed in 1964. Their line-up was Syd Barrett (guitar), Roger Waters (bass), Richard Wright (keyboards) and Nick Mason (drums). Initially inspired by blues music, the band, thanks to Barrett's wayward and unique songs, became the figurehead of the mid-60s psychedelic craze in London and had hit singles such as 'Arnold Layne'. They also released their debut album *The Piper at the Gates of Dawn*. Barrett's reckless use of LSD saw him leave the band in 1968. Waters took over songwriting duties, and David Gilmour replaced Syd. They quickly established a new musical direction, which relied on lengthy, carefully plotted musical explorations to seduce the listener. This style reached its commercial zenith in 1973 with *The Dark Side of the Moon*, which has sold more than 45 million copies. Subsequent albums include *Wish You Were Here*, *Animals* and *The Wall*. In the mid-80s tensions between Waters and Gilmour tore the band apart. They re-formed in 2005 for Live 8. Pink Floyd, they declared, still existed and would appear at very special occasions.'

THE SEX PISTOLS

the filth and the fury

DATE 1 December 1976, Thames TV Studios, London

Punk rock was still an underground movement in 1976, the preserve of the young and the hip. In small clubs, punk bands screamed and shouted over loud fast guitars, and their audiences responded in kind. Many gigs ended in chaos. The world knew little of this anarchic scene – until a certain punk band found themselves on tea-time television.

The mainstream media remained blissfully unaware of punk until 1 December 1976. On this day, the pomp-rock band Queen were due to be interviewed on the *Today* programme by chat-show host Bill Grundy but they pulled out at the last minute. Queen's record company, EMI (or, as someone once dubbed them, Every Mistake Imaginable) quickly looked around for a replacement. They settled on The Sex Pistols, a band that they had signed two months previously, and whose controversial new single 'Anarchy in the UK' had just been released.

THE NEWSPAPER DID WHAT ALL PAPERS DO TO BANDS WHO SWEAR AND BEHAVE WITH ABANDON: THEY ATTACKED THEM. AFTER THAT THE BAND WAS SET FOR LIFE

Given what then transpired, this was plain stupidity – or else it was one of the most inspired PR decisions ever. The Pistols argued with Grundy, swore and generally scandalized the television-watching British public. Present that day were Johnny Rotten, Steve Jones, Glen Matlock and Paul Cook. Accompanying the Pistols were the 'Bromley contingent', Siouxsie Sioux, Steve Severin, Simon Barker and a punk rocker by the name of Simone.

Although the show was broadcast only in London, The Sex Pistols and punk rock were national news by the next morning, the whole of the country talking about nothing else. In the grand tradition of rock outrage, parents were shocked and their young exhilarated.

Yet, when one actually reads the whole transcript (see overleaf) an irony emerges. Bill Grundy, the middle-aged chat-show host, acts far more punk than the Pistols. Live on TV he admits to being drunk, he make suggestive comments to a very young Siouxsie Sioux and he urges the band to

Transcript of Bill Grundy's interview with the Sex Pistols, 1 December 1976

GRUNDY *They are punk rockers. The new craze, they tell me. Their heroes? Not the nice, clean Rolling Stones... you see they are as drunk as I am... they are clean by comparison. They're a group called The Sex Pistols, and I am surrounded by all of them...*

JONES *[Reading the autocue] In action!*

GRUNDY *Just let us see The Sex Pistols in action. Come on kids...*

[Film of The Sex Pistols in action is shown; then back to Grundy.]

GRUNDY *I am told that that group [hits his knee with sheaf of papers] have received £40,000 from a record company. Doesn't that seem, er, to be slightly opposed to their anti-materialistic view of life?*

MATLOCK *No, the more the merrier.*

GRUNDY *Really?*

MATLOCK *Oh yeah.*

GRUNDY *Well tell me more then.*

JONES *We've fuckin' spent it, ain't we?*

GRUNDY *I don't know, have you?*

MATLOCK *Yeah, it's all gone.*

GRUNDY *Really?*

JONES *Down the boozer.*

GRUNDY *Really? Good Lord! Now I want to know one thing...*

MATLOCK *What?*

GRUNDY *Are you serious, or are you just making me, trying to make me laugh?*

MATLOCK *No, it's all gone. Gone.*

GRUNDY *Really?*

MATLOCK *Yeah.*

GRUNDY *No, but I mean about what you're doing.*

MATLOCK *Oh yeah.*

GRUNDY *You are serious?*

MATLOCK *Mmm.*

GRUNDY *Beethoven, Mozart, Bach and Brahms have all died...*

ROTTEN *They're all heroes of ours, ain't they?*

GRUNDY *Really... what? What were you saying, sir?*

ROTTEN *They're wonderful people.*

GRUNDY *Are they?*

ROTTEN *Oh yes! They really turn us on.*

JONES *But they're dead!*

GRUNDY *Well suppose they turn other people on?*

ROTTEN *[Under his breath] That's just their tough shit.*

GRUNDY *It's what?*

ROTTEN *Nothing. A rude word. Next question.*

GRUNDY *No, no, what was the rude word?*

ROTTEN *Shit.*

GRUNDY *Was it really? Good heavens, you frighten me to death.*

ROTTEN *Oh all right, Siegfried...*

GRUNDY *[Turning to those standing behind the band] What about you girls behind?*

MATLOCK *He's like yer dad, innit, this geezer?*

GRUNDY *Are you, er...*

MATLOCK *Or your granddad.*

GRUNDY *[To Sioux] Are you worried, or are you just enjoying yourself?*

SIOUX *Enjoying myself.*

GRUNDY *Are you?*

SIOUX *Yeah.*

GRUNDY *Ah, that's what I thought you were doing.*

SIOUX *I always wanted to meet you.*

GRUNDY *Did you really?*

SIOUX *Yeah.*

GRUNDY *We'll meet afterwards, shall we? [Sioux does a camp pout]*

JONES *You dirty sod. You dirty old man!*

GRUNDY *Well keep going, chief, keep going. Go on, you've got another five seconds. Say something outrageous.*

JONES *You dirty bastard!*

GRUNDY *Go on, again.*

JONES *You dirty fucker! [Laughter from the group]*

GRUNDY *What a clever boy!*

JONES *What a fucking rotter.*

GRUNDY *Well, that's it for tonight. The other rocker Eamonn, and I'm saying nothing else about him, will be back tomorrow. I'll be seeing you soon. I hope I'm not seeing you [the band] again. From me, though, goodnight.*

The signature tune plays (later copied and incorporated into the beginning of Television Personalities' 'Where's Bill Grundy Now?' song), and the credits roll. Rotten looks at his watch, Jones starts dancing to the music, and Grundy mutters an off-mike 'Oh shit!' to himself.

behave badly. For example, when Johnny Rotten first swears, the singer apologizes. It is Grundy who eggs him on.

The impact of the Pistols on this show cannot be underestimated. The *Daily Mirror* reported the incident under a headline that read 'The Filth and the Fury' (the phrase was recycled many years later as the title of Julian Temple's documentary about the band). The *Mirror* did what all national newspapers do to decent rock bands who swear and behave with abandon: they attacked them with false moral outrage. After that the band was set for life.

After the Grundy incident the Pistols went on tour, supported by The Clash and The Heartbreakers. But many of the gigs were cancelled by offended local authorities. Of twenty scheduled gigs, only seven took place. By January of 1977 the band were a national disgrace. Even their record company turned against them: workers at the EMI record plant refused to handle the band's single, thus making the original version a true collector's item.

Not surprisingly, the band left EMI in March 1977 and by June of that year were at number one with their anti-royalist single 'God Save the Queen'. Their debut album, *Never Mind the Bollocks, Here's the Sex Pistols* was released in October 1977 and is now considered by luminaries such as Noel Gallagher to be one of the greatest rock albums ever. Four months after its release, the band broke up.

The Sex Pistols were formed in 1975. They were managed by Malcolm McLaren who did much to get the band noticed. By the summer of 1976 they had been banned from London venues such as The Nashville and The Marquee. In October 1976, as punk rock began to gather pace, they signed to EMI Records. They released their debut single 'Anarchy in the UK' in November. Their televised interview with Bill Grundy brought them national notoriety. In March 1977 they signed to A&M Records, and after the signing ceremony outside Buckingham Palace they trashed the record company's offices. They were dropped and then picked up by Virgin Records. Their huge-selling single 'God Save the Queen' was banned. Rotten boasted that it was 'the most heavily censored record in history'. Their debut album went straight to number one. By now, bassist Glen Matlock had left to be replaced by Sid Vicious. The Pistols were considered punk's premier band. They have reformed a couple of time since their break-up for lucrative concert appearances.

BOB MARLEY'S

One Love Peace Concert

DATE 22 April 1978, Kingston, Jamaica

O n 3 December 1976 two cars drove into the gardens of Bob Marley's house on Hope Road in Kingston, Jamaica. A number of armed men got out the cars, trained their rifles on the house and opened fire. Marley was in the kitchen at the time, eating a grapefruit and talking with his manager Don Taylor. Also present were members of Marley's band and his wife Rita. When the bullets started flying, everyone hit the ground. Taylor was the unlucky one. He took five bullets, four to his leg and one to his back.

Rita Marley was seriously wounded by a bullet to the head. Bob got away with minor injuries to his chest and arms. Given the quantity of bullets that poured into the house that night, it is a miracle anyone survived the attack.

If Marley had died in that shooting, he would not have been the first man of peace to go out in a hail of bullets. Bob Marley's music was dedicated to forging unity amongst all peoples. A strict Rastafarian, Marley preached a doctrine of equality, tried to build a world where the colour of a man's skin would be no more important than the colour of his eyes. His mixed-race background does much to explain his vision of togetherness between peoples.

Marley recorded his first song when he was 16. It was called 'Judge Me Not'. In 1964 he formed a band called The Wailing Wailers with Peter Tosh and Bunny Wailer. In 1967 he came under the influence of the Rastafarian religion, which changed his life and his music. By the early 70s he had written a number of songs dealing with spirituality, poverty and injustice.

It was Marley's ability to create striking reggae music and universalize the suffering

MARLEY PREACHED A DOCTRINE OF EQUALITY, TRIED TO BUILD A WORLD WHERE THE COLOUR OF A MAN'S SKIN WOULD BE NO MORE IMPORTANT THAN THE COLOUR OF HIS EYES

he saw in Jamaica that allowed him huge worldwide success. 'The different people of the earth are the different flowers of the earth,' he once said. He also had behind him a canny record label, Island Records. Founded by Chris Blackwell, Island had given Marley a bright and accessible sound that saw him sell over 20 million records in his lifetime.

Yet Marley's success was in stark contrast to the strife affecting Jamaicans in the 70s. Jamaica was in turmoil as the two main political parties, the JLP and the PNP, employed gangs of gunmen in a bitter struggle to gain control. Both parties turned to Marley for his support. His standing in the country was immense, and his endorsement would have been hugely valuable. But Marley played it clever, and proved adept at keeping both factions happy but never siding with either one,

In 1976 the leftwing PNP Party persuaded Marley to appear at a free outdoor concert. The festival would not be political but dedicated to peace on the island. It was two days before that concert that the gunmen entered Marley's house an opened fire.

Marley was now determined to fulfil his engagement. Under the gaze of Jamaica, with his assailants no doubt looking on, Marley gave a performance that stunned onlookers with its depth of passion and meaning. You can shoot me, he was saying, but you will never defeat me, for I have music and love, and they are my weapons.

The next day he boarded a plane. First he travelled to the Bahamas where he spent a month recuperating. Then he flew on to Britain where he would record his biggest selling album, *Exodus*.

IT WAS A BRILLIANT GESTURE, AND ALTHOUGH BOTH POLITICIANS LOOKED UNCOMFORTABLE THE CROWD ROARED THEIR APPROVAL. FOR THAT NIGHT JAMAICA WAS UNITED

Marley did not set foot in Jamaica for two years, but it was a remarkable sequence of events that brought him home. One day the leaders of the political parties' two rival gun gangs – Claudius 'Claudie' Massop and Aston 'Bucky' Marshall – found themselves sharing the same jail cell. The two men started talking, and within the hour had made a pact to stop the violence. Their first step would be to organize a concert that would unite the country. The musician they asked to headline was, of course, Bob Marley. Their invitation gave the homesick musician the perfect opportunity to return to Jamaica.

The One Love Peace Concert took place on 22 April 1978. Many big-name artists performed. Jacob Miller appeared on stage with a huge spliff that he flaunted in front of the two party leaders, Michael Manley and Edward Seaga. And Peter Tosh (formerly of The Wailers) spent most of his time on stage berating the two men for not legalizing marijuana.

Just after midnight Bob Marley and the Wailers took to the stage to rapturous applause. Halfway through his huge hit 'Jamming' Marley invited Manley and Seaga on to the stage. He took their hands and joined them. 'I just want to shake hands and show the people that we're gonna make it right, we're gonna unite...'

It was a brilliant gesture, and although both politicians looked distinctly uncomfortable shaking hands, the 32,000 strong crowd roared their approval. For that night Jamaica truly was united. Marley had once again worked his magic.

Unfortunately the concert did little to quench the violence. A few weeks after the event Manley called an election, which he won by a large margin, and another round of shooting began. Within two years of the concert both Massop and Marshall, the men who had organized the concert, were dead, shot down by the bullets they had once lived by.

Tragically, Marley was diagnosed with cancer, and on 11 May 1981 he passed away. Ironically, it was at Marley's funeral that Manley and Seaga again met – and this time they shook hands with ease and comfort. Bob Marley's search for love had not been in vain.

BOB MARLEY 1945–1981

Robert Nesta Marley was born on 6 February 1945 to a white father and black Jamaican mother. His father left soon after his birth, and Marley was raised in the Jamaican village of Nine Mile. He left school at the age of 14 and began playing music. By 1966 the band he was in had settled down to a three-piece comprising Marley, Bunny Wailer and Peter Tosh. They were known as The Wailers, and garnered some success both in Jamaica and abroad. In 1972 The Wailers were signed to Island Records. Albums such as *Catch a Fire* and *Exodus* made Marley an iconic figure for many. Although his music was rooted in the reggae tradition, his openness to other influences and the ability of his record company to sell him as a rock act, gave Marley wide and deep success. Marley was a follower of the Rastafarian religion, and his message of unity amongst all people inspired many. This message was cut short by his tragic death from cancer on 11 May 1981. Marley's body was taken back to his birthplace in Nine Miles where it now rests in a mausoleum.

The murder of Nancy Spungen and the death of
SID VICIOUS

DATE 12 October 1978, The Hotel Chelsea, New York

He wakes up in Room 100 of New York's infamous Hotel Chelsea feeling so groggy. The night before he swallowed a large dose of the drug Tuinal and passed out. Now he is paying the price, as he does every morning of every day. He raises himself from his bed, and that is when he notices the blood – on the sheets, on the mattress, on the floor.

Sid Vicious follows the blood trail to the bathroom, where he finds Nancy Spungen. His girlfriend is lying on the floor in her black underwear. There is also a big wound in her abdomen. At some point in the early hours of 12 October 1978 Nancy Spungen has been stabbed and has bled to death. Doctors later estimate that it would have taken her three hours to pass away.

Sid wonders what to do next. He searches his mind to try to put together what happened last night but all is blank. Who would do this to Nancy? Did he do it?

SID LOVED NANCY, AND NANCY LOVED SID. OH, THEY FOUGHT AND BITCHED AND THERE WAS VIOLENCE, BUT THEY KNEW THAT WHATEVER HAPPENED THEY HAD TO BE TOGETHER

For the rest of his life, he will vehemently deny the charge. She was his life, he would scream at people, he would never harm her in such a way. Who then? This was a story of murder and suicide and overdoses, a tale of everlasting love, heroin and junkies, the rock'n'roll lifestyle taken to limits that no one should take it to. Sid and Nancy did.

Sid loved Nancy, and Nancy loved Sid. Oh, they fought and bitched, and there was violence amongst the love, but they knew that whatever happened they had to be together. The world sneered at them – the loudmouthed groupie with the self-destructive Sex Pistol. But they sneered right back, for only they knew the truth about each other...

As the police began their investigation, conflicting stories emerged from the junkies and dealers and chancers. One witness, Leon Webster, gave his statement to the police then sold his story twice, once to the *New York Post* and again to the *Soho Weekly News*. All three accounts differed. A drug dealer, Rockets Redglare, said he had been with Sid at dawn, contradicting the professional medical opinion that Vicious had been asleep since four that morning. Even the hotel staff could not get their stories straight. Some said they saw Nancy in the lobby at three in the morning, others that they were around at that time and never saw either of the doomed pair.

When Vicious was taken in for questioning, it was discovered that the knife he owned fitted the profile of the knife that killed Nancy. A murder suspect, he was placed in Rikers Island prison. Malcolm McLaren, the Pistols' former manager, flew to New York to help. He knew Vicious needed a good lawyer, and that meant money, serious money, had to be found. On Friday 21 Vicious was released on $50,000 bail, the money paid by Virgin Records. Vicious told McLaren that he had been treated like a hero in prison.

Meanwhile Vicious's mother, Anne Beverley, flew in to New York. Sid had to report every morning to a police station and provide urine samples for drug testing. McLaren impressed on Anne the urgent need for Sid to keep a very low profile and stay out of the media spotlight.

Two days later Sid Vicious tried to commit suicide. His mother called McLaren who arrived to find Vicious dripping with blood and screaming: 'I want to die, I want to go to Nancy now!' Sid had used broken light bulbs to lacerate his arms and wrists. His mother had bruising on her face. The police came, and Sid was

VICIOUS WAS DRIPPING WITH BLOOD AND SCREAMING: 'I WANT TO DIE, I WANT TO GO TO NANCY NOW!' SID HAD USED BROKEN LIGHT BULBS TO LACERATE HIS ARMS AND WRISTS

taken to the Bellevue Hospital and put into a straitjacket. McLaren left for London, but before he went he hired a team of private investigators to discover Nancy's murderer. They never did.

Back in London, The Clash put on a benefit gig to raise money for Sid's trial. But most people, including John Lydon, wanted nothing to do with it. On 28 November Vicious was released from Bellevue. A few weeks later he had a new girlfriend, Michelle Robinson, whose apartment he moved into. Robinson soon discovered that being Sid Vicious's girlfriend was a major task. The man was constantly surrounded by groupies and drug dealers.

His name carried a huge cachet by dint of his time with The Sex Pistols. When that band fell apart on tour in America, Vicious signed a solo deal and hit big with his punk version of the Paul Anka song 'My Way'. His wayward lifestyle and heavy drug abuse prevented a follow-up, yet he was still able to trade on his name. The week before

Nancy's death he had played three shows at Max's Kansas City, the famed New York venue. He had been awful, so smacked out of his head that he could not finish most the songs. Didn't matter. Thousands had queued up to see him, and this allowed him enough money to feed his habit.

For Robinson, keeping up with Sid became a nightmare. She had a nervous breakdown and went into hospital. When she came out, Vicious was back in Rikers Island prison. At a club one night Vicious had smashed a glass into the face of Patti Smith's brother Todd. In prison, Vicious was put into a detoxification ward and spent the Christmas season clean. He was released on bail on 1 February, and a party was held to celebrate at his girlfriend's apartment. After dinner a dealer arrived at the house and sold heroin to some of the guests. Vicious had not taken the drug for at least two months. He could not resist.

The next morning he was discovered dead. A few days after his funeral his mother Anne discovered a suicide note in his jacket. It read: 'We had a death pact and I have to keep my half of the bargain. Please bury me next to my baby in my leather jacket, jeans and motorcycle boots. Goodbye.' His last wish could not be granted. Nancy was Jewish, and buried in an exclusively Jewish cemetery. So his ashes were sprinkled secretly on her grave. As in life, so in death: the star-crossed junkies were now together forever.

SID VICIOUS 1957–1979

John Simon Ritchie was born in the London suburb of Lewisham on 10 May 1957. His mother Anne was in the RAF, and his father was a guardsman at Buckingham Palace. Shortly after John's birth his mother took him to live on the Mediterranean island of Ibiza. His father was due to join them, but he never showed up. Anne subsequently remarried, but three years later the boy's stepfather died of cancer. From the age of 11 he grew up with just his mother. He left home as a teenager and lived in various squats. It was at this time that he met Jah Wobble and John Lydon, who gave him his nickname, Sid Vicious. In 1976 he joined the band Flowers of Romance as bass player. After Glen Matlock's departure from The Sex Pistols, Sid took the vacant position. A year later the band split whilst on tour in the US. Sid stayed on in America with his girlfriend Nancy Spungen. He died of a heroin overdose on 2 February 1979 following Nancy's murder. Sex Pistols manager Malcolm McLaren later said of him: 'If Johnny Rotten was the voice of punk, Sid was the attitude.'

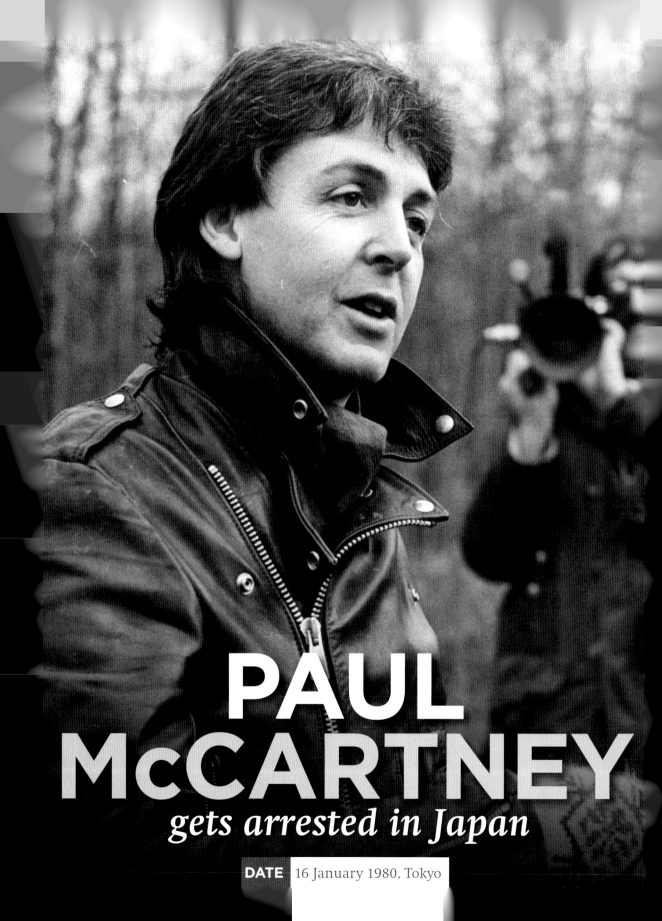

PAUL McCARTNEY

gets arrested in Japan

DATE 16 January 1980, Tokyo

When it was all over, and Paul McCartney was preparing to leave the country that had incarcerated him, the world's most successful songwriter said: 'I spent my time in a Tokyo jail making a mental list of all those drugs which are legal but dangerous. We're all on drugs – cigarettes, whisky and wild wild women. Society thinks alcohol is terrific, yet it kills. Cigarettes can kill. They are worse than marijuana. It's just not true that marijuana can kill. What about the little old ladies on Valium? Think of aspirin's danger to the stomach.'

McCartney was again making the case for marijuana, a cause he has been involved in for most of his life. He began smoking it regularly in 1964, and in July 1967 he signed a full-page advert that appeared in *The Times* calling for the decriminalization of pot. The other Beatles also signed the ad as did their manager, Brian Epstein.

McCartney subsequently joined the Legalise Cannabis campaign. In 1972 he was busted twice for possession, once in Sweden and once in Scotland where he was then living. A year later he was caught again and fined £200 for growing the drug on his farm. Entertainingly, McCartney told a newspaper that a fan had sent him some seeds in the post and he, having no idea what they were, had innocently planted them.

As a consequence of these incidents, Japan had always refused McCartney a permit to tour the country. In many Far Eastern societies, drugs are very much frowned upon. It was only after years of pressure that McCartney was allowed to undertake an 11-date tour with his band Wings.

MCCARTNEY DECIDED TO TAKE THE DRUG THROUGH IN HIS SUITCASES BECAUSE NO ONE WOULD THINK TO SEARCH HIM. THE JAPANESE POLICE WERE WAITING FOR HIM

McCartney arrived in Japan with his band on 16 January 1980. He had in his personal luggage half a pound of pot. Normally, musicians get their roadies to hide such substances in amplifiers, speakers, drum sets, guitar cases... McCartney decided he would get cute. He would just take the drug through in his suitcases, because no one would think to search him. He had forgotten one thing. Thanks to his previous drug offences, the Japanese police were waiting for him.

MCCARTNEY TOLD THE PRESS THAT A FAN HAD SENT HIM SOME SEEDS, AND, HAVING NO IDEA WHAT THEY WERE, HE INNOCENTLY PLANTED THEM

'I didn't try to hide the pot,' McCartney said later. 'I had just come from America, and still had the American attitude that marijuana isn't that bad. I didn't realize how strict the Japanese attitude was. I had all this really good grass, and I knew I wouldn't be able to get anything over there. The stuff was too good to flush down the toilet so I thought I'd take it with me.'

After the discovery of the drug, McCartney was taken from the airport to a government office and interrogated for five hours. After his first night in jail he was taken to the main narcotics headquarters where he says he was handcuffed and had a rope tied around him. He was interrogated for six more hours. He claimed throughout that the drug was simply for personal use.

As he answered questions inside, his fans gathered outside. When officials tried to return him to prison, the fans blocked their way and riot police had to be called. The next day McCartney was given bad news. A judge had granted Tokyo's public prosecutor permission to keep him in jail for at least ten days whilst they conducted their inquiries. McCartney had no choice but to settle into the routine of prison life.

He was awakened at six o'clock each morning and made to sit cross-legged as the morning roll-call was made. When his number 22 was read out, he would have to shout back '*Hai*'. For breakfast he was given seaweed-and-onion soup, which was followed by 20 minutes of exercise. At lunchtime he was given bread and jam, and then taken for another interview, or for a consultation with his lawyers, or allowed a visit from his wife Linda. Lights out was at eight o'clock each night.

McCartney asked for permission to have his guitar brought to him, but that request was refused. However, his entourage was allowed to bring him extra blankets and hot food. 'At first, I thought jail was barbaric,' he later recalled. 'But underneath their inscrutable exterior the guards were quite warm. We joked and we had a few sing songs. I also got requests for "Yesterday", which I would sing and they clapped along to. It was a bit of a laugh... But I have no complaints. All in all I was very well treated.'

'THE STUFF WAS TOO GOOD TO FLUSH DOWN THE TOILET SO I THOUGHT I'D TAKE IT WITH ME'

McCartney's lawyer and father-in-law Lee Eastman flew in to Tokyo to help with the defence. But on 25 January, the authorities released McCartney from jail and deported him back to Britain. The episode had cost him many thousands in lost tour revenues, compensation to the promoter and legal fees.

Of course, McCartney was not the first musician to have spent time inside, not by a long chalk. He joined a long list of luminaries that now includes Johnny Cash, Merle Haggard, Chuck Berry, Boy George, Ian Brown, Mick Jagger, Keith Richards, Tupac Shakur, 50 Cent, Lil Wayne, Lil' Kim, Leadbelly and more. But McCartney was surely the first musician to be imprisoned in a country where he was about to perform songs from an album called *Band on the Run.*

James Paul McCartney was born on 18 June 1942. His mother was a nurse and his father a musician. He has a brother, Michael, who as Mike McGear played with The Scaffold. Paul met John Lennon at the Woolton Church Hall Fete when he was 15, and they began writing songs together. After The Beatles split in 1970 McCartney released two well-received solo albums and then formed the band Wings. In 1969 he had married Linda Eastman and together they had three children, Mary, Stella and James. He also adopted Linda's daughter Heather. Their albums include *Band on the Run* and *Venus and Mars.* Wings lasted ten years with various line-ups. After its demise, McCartney made many solo albums. He has written classical pieces, published poetry and drawings and been active in numerous charitable causes, especially those that promote animal welfare and vegetarianism. In 2009 McCartney launched a Meat Free Monday campaign. After Linda died of breast cancer, he married (and later divorced) Heather Mills, who bore him another child, Beatrice.

DEXYS
steal the master tapes for their debut album

DATE April 1980, Chipping Norton, Oxfordshire

No one saw it coming, least of all the record company. After all, no one had ever stolen the tapes of their debut album and refused to hand them over until the contract was renegotiated. But that is precisely what Dexys Midnight Runners did to EMI Records. It was an extraordinarily audacious stunt, pulled off by an extraordinary band.

The story begins in 1978 with the disbandment of a punk band called The Killjoys and the drive and ambition of that band's singer, Kevin Rowland.

Born in Wolverhampton on 17 August 1953, Rowland was a working-class boy who in his teens moved around the country quite a lot. His first band was called Lucy and the Lovers, and was influenced in part by the Liverpool band Deaf School and by Roxy Music. The Killjoys were Rowland's next band. They made a single entitled 'Johnny Won't Go to Heaven' that did nothing. This failure, coupled with the alienation he felt from the fading punk scene, made Rowland determined to stop following trends and to follow his own sense of individuality.

The result of that desire was Dexys Midnight Runners, a nine-piece, soul-influenced band that spent the first year of its existence writing songs and relentlessly rehearsing, day in, day out. Rowland insisted on acting as the leader in all matters. This included the clothes.

Rowland's admiration of Bryan Ferry's highly intelligent use of style and imagery would be a major factor here.

Early photos of the band wearing make-up and with one-off haircuts make it clear that Dexys were at least one year ahead of the New Romantic movement. However, having been offered a tour slot with The Specials, and fearing their radical image would alienate people, Dexys opted for a safer male look based around woollen hats and donkey jackets. As soon as they

PHOTOS OF THE BAND WEARING MAKE-UP AND ONE-OFF HAIRCUTS MAKE IT CLEAR THAT DEXYS WERE AT LEAST ONE YEAR AHEAD OF THE NEW ROMANTIC MOVEMENT

started touring, it became obvious that this band was one of the most powerful around. They put their all into every live show, Rowland in particular creating a new soul vision. His performances were stylized but highly effective. Dexys did not conform to the norm. They gave interviews in which they expressed disgust for drinking at gigs. 'We want our performances to be special,' they said, and distanced themselves from every other band.

YET ROWLAND WAS NOT HAPPY, FAR FROM IT. HE LATER CONFESSED THAT HE THOUGHT APPEARING ON TOP OF THE POPS WOULD CURE ALL HIS ANXIETIES. INSTEAD THEY ADDED TO THEM

They secured a deal with EMI records and their first single, 'Dance Stance', scraped into the top 40. But it was their paean to US soul singer Geno Washington, 'Geno', that smashed its way to number one. Yet Rowland was not happy, far from it. He later confessed that he thought appearing on *Top of the Pops* would cure all his anxieties. Instead they added to them.

Dexys now headed into a studio in Oxfordshire to record the debut album.

The producer was Pete Wingfield, whose 1975 hit solo single, 'Eighteen With a Bullet', Rowland much admired. Wingfield and the band worked well together. The producer knew that the band was brilliant in a live context, and the success of the album would lie in his ability to capture that intensity on record. The sessions took about 12 days with producer and band bouncing ideas off each other at regular intervals, all of them working towards a truly outstanding debut album.

At the same time Rowland was acutely aware that the contract the band had signed with EMI was heavily weighted in favour of the company. Dexys were to receive royalties of six per cent; most bands get ten to twelve per cent. After the success of 'Geno' the band reopened negotiations with EMI but failed to persuade their paymasters of the justice of their cause. Even producer Pete Wingfield thought the deal was terrible.

It was during the recording sessions for the album that Rowland put forward the idea of holding EMI to ransom by stealing the master tapes. 'I think I am one of those guys who like a battle to fight, a cause,' he later said. 'I got into this thing: big record company is not going to screw us; it's us against EMI.'

As the last song of the album was being given its final mix, and with Wingfield out of the studio, the band leapt into action. They locked the studio door, held back the engineer and took every tape they could lay their hands on. Then they ran to their waiting cars and took the tapes to Rowland's parents' house in Birmingham.

EMI furiously demanded the return of the tapes. Dexys refused and headed off on a nationwide tour. EMI were in a corner. They agreed to up the band's royalty to nine per cent, and the tapes were delivered back to the company – albeit in a lucky fashion. The group took the tapes on to the London Underground, which in itself could have demagnetized them and wiped everything. Fortunately, the tapes survived the journey.

THE BAND LEAPT INTO ACTION. THEY LOCKED THE STUDIO DOOR, HELD BACK THE ENGINEER AND TOOK EVERY TAPE THEY COULD LAY THEIR HANDS ON

When the album, *Searching for the Young Soul Rebels*, appeared in July 1980 it was to rave reviews and a top-ten chart placing. EMI, however, did not forget the band's daring actions, and Dexys were off the label inside the year. They signed to Phonogram where they scored their biggest chart hit with 'Come On Eileen'. 'We always were drama queens,' Rowland later noted.

Dexys Midnight Runners were formed in 1978. The line-up changed many times over the years, but key players include Al Archer, Pete Williams, Mick Talbot, Billy Adams, Helen O'Hara, Big Jim Patterson and Seb Shelton. They were signed to EMI in 1979. Their second single, 'Geno', was a number-one hit, and their debut album, *Searching for the Young Soul Rebels,* was a critical and commercial smash. In 1981 the band moved to Phonogram Records and changed their image and music. The resulting single, 'Come On Eileen', and album, *Too-Rye-Ay*, sold millions both in Great Britain and in America. After an extensive period of touring Rowland retreated from the spotlight. When the band re-emerged in 1985 with their third album, *Don't Stand Me Down*, they had again changed their image and sound. The album had taken an extremely long time to write and record, and unfortunately failed to match the success of its predecessors. Dexys fell apart within a year, and Kevin Rowland became a solo artist. In 2006 the band re-formed for a well-received British tour.

The killing of
JOHN
LENNON

DATE 8 December 1980, New York

He got his wish. Mark Chapman made sure that whenever someone in the world thought of John Lennon, his own name would not be far behind. Chapman and Lennon, Lennon and Chapman, bound together in senseless tragedy. Now Chapman sits in prison and will remain there all his life. As for Lennon, he is on sale again, and will be forever more.

On 8 December 1980 four bullets entered John Lennon's body as he made his way to the entrance of his New York apartment. The world stopped in shock as Lennon fell to the ground. He remained conscious for about 30 minutes, and then passed away.

His killer was Mark David Chapman, born in 1955 in Fort Worth, Texas. He said he had done it because the voice in his head told him to. After killing Lennon,

> ## HE WAS OBSESSED WITH THE CATCHER IN THE RYE. 'I'M SURE THIS LARGE PART OF ME IS HOLDEN CAULFIELD,' HE SAID IN THE BACK OF THE POLICE CAR. **'THE SMALL PART OF ME MUST BE THE DEVIL'**

Chapman dropped his gun and stood reading *The Catcher in the Rye,* awaiting the police. When they arrived, his first words were: 'I acted alone.'

In the back of the police car, as two incredulous officers questioned him, Chapman revealed, 'I'm sure this large part of me is Holden Caulfield, who is the main person in the book. The small part of me must be the devil.'

As thousands gathered together outside Lennon's building in shock, the police and journalists started digging into Chapman's background. What they found was highly disturbing. His childhood was unhappy. The father abused his wife and his son. At school Chapman's unhappiness was a weakness, and the other kids smelt it. They bullied and teased him continually and without mercy.

Then one day he heard a Beatles song on the radio, and like millions of others was transfixed by their music. By the ninth grade Chapman was dressing like Lennon and ignoring school. At 14 he had his first

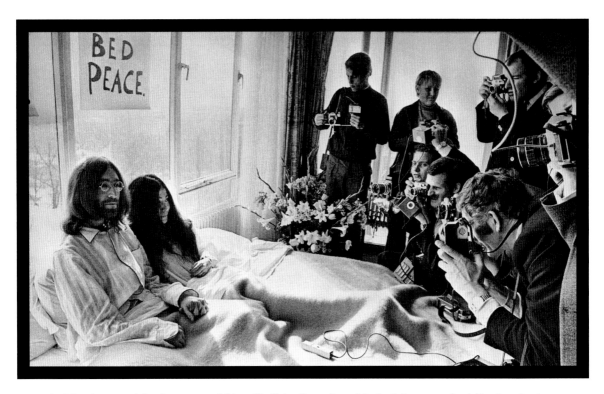

In March 1969 John Lennon and his wife Yoko Ono stayed in bed for a week at the Amsterdam Hilton. It was one of a series of stunts designed to raise awareness of world peace.

run-in with the cops. He was on LSD, they weren't. He spent a night in jail. There were two more years of drugs and aimlessness until one day, in a fit of personal despair, he threw his hands to the sky and asked Jesus to save him. And Jesus filled him with a new spirit, and Chapman's life changed. He threw away his rock'n'roll clothing and started attending church. He went to school and asked people if they had heard the good news.

With Jesus in his mind Chapman turned his attention back to The Beatles and in particular to Lennon's massive hit 'Imagine'. How could a multimillionaire sing about having no possessions? Surely John Lennon was a phoney. That was the word Holden Caulfield used countless times in Chapman's favourite book, J.D. Salinger's *The Catcher in the Rye*. If someone was bad, they were a phoney. Chapman was obsessed with that book, and it got to the point where he had to have a copy with him at all times. If he didn't, he would scour the area for a bookshop and buy a new one.

Chapman began work as a YMCA summer-camp counsellor. The children liked him enormously, called him Nemo, and he went on to win an Outstanding Counsellor award. His roommate David Moore would later recall that 'he was one of the most compassionate staff members we ever had'. Chapman's kind nature attracted a girl named Jessica Blankenship, and they began dating.

Chapman, it seemed, had turned his life right around. But there were signs of great inner pain. He sent a tape to a friend and described it as 'a picture of a soul in pain'. The unravelling of his mind started to gather pace. He enrolled in an evangelical college with his girlfriend but soon dropped out. Jessica left him, and he tried to commit suicide. He spent time in hospital, and on his release was given part-time work there, playing his guitar to patients. A year later he put all his money into a trip round the world. He saw Tokyo, Seoul, Hong Kong, Singapore, Bangkok, Delhi, Israel, Genoa, London, Paris and Dublin. He came home, met a Japanese-American woman named Gloria Abe, and on 2 June 1979 they were married.

> ## THERE WERE SIGNS OF **GREAT INNER PAIN.** THE UNRAVELLING OF CHAPMAN'S MIND STARTED TO GATHER PACE

He worked in various dead-end jobs to support Gloria, and at the same time rediscovered his passion for getting high and hitting the bottle. His wife despaired at this self-destruction but she could not stop him. One day the idea that he would kill someone famous planted itself in his brain. It is said that Chapman now went to his local library, stood in the biography section, closed his eyes, reached out and took a book from the shelf. Whoever this book is about, he has said to have reasoned, I will kill them. He opened his eyes. It was a book about John Lennon.

Lennon lived in New York City and had done so since 1971. He had left The Beatles in 1970, he and Paul McCartney spitting fire at each other. He was tired of being a commodity, tired of being called a Beatle and a Beatle only. He determined a radical course of action that was designed to use his fame to further the causes he believed in so strongly. He spent a week in bed with his wife Yoko for world peace, hung out with militant radicals such as the Black Panthers, attacked American involvement in the Vietnam War, stubbornly battled the authorities until he was allowed American residence, wrote furious songs about discrimination against women, the Irish and black people.

Yoko sent Lennon to LA with their secretary May Pang for what was later described by Lennon as his Lost Weekend. He and May, with Yoko's blessings, became a couple, Lennon drank himself silly, tried to make some music and after 18 months of debauchery he came running home to Yoko. She took him back, and their son

Sean was born on 9 October 1975. Sean was Lennon's second son. His first son Julian had the misfortune to arrive in the middle of Beatlemania, and Lennon could not be both a Beatle and a father. He chose the former, ignored Julian and later regretted his actions. He realized he had been absent from Julian's life, just as his own father had been absent from his when he was growing up in Liverpool. With Sean, no such mistake would be made.

JOHN LAY NAKED IN THE FOETAL POSITION ON HIS WIFE'S CLOTHED BODY, AND LEIBOVITZ TOOK ONE OF THE GREAT PHOTOS OF HER CAREER

Lennon gave up everything – music, carousing and chemicals – and became a house-husband. He dedicated himself to raising his son. During that time he often looked at a strange toy guitar that he had purchased just before his reconciliation with Yoko. John was amused by the instrument, and as the years rolled by he began wondering how it would sound on an album or indeed in a live context... Finally, he picked it up and began writing.

In 1980 he began writing the songs that would appear on his and Yoko's *Double Fantasy* album. He no longer had any illusions about his standing in the music world. His days as an innovator were over. Instead, the work would be a musical letter to his fans, asking questions such as: Did you survive the 60s? Did you get on with the 70s? How you feeling 'bout the 80s? In August, with Jack Douglas at the helm, John and Yoko began recording *Double Fantasy*. By December the album was in the shops and receiving good reviews.

On 8 December, John got out of bed and began the last day of his life. It started with a photoshoot by photographer Annie Leibovitz. At the session she asked John and Yoko to undress. John complied, but Yoko didn't. So John lay naked in the foetal position on his wife's clothed body, and Leibovitz took one of the greatest photographs of her career.

John and Yoko then gave an interview to journalist Dave Sholin. In the course of the discussion, Lennon reaffirmed his commitment to world peace and later added, ominously: 'We're going to live or we are going to die. If we're dead, we are going to have to deal with that...'

The interview lasted three hours. Lennon and Yoko then left their apartment in the Dakota Building and headed for the recording studio. By the building's front door Lennon was approached by a young man with glasses. He shook the man's hand – it was Mark Chapman – and signed his copy of *Double Fantasy*. Another fan, Paul Goresh, took a photo of Lennon and Chapman together. 'Do you want anything else?' Lennon asked Chapman, handing back the album. 'No,' he said, so Lennon walked off to his limo, to his fate.

'At that point my big part won, and I wanted to go back to my hotel,' Chapman later confessed, 'But I couldn't. I waited until he came back. He knew where the ducks went in winter, and I needed to know this.' This was a reference to a question Holden asks himself throughout the book.

THAT WAS JOHN LENNON'S FINAL WISH ON EARTH – TO SPEND SOME TIME WITH HIS SON

At the studio Lennon added some finishing touches to a Yoko song called 'Walking on Thin Ice'. They worked on the song until ten o'clock, then made arrangements to go out for dinner with producer Jack Douglas. They left the studio and got in the limo. 'Do you want to go out for dinner?' Yoko asked John as they neared home – but he seemed to have changed his mind. 'I want to get back and see Sean,' Lennon replied. That was John Lennon's final wish on earth – to spend some time with his son.

John Winston Lennon was born on 9 October 1940. His father was a seaman, absent for most of his life, and Lennon was raised for the most part by his Aunt Mimi. When he was 17 years old his mother was killed in a car accident. By now he was playing in various bands, and in 1957 he met Paul McCartney. Lennon married his teenage sweetheart Cynthia in 1962, and they had one child, Julian. They separated in 1968, and John took up with the Japanese artist Yoko Ono. In 1970 he left The Beatles to embark on a solo career. Lennon's early work apart from The Beatles was marked by its intensity and rawness. He developed strong leftwing views and campaigned for world peace, using his fame to further the causes he believed in. His major solo songs include 'Imagine', 'Give Peace a Chance' and 'Jealous Guy'. After his murder, a section of Central Park was named Strawberry Fields after one of his celebrated songs, and in his hometown of Liverpool the airport was renamed in his honour. Lennon remains a towering figure in contemporary music.

JOE STRUMMER

goes missing

DATE April 1982, Paris

Throughout their career, chaos dogged The Clash like a hellhound, always snapping at their heels. Gigs ended in riots, band members screamed and pouted at each other, record company rows were frequent. Being a member of The Clash was no picnic, and it often it extracted a very heavy price, as singer and band leader Joe Strummer was about to discover.

The Clash appeared in 1977, cut through with style and image and genuine bravado. They were top-three material, older than the other punk bands, more talented, more rock'n'roll. They were madly in love with music and its attendant mythology. And from that mythology each member's character emerged.

> HE TOOK IT UPON HIMSELF TO LOOK AFTER THE FANS, SLIDE THEM FREE TICKETS, GET THEM BACKSTAGE. **HE DROVE THE BAND FORWARDS POLITICALLY,** PUTTING HIS ANGER INTO HIS SONGS

Topper Headon was the drummer, looked like the buddy you would have a drink with at the bar – an illusion that neatly covered up his raging heroin addiction. Paul Simonon, the bassman, was the good-looking guy, the magnet for the models. Mick Jones on guitar – he was the rock star with the tousled hair and a penchant for cocaine. And Strummer? Well, Joe Strummer was the soul of the band. He was the one who took it upon himself to look after the fans, slide them free tickets, get them backstage. He drove the band forwards politically, picking up on oppression all over the world and putting his anger at injustice into songs.

It had all started so well, The Clash dominating the punk scene in Britain by spitting out three-minute gems. They were a true English garage band, all the way from Notting Hill – at the time, that most metropolitan of London areas. But they were too old, too seasoned to let one musical style tie them down. For their second album they tried American rock, and, apart from one blistering track, messed up totally. They regrouped and devised a new blueprint – clever bands do this – then went into the studio and produced the brilliant *London Calling*, which musically zoomed all around the room, taking in dub and reggae and soul and pop. It is now considered a classic work, always popping up in best-ever album lists.

Yet everywhere they went the press were on their backs. 'What do they see when they look in the mirror?' asked the *New Musical Express*. 'Third-world guerrillas with quiffs?' In public Strummer remained unrepentant. 'I know what I'm doing,' he shot back. In private he thought: Do I really need all this?

SUDDENLY, THERE WAS NO HIPPER BAND IN NEW YORK THAN THE CLASH. THE BAND EVEN FILMED A CAMEO IN A SCORSESE FILM, AND HUNG OUT IN BARS WITH ROBERT DE NIRO

In 1981 Strummer reached back into his past and asked original Clash manager Bernie Rhodes to take back the reins. Rhodes was the classic pop manager, full of scams, moves and disguises. Strummer figured – correctly – that he was the man to get them back on track. Rhodes got to work on CBS, got them to start putting out material to keep the band in the public eye. Good move. Hit singles such as the 'The Magnificent Seven' and 'Radio Clash' helped stabilize the band's fortunes. Rhodes also organized a month of live dates in Italy, France and Spain, then the band headed to New York for a six-week residency in a Times Square club.

When the New York Fire Department closed the club after just one night, The Clash were pushed right onto the front of all the papers. New York radio responded by picking up on 'The Magnificent Seven' and began playing the cut to death. Suddenly, there was no hipper band in New York than The Clash. The band even filmed a cameo part in Martin Scorsese's dark film *The King of Comedy*, and hung out in bars with Robert De Niro.

In September they played a week's residency in Paris, did the same at the Lyceum in London. At all their shows they were taken by the crowd's obvious love and respect for their music, their stance, their politics. They had believed the press, thought the world hated them. Now they knew different.

Fired up, they began to make some tentative recordings, but this was The Clash, and they had to shoot themselves in the foot. Two factors would stymie them: Topper Headon's growing drug addiction and Mick Jones's insistence that he produce the album and record in New York. Jones was in love with the Big Apple at that point. He was very taken by the hip-hop sound

Clash members Paul Simonon, Joe Strummer and Mick Jones in May 1982. Unfortunately, the band's US success could not mask their dissent, and The Clash began to fall apart.

emerging from the New York ghettos; he regularly had tapes of hip-hop radio shows sent over to him in London. And, of course, there was a woman. There is always a woman. Her name was Ellen Foley, she lived in New York, and Mick wanted to be with her.

Jones got his way. In November the band flew out to New York to start recording. Meanwhile, Topper's heroin use was spiralling out of control. Voices were raised in his direction. Clean up or clear out. The band worked in New York until Christmas. On their return Topper was busted for heroin possession. By January 1982 the band should have finished the

album. Instead they were still recording, with a Far East tour to complete at the end of the month.

Just before departure Mick Jones presented the others with his mix of the album. It now stretched to 65 minutes and carried 15 songs. They were appalled by his work, and after the tour they pulled in producer Glyn Johns to help. Good choice. Johns certainly knew about salvaging albums. Joe and he now set to work, giving the songs a much more radio-friendly sound, cutting down their length, dumping a few of the tracks. Joe was out to break America again, and no one in the band was going to stop him. He wanted the band to stop acting like 'priests', with a devoted but cult following, and reach out to the rest of the world.

In April, finally, the finished tapes were delivered to CBS Records. The company went into overdrive and scheduled a single, 'Know Your Rights', for late April and the album itself – *Combat Rock* – for mid May. A tour was announced. First two dates were in Scotland. The tickets went on sale… and no one bought them.

At this point Bernie Rhodes went to see a whacked-out Joe with an idea both to sell the tour and salvage the band. 'It was on the eve of the tour,' Strummer recalled in a 1988 TV interview, 'and the tickets were not selling, and there were three days to go. So Bernie Rhodes, who along with Malcolm McLaren liked the odd scam, said: "Look, you got to disappear. Okay?" I said, "Okay Bernie, if you really think I should disappear, I will. Where do you want me to disappear to?" He said, "I don't know. Go to Austin, Texas. You know that fellow there, that country singer Joe Ely. Stay with him, but ring me every morning at ten a.m." I said, "Okay Bernie, I will be seeing you." But I took the boat train to Paris instead. And I got to Paris, and I thought it would be a good joke if I never phoned Bernie at all because he thought he would be acting – "Oh, where has Joe gone?" – but after a few weeks he really *was* going: "Oh no, where has Joe gone?"'

And they didn't know where Joe had gone, not for a month at least. Rhodes had played right into Joe's hands. When he made his idea known Strummer was exhausted and tired and highly irritable. The last two years had been wildly hectic, the band besieged by all kinds of problems, from money worries to a cynical press hounding their every move. It had left Strummer burnt out with exhaustion, unhappy with his life and its future. Now he saw a way of escaping from this nightmare, and he took it.

WITHIN HOURS KOSMO WAS BANGING ON JOE'S DOOR, 'DRESSED LIKE RAMBO FOR SOME REASON', STRUMMER RECALLED

The two men had agreed he would go to Texas but then Joe and his longtime partner Gaby switched the cars and hopped it to Paris instead. They stayed with a friend and forgot the world. They were free. They visited art galleries and museums, they walked tree-lined streets, took coffee in cafés, drank French beer.

Producing and touring and fighting his corner and dealing with a smacked-out drummer and a prima-donna guitarist, had done for the man. Now all he wanted was peace, and Paris delivered it unto him.

Back in Britain the papers were full of reports about his disappearance.

Every week lengthy articles discussed this remarkable turn of events. Rumours persisted. Joe was in Scotland, Joe was in New York, Joe had just been fished out of a river...

Although closely associated with rock mythology, Strummer kept himself fit. The year before he had run the London Marathon, and in Paris he gladly took on that city's run, completing the 26-mile course without any training whatsoever. Then, six weeks into this idyllic sojourn, Joe made his mistake. He went to a bar and was spotted by a Dutch journalist, who then called band's press officer Kosmo Vinyl in London. Within hours Kosmo was banging on Joe's door 'dressed like Rambo for some reason', Strummer recalled.

Joe and Gaby returned to London, faced the press, faced the music. Strummer was delighted to discover that the band's new single had been rapturously received as had the album. In a position of strength now, Strummer called the shots. Topper was sacked and the band's original drummer, Terry Chimes, brought back into the fold. Ironically, the band's next single, 'Rock the Casbah', had been written by Topper, and such was its popularity it helped the band crack America.

Combat Rock was similarly successful. It went on to sell two million copies worldwide, and The Clash were never more popular. Strummer had acted with his heart and got his glory. It was a lesson he would never forget.

John Graham Mellor was born on 21 August 1952 . His father was a diplomat, and the family lived in many different countries before settling in London. At age ten John and his brother David (who would later commit suicide) were sent to boarding school. After quitting education Strummer moved to Wales and began playing in various bands. He then moved back to London, and by 1975 was installed in a band called The 101ers. The band made a bit of a name on the London pub-rock scene. In 1976 Strummer (so-called due to his style of guitar playing,) was poached by Bernie Rhodes (manager) and Mick Jones (guitarist) and asked if he would front a new band, The Clash. The band made their debut supporting The Sex Pistols in July 1976 and by January 1977 were signed to CBS records. Their debut album *The Clash* was enthusiastically received as was their third album, *London Calling*. Strummer left the band in the mid-80s to pursue a solo career; he also appeared in various films and documentaries. On 22 December 2002 he died at home of a heart attack.

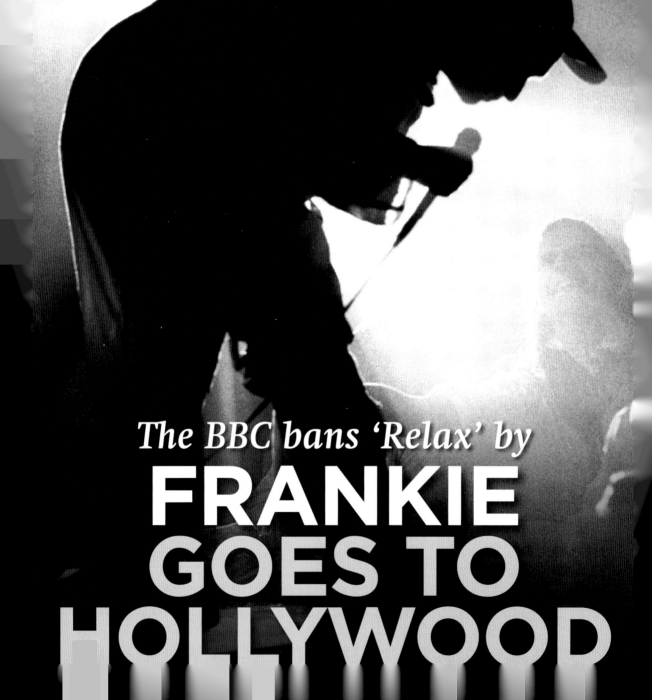

The BBC bans 'Relax' by

FRANKIE
GOES TO
HOLLYWOOD

At first, Britain did not want to know about 'Relax'. The debut single of Frankie Goes to Hollywood, released in November 1983, sold very little. It came into the charts at 67 and took seven weeks to struggle to 35. Perhaps the advertising had done for it. 'Relax' was promoted by adverts featuring the band's two front men, Holly Johnson and Paul Rutherford. Beneath head-and-shoulder shots of both men was placed the strapline 'All the Nice Boys Love Sea-Men'.

Early in January 1984 the cards fell the band's way. After an appearance on the TV music show *The Tube* they were asked to perform the song on Britain's leading pop show, *Top of the Pops*. The show aired on 5 January, and the following week the song shot to number six in the charts.

As the band embarked on a hectic promotional tour, the producer of BBC1's *Mike Read Show* went home to find his children endlessly playing the song's risqué video. The following day he urged Read to publicly boycott the record. Read agreed, and on air that day he castigated the song, labelling it obscene.

'People might now say "fancy banning that", but you're talking 1984,' Read later said in his defence. 'At the time I had a high profile. I was the face of children's TV. There was a picture of a phallus on the back of the sleeve. But the real reason it was banned was because of the video, which featured simulated buggery and urinating into people's mouths.'

What made this ban so significant was that the BBC had already decided to remove the record from their playlists before Read's announcement. But after past embarrassments they did not want

AS SOON AS THE BBC BANNED THESE RECORDS THEY SHOT TO NUMBER ONE, A POSITION THEY STAYED AT FOR LENGTHY PERIODS SIMPLY BECAUSE THOUSANDS RUSHED OUT AND BOUGHT THEM TO FIND OUT WHAT ALL THE FUSS WAS ABOUT

to make their position public. Banning records, as they knew to their cost, was a dangerous business...

In the 30s the British Broadcasting Corporation had set up a panel of men who would decide what was acceptable for the airwaves and, consequently, for public morality. 'No one is more alive than I,' said one member, 'to the need to buttress the forces of virtue against the unprincipled elements of the jungle.'

This attitude led to some pretty crazy decision-making. The BBC censors introduced a ban on any song that linked heaven or God to human love. Don Cornell's 1954 number-one single 'Hold My Hand', for example, was banned because it likened holding hands with a woman to the kingdom of heaven. Furthermore, no record was allowed to adapt a classical tune for pop purposes, so goodbye to Perry Como's 'I'm Always Chasing Rainbows', which had the nerve to adapt Chopin's *Fantaisie Impromptu*. Naughty boy.

In the 60s, as a culture of sex and drugs developed, records began reflecting the seismic changes taking place in British society. Some of these served to confuse rather than shock the BBC. For example, the Small Faces' innocuous single 'I Can Make It' was banned because the BBC thought that the title was a euphemism for sex. On the other hand, the band's overt tribute to amphetamines, 'Here Comes the Nice', which included a line about needing speed, escaped censure. You go figure.

Other songs were even more brazen. Max Romeo's single 'Wet Dream' and Jane Birkin's 'Je T'Aime... Moi Non Plus' single with Serge Gainsbourg, where the glamorous pair exchanged sighs of a very sexual nature over a haunting theme, were hardly out of their sleeves before they were prevented from polluting the airwaves.

The trouble with both these records is that as soon as the BBC banned them, they shot to number one, a position they stayed at for lengthy periods, simply because every week thousands rushed out to buy the singles to discover what the fuss was all about.

FOR YEARS THE BAND PROTESTED THEIR INNOCENCE, REFUSING TO ADMIT THAT THE SONG'S LYRICS WERE SEXUAL. FINALLY, A BAND MEMBER SAID: 'REALLY IT WAS ABOUT SHAGGING'

Lou Reed's 1973 single 'Walk on the Wild Side' also got the chop thanks to its 'giving head' line. Which brings us back to Mike Read. Years after the Lou Reed song was banned, Mike Read innocently played it on his show, and was reprimanded for doing so. Read was shown the offending lyric, which he confessed he did not understand. 'Talk about Mr Naïve,' he later said. 'I had to go and ask somebody what it meant. I mean, I knew about the action but I hadn't heard anyone use that phrase.'

With the BBC ban of 'Relax' the buying public conformed to type and sent it straight to number one – where it stayed for five weeks. Every week on *Top of the Pops*, the show had to cut to a picture of the band before playing another artist in its place.

Some DJs within the BBC – notably David Jensen and John Peel – refused to toe the line and played the record regularly. As did the BBC's competitors, the commercial radio stations, who, sensing the BBC's discomfort and the song's huge popularity, placed 'Relax' on heavy rotation.

For years the band protested their innocence, refusing to admit that the song's lyrics were in any way sexual. Finally, a Frankie band member confessed: 'We used to pretend it was about motivation, but really it was about shagging.'

The song is the seventh-bestselling UK single ever, and deservedly so. Trevor Horn's production is brilliant, and Holly Johnson's vocal – which was captured at four in the morning when the singer was high on Nepalese hash – captures the song's intent beautifully. The song would go on to be used in various film soundtracks and hit the top ten again when it was re-released in September 1993. It has spent a combined total of 59 weeks in the UK chart. And thanks to censorship its popularity will never die.

Frankie Goes to Hollywood emerged from the late-70s Liverpool punk scene. They toured locally for a number of years and appeared on John Peel's influential radio show. In 1983 they were signed to Trevor Horn's new record company ZTT, and a year later were huge stars with their singles 'Relax' and 'Two Tribes'. Their debut album *Welcome to the Pleasure Dome* was equally successful. Providing a suitable follow-up to that album proved beyond them. Poorly attended tours and bad record sales damaged the band considerably, as did Holly Johnson's distancing from his fellow members. In 1987 the band split, and Johnson signed to MCA Records. ZTT took Johnson to court, claiming they had exclusive rights to all solo material. After two years of wrangling a judge ruled in Johnson's favour and the singer released two solo albums, which sold well. In 1993 he was diagnosed with HIV and later published his well-received biography, *A Bone in My Flute*. In later years the band would attempt to reform, but would always be undone by legal wrangling.

The shooting of
MARVIN
GAYE
by his own father

DATE 1 April 1984, Los Angeles

Hard to fathom, but there are some who believe that Marvin Gaye engineered his own death, that in essence he handed a gun to his father and instructed him to murder him. It's not clear if the death of Marvin Gaye was actually a kind of suicide, but it is a fact that on that terrible morning Marvin Gaye Snr shot a bullet into the heart of his son.

Marvin Gaye's father was a preacher who ranted against all unnatural vice. He was also a cross-dresser who drank copious amounts of vodka, beat his wife Alberta and their four children and ruled the house with violence and intimidation. His children lived in terror of him. Especially Marvin. 'From the time he was seven until he became a teenager,' his sister Jeanne says, 'Marvin's life at home consisted of a series of brutal whippings.'

Music came to Marvin's rescue, became his comfort, his refuge. He picked up the piano and drums very quickly. He had a natural ear. His father remained unimpressed. To get away from him, Marvin joined the air force but found no solace there. Just a string of colonels who liked to assert authority over him. He faked madness, and was given a discharge.

On his return to his home town of Washington he began singing doo-wop music with local bands, eventually ending up with The Moonglows led by one Harvey Fuqua. It was Fuqua who in 1960 took Gaye to Detroit to meet Berry Gordy and the Motown company. Gaye signed to Motown. He would stay there for 22 years, release several hit singles, create *What's Going On* and constantly argue with Gordy.

His time with Motown ended with a host of personal problems. By 1980 Gaye was addicted to cocaine and pornography, and he was anxious to leave America, where he owed millions of dollars in tax. He moved to London with his Dutch girlfriend Eugenie Vis, making dark demands of her as he sank further into his addictions.

'FROM THE TIME HE WAS SEVEN UNTIL HE BECAME A TEENAGER,' HIS SISTER JEANNE SAYS, 'MARVIN'S LIFE AT HOME CONSISTED OF A SERIES OF BRUTAL WHIPPINGS'

A saviour for Marvin arrived in the most unlikely guise. Freddy Cousaert was a Belgian promoter who adored Gaye's music. He persuaded the singer to come and stay with him in his house in Ostend. Marvin agreed and on his arrival began a programme designed to regain health and sanity. Marvin took to running, taking long walks, early nights. In the meantime CBS stepped in and put him back on track financially. He began writing a new album that he would call *Midnight Love*.

> 'THERE WAS MORE COKE ON THAT TOUR THAN ON ANY TOUR IN THE HISTORY OF ENTERTAINMENT.' THE COKE PLAYED HAVOC WITH HIS SEX INSTINCTS. GROUP ORGIES WERE COMMON. ON STAGE MARVIN WOULD STRIP DOWN TO HIS BRIEFS

Gaye also embarked upon writing an autobiography with the help of an author named David Ritz. One day, observing Marvin's collection of sadomasochistic pornography, Ritz observed that he needed 'sexual healing'. Within a week Gaye had put together the single that would return him to the public spotlight and win him two Grammy awards.

It was around this time that Marvin's mother Alberta suffered a stroke. He returned to the US to be near her. In April 1983 he began a four-month American tour which reignited his cocaine addiction. One participant said: 'There was more coke on that tour than on any tour in the history of entertainment.' The coke played havoc with his sex instincts. Group orgies were common, whilst on stage Marvin would sometimes strip down to his briefs.

At the tour's conclusion Marvin retreated to the house that he had bought his mother in Los Angeles. His brothers and sisters lived there too. 'I never saw Marvin in such bad shape,' said Alberta. 'He was exhausted. He should have checked into a hospital.' In October Marvin Snr moved back in with the family and berated his son for his seedy lifestyle. Marvin dismissed him. 'If he touches me,' he told his daughter Jeanne, 'I'll kill him.' Then for Christmas he gave his father a gun, an unregistered .38-calibre Smith and Wesson.

Three months passed, three months of tension between father and son. Despite all the success and the achievements, Marvin Gaye's father refused to give his son the unconditional love he so desperately sought. Instead, they argued and fought and humiliated each other. There was no respite and there was no love.

Two days before Gaye's 45th birthday came the tragic denouement. On 31 March mother and father quarrel. Son intervenes, tells father to lay off mother. Father wisely retreats. The next day father starts yelling that he is missing an insurance policy. Son calls father to his bedroom. Father refuses to go. Son verbally threatens him, and father walks in. Son physically attacks father. Mother rushes in and pulls the men apart. Son tells mother he is leaving the house. Son stays in bedroom. Father re-enters bedroom. With a gun. And he kills son with two bullets.

Brother Frankie and wife hear shots, run towards the house. Wife finds mother screaming: 'He shot my son.' Frankie runs upstairs, finds Marvin dying. Paramedics arrive to find father sitting on the porch, staring into space. Too late. By the time they get to Marvin he is barely alive. One of the greatest singer-songwriters of the 20th century is dead on arrival at the hospital.

Marvin Gaye Snr was charged with first-degree murder. That charge was reduced to manslaughter before the case came to court. In June he went on trial for the killing of his own son. His wife Alberta had posted bail. In November he was given a six-year suspended sentence and five years' probation.

Marvin Gaye's father said at his trial: 'If I could bring him back, I would. I was afraid of him. I thought I was going to get hurt. I didn't know what was going to happen... I'm really sorry for everything that happened.' It had taken him six months to apologize for killing his son.

Marvin Pentz Gaye was born on 2 April 1939. By the time he reached his teens Gaye could play drums and piano and was displaying a voice that was remarkable for its purity and four-octave range. He signed to Motown in 1963 and soon had a succession of hit singles such as 'Stubborn Kind of Fellow' and 'Can I Get a Witness'. In 1964 he married Anna Gordy (Berry's sister) and by 1967 he was singing duets with the singer Tammi Terrell. In 1971 he released *What's Going On*, regarded as one of the greatest albums ever. Albums such as *Let's Get It On* and *I Want You* made Marvin a sex symbol. Unhappy with such a categorization, Gaye fought numerous times with Gordy over musical direction and image. In the early 80s, with his record sales at an all-time low, Gaye left Motown, signed to CBS Records and resuscitated his career with the worldwide hit single 'Sexual Healing' and the album *Midnight Love*. Just as he was planning to record a follow-up, he was shot by his father at the family home in Los Angeles. It was the day before his 45th birthday.

LIVE AID

Geldof's gift to Africa

DATE 13 July 1985, Wembley Stadium, London

He sits in front of the TV, depressed and worried. It is 23 October 1984, and these are not the best of times for Bob Geldof or his band, The Boomtown Rats. They have a new album and a single waiting to go, music they think will revitalize their career. Big problem, though. Their record company are not prepared to back them. Single after single has flopped, and the company is wary of pouring money into a sinking ship. No hit, no tour; no tour, no band. No wonder Geldof is worried.

The Boomtown Rats, the band whose refusal to play image games has annoyed the music press no end and the band that had conquered most of the world with the single 'I Don't Like Mondays' is now on its knees. Oblivion beckons.

Geldof is at home brooding, thinking what to do, and with him is his partner, the TV presenter Paula Yates. Upstairs sleeps their baby Fifi. The voice on the TV announces the arrival of the news. The BBC journalist Michael Buerk appears on screen, and suddenly the world twists and Geldof's life changes forever – and so do those of many, many others.

Buerk is in Ethiopia reporting on a famine so severe he refers to it as 'biblical'. The screen is filled with emaciated faces and bodies, pleading eyes, desperation. The images are shocking. And this is not a handful of people Buerk is talking about. It is thousands upon thousands upon thousands of human beings wasting away. Geldof watches in horror, and cannot shake the images from his mind. They haunt him until morning light.

THE IMAGES ARE SHOCKING. AND THIS IS NOT A HANDFUL OF PEOPLE. IT IS THOUSANDS UPON THOUSANDS UPON THOUSANDS OF HUMAN BEINGS WASTING AWAY. GELDOF WATCHES IN HORROR

As part of his deal with Phonogram Records Geldof has been given his own office from which to conduct Boomtown Rats affairs. As he travels to work that day he wonders how he can help the people of Ethiopia. He can send money. But that would be a pittance against what is needed. He could persuade the band to give all the royalties from their next single to the famine fund, but that too would be a pittance, given their current popularity.

> U2 CAUSE THE FIRST RUCKUS OF THE DAY, BONO DIVING INTO THE AUDIENCE TO DANCE WITH A GIRL. MOST PEOPLE THINK IT IS A STUNT, A CHEAP STUNT, UNTIL IT IS LATER REVEALED THAT **THE GIRL WAS BEING CRUSHED TO DEATH**, AND BONO HAD JUMPED OFF THE STAGE TO SAVE HER

Then again, he could get the band to record a single specifically to raise money for Ethiopia. That might work. He arrives at his office. Two doors down there are four girls who work in the press office. He slides into their space and tentatively mentions the idea of a charity single to them. Their enthusiastic response hits Geldof. He knows that the Rats alone will not shift many copies. But maybe they get some star guests in. He calls his wife Paula who is recording *The Tube*, a TV pop show. Is there anyone she could approach with the idea of a charity single? Yes, she replies, Midge Ure is here. Put him on, says Geldof. The men talk. Ure asks Geldof if he has a song ready to record? Fragments of one is the Irish singer's reply. We will work on something tomorrow, Ure replies. Geldof puts down the phone, thinks and calls Sting. Will he help? Absolutely, says the Police frontman, I'll come in.

So will Simon Le Bon, Frankie Goes to Hollywood, Paul Young, Phil Oakey, Boy George – and even Paul Weller who Geldof knows despises him and the Rats. No problem, tragedy has rendered pop prejudice absurd.

Geldof is overwhelmed by the support. He now calls a meeting with the top people at Phonogram. They agree to print up the record, get it distributed. Geldof contacts pioneering artist Peter Blake who agrees to produce a cover. Geldof talks to George Michael's manager, Simon Napier-Bell, who tells him that even if they sell half a million copies it is still not much money. To really help, he needs to get the big stores not to take a profit on the record.

Geldof listens, Geldof acts, Geldof achieves. Everyone selling the record agrees not take a penny. The only tax to be paid is VAT, a position that the Tory government refuses to budge on. Until Geldof confronts Thatcher who, sensing a huge banana-skin mistake, waives the tax.

Midge Ure sends Geldof a tape with some music. Geldof meshes it with some lyrics, and a rough version of the song 'Do They Know It's Christmas' is made. Then a surprise: Paul Weller volunteers to play guitar. On the Saturday, Weller records his part, but his guitar rubs against Ure's electronic music, and Weller's contribution is left on the cutting-room floor. However, Sting and John Taylor from Duran Duran come and record the bass, and backing vocals are added.

MORE HELP IS NEEDED. THEY HAVE MADE A RECORD, GELDOF PRIVATELY THINKS. PERHAPS THEY NEED TO PLAY LIVE

The next day, Sunday 25 November 1984, a unique event is held. A host of British recording stars turn up at the Basing Street Studios in Ladbroke Grove and record 'Do They Know It's Christmas'. The line-up is staggering, and the group will be known as Band Aid. Bono, Phil Collins, George Michael, Boy George, Frankie, Status Quo, Kool and the Gang, and many more. David Bowie and Paul McCartney, unable to make the session, send tapes that are to be used on the B side. The record is finished at seven the next morning.

It is just over a month since Geldof sat in front of his TV. Advance orders for the single rise to 500,000. A week later the single is number one. In the first week alone it sells a million copies. It stays at number one for weeks, eventually selling three million copies. Geldof now travels to Ethiopia, is welcomed as he should be. A great thing has been achieved. But there is more to be done. Much more. He meets Mother Teresa, is appalled by the conditions and the two civil wars that are tearing the country apart, killing thousands of innocent children.

More help is needed. They have made a record, Geldof privately thinks. Perhaps they need to play live. Geldof receives a phone call from Ken Kragen. An American Band Aid style record is being planned. Michael Jackson and Lionel Richie have written a song entitled 'We Are the World'. Quincy Jones will produce, the *crème de la crème* of American music will take part. The band will be called USA for Africa.

Geldof flies to the studio in Los Angeles. He meets them all: Bob Dylan, Michael Jackson, Diana Ross, Stevie Wonder, Ray Charles, Dionne Warwick, Paul Simon, Lionel Richie, Bruce Springsteen, Smokey Robinson, Tina Turner… He makes a speech about his experiences in Ethiopia and other parts of Africa. At the end of his passionate speech, he mentions the possibility of a live concert…

Harvey Goldsmith is one of Britain's most famous promoters. Geldof contacts him with the idea for a twin concert, one starting at Wembley and then later on in the day a concert in the US. It is an outrageous plan but typical of Geldof's fierce drive. In discussions with Goldsmith

GELDOF GOES BACKSTAGE, AND IS INTERVIEWED LIVE. HE BERATES THE NATION FOR NOT DIGGING DEEPER. WITHIN AN HOUR THE SUM RISES TO £3 MILLION. WHEN THE MONEY IS COUNTED, IT IS IRELAND, GELDOF'S HOME COUNTRY, THAT LEADS THE WAY

he decides that British and American TV should transmit both events live. Bands will only get an allotted amount of time and will be expected to play their big hits to make maximum impact. As the bands play, viewers will pledge money. It will be the biggest TV fundraiser ever, a global jukebox of massive proportions.

Geldof gets on the phone. McCartney, Bowie, Jagger, Sting, U2, Queen, Adam Ant, Style Council, Status Quo, George Michael and Elton John, Boy George... the list gets bigger and bigger. In America, The Beach Boys, Paul Simon. Other countries, other networks now come in. But then bands and individuals start coming up with demands. 'I want to be on at this time' and suchlike. It is a minefield of delicate negotiations that Geldof has to tread through, all the time arguing that people are dying, and that means that your problem just fades into insignificance.

As millions are pledged by the TV companies and the sponsors, Geldof goes broke. His contract with Phonogram is up. He has to keep on borrowing from his wife to keep going. But then things swing Geldof's way. Dylan agrees to play: he will headline the American concert and finish with 'Blowin' in the Wind'. Mick Jagger and David Bowie will shoot a video of the Motown classic 'Dancing in the Street'. Whilst Bowie will play Wembley, Jagger will be at Philadelphia. Phil Collins agrees to play both gigs by flying between continents on the day.

On and on it goes, phones constantly ringing, a million questions, a hundred million inquiries directed at Geldof and his team. And then suddenly the day is

Millions were raised for Ethiopia when Bob Geldof persuaded fellow artists to play for free in both Britain and America one glorious July day. The concerts gave Geldof the platform to bring about real change in Africa.

upon them, a beautiful summer's day: 13 July 1985. Status Quo kick off the concert, Prince Charles tapping his feet in the royal box to the band's huge hit 'Rockin' All Over the World'. Style Council, The Boomtown Rats, Adam Ant, Ultravox and Spandau Ballet all perform.

Then an announcement: Philadelphia has just gone live. Bernard Watson, Joan Baez, The Hooters, Four Tops, Billy Ocean, Black Sabbath, Run DMC, Rick Springfield and REO Speedwagon take up the first few hours. Back in the UK, Elvis Costello, Nik Kershaw, Sade, Sting, Phil Collins, Howard Jones, Bryan Ferry and Paul Young give their performances.

FINALLY, PAUL MCCARTNEY STRIDES OUT ON STAGE FOR THE FIRST TIME IN EIGHT YEARS, INVITING ALL THE OTHER ARTISTS TO SING HIS SONG 'LET IT BE'

U2 cause the first ruckus of the day, Bono diving into the audience to dance with a girl. Most people think it is a stunt, a cheap stunt, until it is later revealed that the girl was being crushed to death, and Bono had jumped off the stage to save her. His intervention means that the band are unable to play their single 'Pride'.

No problem, the band are catapulted into the charts the following week, and Bono subsequently dedicates much of his time to famine issues in Africa.

Princess Diana gets her wish when her favourite band Dire Straits appear. Over in Philadelphia, the names are starting to get bigger and bigger – Crosby Stills and Nash, Judas Priest, Bryan Adams, The Beach Boys, George Thorogood and the Destroyers, Simple Minds, The Pretenders, Santana, Ashford and Simpson along with singer Teddy Pendergrass (his first live concert since being confined to a wheelchair), Kool and the Gang, and Madonna. London retaliates with a performance from Queen that was later voted one of the best live performances ever; and with Bowie, who dedicates his 'Heroes' to 'all the children in the world'.

Around this time Geldof asks the office how much the UK has pledged so far. He is told: £1.2 million. He is devastated. He figured much more would be coming in. He goes backstage and is interviewed live on TV, where he berates the country for not digging deeper into their pockets. Within an hour the sum rises to £3 million. When all the pledges are counted it is Ireland, Geldof's home country, that leads the way. The biggest single donation is from Dubai, whose ruling family donate £1 million.

The show goes on. A ragged The Who, simmering with tension, are cut off halfway through their anthemic song 'My Generation'. Then, finally, Paul McCartney strides out on stage for the first time in eight years, inviting all the other artists to sing his song 'Let It Be'. The concert finishes with a version of 'Do They Know It's Christmas', all the artists now on stage for the conclusion to an amazing day, a historic day.

But the music plays on in Philadelphia: Tom Petty and the Heartbreakers, Kenny Loggins, The Cars, Neil Young, Power Station, Thompson Twins, Eric Clapton, a unique set from Plant, Page and Jones, Duran Duran, Patti LaBelle, Hall and Oates. Mick Jagger performs 'It's Only Rock 'n' Roll' with Tina Turner, and rips part of her dress off. Then Bob Dylan appears with Ron Wood and Keith Richards, looking like they have been up all night drinking not rehearsing. Dylan breaks a string, so Ron Wood hands him his guitar, and as he waits for a replacement Wood air-guitars his part. Dylan finishes on 'Blowin' in the Wind', and then everyone takes to the stage to sing 'We Are the World'.

It is estimated that more than £150 million was raised as a result of these two concerts. Similar events would later be staged, with bands either performing at concerts or on charity records. It is ironic to think that when he first appeared on London's punk scene, Geldof and The Boomtown Rats were considered a sham, a bunch of jokers. Yet it is arguably the hotheaded Irishman who has done more than any other punk performer to truly change the world.

BOB GELDOF
1951–

Robert Frederick Zenon Geldof was born in Ireland on 5 October 1951. He attended Blackrock College, a private school, where he was often bullied. He left school and took on various jobs before relocating to Canada and working there as a music journalist. On his return to Ireland in 1975 he became the frontman for The Boomtown Rats, adopting a punk sound and style. In 1979 their song 'I Don't Like Mondays' (written by Geldof) became a huge international hit. The band spent much of the early 80s touring and recording. Unable to sustain their success, the band fell apart in the late 80s. By then Geldof was a highly respected figure thanks to his work in putting together the Live Aid records and concerts, which have raised millions of pounds for Africa. Geldof has been bestowed with many honours for his charity work, including the Freedom of the City of Dublin and the Man of Peace award. He also runs a successful television company. He married presenter Paula Yates and they had three daughters: Fifi, Peaches and Pixie.

The press turn on

BOY GEORGE

DATE April 1986, London

Famously, he told the nation that he would rather have a cup of tea than sex. He was lying through his teeth, of course. Judging by his autobiographies, George O'Dowd was always a highly sexed man who got more than his fair share.

George O'Dowd's alter-ego, Boy George, was a whole different boudoir, however. Boy George was the androgynous singer who fronted Culture Club. He sang very pretty pop songs, challenged people's prejudices, and kept his sexuality secret. He had to if he wanted to be very famous. The world loves a man who dresses up, who slaps on the make-up. As long as he keeps it pantomime. Boy George, the pin-up poster on the young girl's bedroom wall, had to remain cuddly and warm and, above all, safe. He was a doll, a fantasy, an illusion that could not be broken.

So when the *Daily Mirror* wrote about his strange behaviour in a story headlined 'What's the Trouble with the Boy?' people were really taken aback. George? Being strange? George is many things: he is witty and wise, an Oscar Wilde type. He wouldn't be doing anything strange, would he?

Then there was a *London Evening Standard* article entitled 'Worried About the Boy'. The piece discussed George's recent appearance on a chat show. They reported that George had been sweating heavily and fell asleep. The subtext was clear – George, cuddly George, was a massive drug-taker. It was some turnaround by the press, because once Georgie was their darling.

When the *Standard* hit the stands George was on heroin, flying high as a kite in his Hampstead mansion. A *News of the World* reporter now banged on his door. Stupidly, given his condition, George

GEORGE WAS SAFE AND HE WAS WITTY, FUNNY BUT VULNERABLE. A PERFECT FIT FOR A FAMILY NEWSPAPER. GRANNIES LOVED HIM, KIDS ADORED HIM

answered. The reporter asked George if he wanted to respond to the article. Having not seen it, he and the journo went and bought a copy of the paper. Enraged by its contents, George asked the journo to drive him to the *Standard* offices. Once there, George demanded to see the writer, whom George knew. He had given him interviews and quotes. They had been

Boy George arrives at court to face charges of possession of heroin. His charming, asexual persona made him seem an unlikely candidate to succumb to the rock'n'roll lifestyle.

chummy. Now he had stabbed him in the back, and George wanted revenge. A journalist named Spencer Leigh (later George's biographer) managed to persuade George to leave the building. Straight away. But the *News of the World* reporter had a real scoop. The following Sunday another story about George's erratic behaviour appeared. George now knew that his once-warm relationship with the press had entered a very dangerous phase. That which had helped make him was now out to destroy him – once and for all.

In the early 80s Boy George and Culture Club were one of the first acts to benefit from the tabloids' decision to take a closer interest in pop music. George was perfect for their needs – he was safe, and he was witty, funny but vulnerable, a perfect fit for a family newspaper. Grannies loved him, kids adored him. He mixed charm and bitchy one-liners beautifully. He was the kind of person whose fame no one begrudged. The teen-pop mags loved him, but then so did the more serious publications. That was George, likeable and lovable, and all things to all men.

Then on New Year's Eve 1984 he swallowed an ecstasy pill, and his life changed forever. George fell in love with ecstasy, the way it dissolved all his fears and paranoia, the way it made him so happy and joyous and sensual. He woke up the next morning, having had great sex with a beautiful man, and ordered a truckload more.

From there he graduated to cocaine. As he writes in his autobiography, one drug led to another like stepping stones across a murky stream. The only thing he cared about was having a good time. And why not? Culture Club were on the wane, and the band were drifting apart. They had lost the ability to communicate with each other, George later noted. Instead of tackling the decline, George pressed the party-mode button. Big time. He partied in New York and in London and in Paris. And it was in Paris that he met the substance that would bring him to his knees.

Again, it was New Year's Eve. George was at a fashion show and desperate to score some cocaine. He asked around and someone slipped him a bag with brown powder in it. 'It could have been any drug,' he writes. 'I didn't care.' He went to the toilets and he snorted heroin. At first he felt sick and ill, and then suddenly a warm glow spread out inside of him, and George had taken his first step towards his addiction. Heroin became a way of life. He had the money, and he had the time. As his addiction deepened, people started making warning noises, but he was a pop star so he ignored them.

Even when a key member of his team, Jo Bailey, quit because of his habit, he simply shrugged his (very broad) shoulders. When the head of his record company, Richard Branson, sent him a letter expressing his concern, George just threw it in the bin. In Stockholm, to meet King Carl Gustaf and Queen Silvia, George found a wrap of heroin in his suitcase. He still wonders if the king and queen realized just how high he was when he met them half an hour later, after having snorted up a line or two.

GEORGE NOW KNEW THAT HIS ONCE-WARM RELATIONSHIP WITH THE PRESS HAD ENTERED **A VERY DANGEROUS PHASE.** THAT WHICH HAD HELPED TO MAKE HIM WAS NOW OUT TO DESTROY HIM – ONCE AND FOR ALL

When the press began to sniff around, George went to Jamaica with his boyfriend Marilyn. They spent so much time doing heroin that they decided on a holiday to get over the holiday. They booked a two-week cruise knowing they wouldn't be able to get any drugs at sea.

Two days into the trip, the withdrawal symptoms were excruciating. So they jumped ship at Guadeloupe, and made it to the airport where they phoned a friend in New York, and begged her to meet them in Paris with heroin. She agreed, and started packing her bags. The boys flew to the connecting airport for Paris, then saw a plane bound for New York. So they jumped on that plane, flew to New York and landed just in time to catch the friend before she boarded the plane to Paris. They then spent two weeks in New York on heroin.

When George got back to London the press were waiting for him, poisoned pens poised. Again he lied through his front teeth. He told them: 'I've always tried to tell kids to stay off drugs. I've never taken them myself, but people think I have been going round taking everything in sight. It's not true and it never will be.'

The illusion had been shattered, but no one could face picking the glass up off the floor. The reporters who once smiled at him and laughed at his jokes no longer had any use for him. Culture Club? Schmulture Club. No one cared about them any more. No one bought their records.

In June 1986 George showed up for the Artists Against Apartheid show. His appearance was shocking. He was dishevelled, ultra-skinny, his face caked in make-up. He sang two songs very badly before quitting the stage. He retained his humour. 'I am a drag addict,' he shouted to the crowd, 'not a drug addict.' Backstage, he talked incoherently with other artists before someone ushered him into a car and he was taken home. To do more drugs.

It was a year and a half since he had taken that first ecstasy pill. At a photoshoot later that summer a photographer named David Levine showed up at the studio. He knew George and he started badgering the singer for drugs. George made a call and a dealer arrived at the studio. The next morning, two *Daily Mirror* reporters arrived on George's doorstep. They have some bad news. On tomorrow morning's front page David Levine would claim George procured drugs for him.

'I AM A DRAG ADDICT,' HE SHOUTED TO THE CROWD, 'NOT A DRUG ADDICT'

George's brother Kevin now went to the papers. He told the *Mirror* that his family believed George had just eight weeks to live. George agreed to go into rehab to wean himself off the drug. Whilst at the clinic George was arrested. 'The British press had me arrested,' George later claimed. 'I was away for a few days, and they started printing stories saying, "Get him! Find him!" I was never caught with heroin, but they made a new law that said, "Because you have admitted taking heroin, we are charging you with possession".'

He was right. The press was on a witch-hunt. George appeared in court and was fined... £250. The press were outraged by what they considered overly lenient treatment, and George walked away smiling. But his life was far from happy. He was still an addict. In August an American friend, a songwriter named Michael Rudetsky, arrived at George's house. He was there to help George write songs. Before they could start work, Rudetsky overdosed on heroin and died in George's house. Although George was cleared of all wrongdoing, and although highly distraught at the loss of a friend, the singer was still in thrall to heroin's dark powers. He kept on using until finally, at Christmas, a second death gave George back his life.

Mark Golding was someone George loved, one of the few people who spoke to George O'Dowd, not to Boy George. Mark, George and another friend went out for a Christmas party and were arrested for marijuana possession. They were kept in the cells for 12 hours. The next day Golding overdosed on methadone and died.

On hearing of his passing George broke down. 'When Mark died, that's when I decided to come off everything,' he said. He found Buddhism, found work as a DJ and eased himself back into life. His relationship with drugs was not quite finished: there would be other incidents with cocaine that would take George into sobriety and the Narcotics Anonymous movement. But he now knew something he had not realized before – if you live by the press, you will probably die by the press.

BOY GEORGE 1961–

George O'Dowd was born on 14 June 1961 to an Irish family living in England. As a young man his outlandish style of dressing caught the attention of ex-Sex Pistols manager, Malcolm McLaren, who brought George into Bow Wow Wow, the band he then managed. After he finished with them, George began putting his own band together. Culture Club was launched in the early 80s and became a worldwide sensation, with singles such as 'Do You Really Want to Hurt Me' and 'Karma Chameleon'. Boy George's androgynous image and witty one-liners endeared him to the public but following faltering record sales the band split in 1986. George went on to have a solo career, scoring a number one hit with his cover of Ken Booth's 'Everything I Own'. He also released underground music and DJ'd all around the world. His battle with drug addictions led him to be arrested in New York, and he also served a prison sentence in the UK in 2009 for kidnapping a male escort. In 2010 the BBC screened a drama about his life, *Worried About the Boy.*

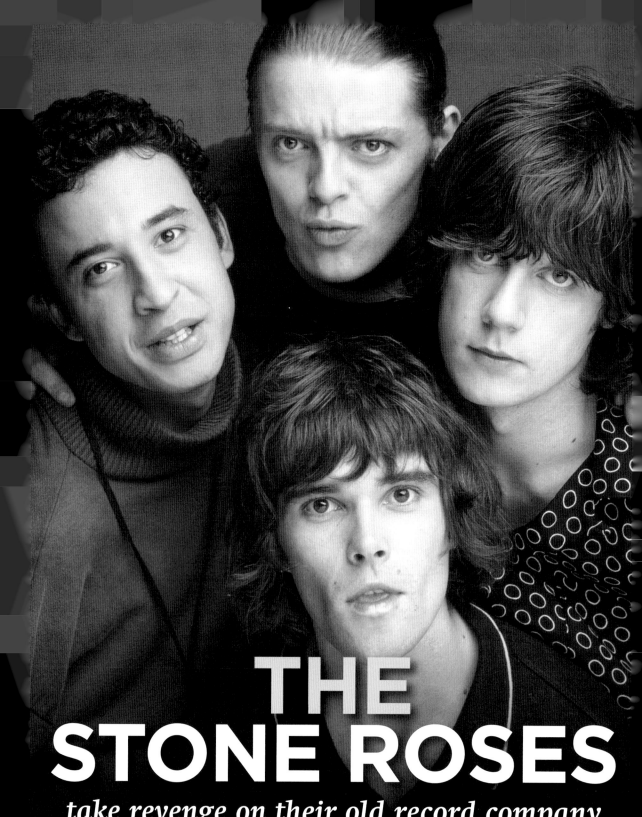

THE
STONE ROSES

take revenge on their old record company

DATE 6 February 1990, Wolverhampton

The Stone Roses are on the road, heading south from their home town of Manchester towards Wolverhampton. But they are not on their way to a gig, and they have none of their musical instruments with them. Instead, the boot of the car is loaded with pots of red and blue paint.

When the band arrive in Wolverhampton, they make their way to the offices of Revolver FM Records, run by Paul Birch and his girlfriend Olivia Darling. They pull into the record company's carpark and get out of the car. They go to the back of the car, remove the paint from the boot, walk over to a stationary Mercedes-Benz and throw paint all over it. They repeat the act with two other cars. Then they walk into Revolver, find the office of Birch and Darling and throw paint all over the shocked pair. They do the same to the office furniture and walls before departing.

The police are called and the band quickly apprehended. After all, locating four paint-splattered Mancunians in a car on a drizzly afternoon in Wolverhampton can't be all that hard. They are taken to the Birmingham Road police station, and placed in cells. Why is the hippest band in Britain at that time acting in such a manner? The answer is: a three-minute pop video.

This band are never going to have a staid and uneventful career. Their very first gig in 1984 is supporting no less a luminary than Pete Townshend. It is an anti-heroin benefit, and after that performance Townshend tells them that Reni, their drummer, is the best he has heard since Keith Moon.

> **THEY GO TO THE BACK OF THE CAR, REMOVE THE PAINT FROM THE BOOT, WALK OVER TO A STATIONARY MERCEDES-BENZ AND THROW PAINT ALL OVER IT**

No one knows it at the time, but The Stone Roses are to take over from The Smiths, whose job in music is now nearly done. At first, the Roses' music is unfocused, unremarkable. In 1985 they release a debut single, 'So Young', and it sounds, in vocalist Ian Brown's wry statement, 'like four lads trying to get out of Manchester'. Too much enthusiasm and not enough thought goes into that record. It is produced by the hip Martin Hannett, and the band promote it by putting on warehouse parties in Manchester. They write new songs, work again with Martin Hannett, yet the finished tapes are still nothing remarkable, still have nothing on them to suggest what is to come.

AFTER THAT PERFORMANCE TOWNSHEND WILL TELL THEM THAT RENI, THEIR DRUMMER, IS THE BEST HE HAS HEARD SINCE KEITH MOON

So The Stone Roses sack management and bring in a loudmouthed, fast-talking man called Gareth Evans, who sets about promoting the band as if they were the Second Coming. He manages a new venue in town called The International, which is where he now installs the band to rehearse by day, and play gigs by night.

It is at a gig at The International that a 16-year-old lad called Liam Gallagher watches Ian Brown and thinks: That's what I want to do. Evans gets the band

a deal with a small label called Black, a subsidiary of Revolver Records, and they record and release their best song to date, 'Sally Cinnamon'. It gets them attention on Britain's indie scene, but the relationship between band and record company falters, and in June the next year they sign to Silvertone Records.

In April 1988 the band makes the breakthrough and puts out 'Elephant Stone', which lays down the blueprint they will now follow: shuffling dance rhythms, funky rock guitar and Brown's melodic and wispy vocals. Meanwhile the Madchester scene is starting to gather pace. The main nightclub, The Hacienda, is getting known for its wild acid-house nights, and a new breed of bands appear to mirror that excitement – Happy Mondays in particular.

The Stone Roses' next single is 'She Bangs the Drums', which creates more momentum for the band. And then in May 1989 comes their debut album, simply entitled *The Stone Roses*. The reviews are ecstatic. 'This record is godlike,' says one paper. The band become the band of their generation, and cement it all by issuing the ultimate indie dance crossover song 'Fools Gold'. And that is it. From then on they are the new kings.

Sold-out gigs, front covers of music papers, fan devotion, money, drugs, all theirs now, and plenty more where it came from. And then Revolver pull their little stroke. They re-release 'Sally Cinnamon' to capitalize on the band's newfound success. And, worse, they shoot a cheap video to accompany its release. It's the video that really gets up the band's noses. Ever conscious of image, the band have forged a new look in their dress and record sleeves. Style is important to them, artistic expression highly important. To see one of their songs accompanied by a film that looks as if it was shot in one hour on a high street somewhere is highly insulting to their sensibilities.

So if the label wants to mess around with their art, what better revenge than to cover the bosses with paint? Perhaps their offices could stand a little artwork à la Roses...

After a night in the cells they appear before a court and are granted bail on the condition that they stay away from Revolver's offices in Wolverhampton and London, and from Birch and Darling. Outside the courthouse Ian Brown quips about his cell: 'It was the worst hotel I've ever stayed in.' Two girl fans wait for them by their car. 'They couldn't have done it,' one of them says, 'they are too sweet.'

The band return to court on 6 March, to be told by the judge that he will not imprison them since that act would give them lifelong notoriety. Instead, the band receive hefty fines and are made to pay compensation. Leaving the court, John Squire, the guitarist, is heard to comment: 'I didn't know abstract expressionism was a criminal offence.'

The Stone Roses rose from the ashes of two other bands, The Patrol and The Waterfront. The Roses' line-up consisted of John Squire (guitar), Ian Brown (vocals), Mani (bass) and Reni (drums). The band built their reputation with various one-off singles and gigs before releasing their debut album in May 1989. The eponymously titled album was seen as the epitome of the Madchester scene and went on to influence numerous bands. Their subsequent shows at Spike Island and Alexandra Palace placed the band at the forefront of British music. A dispute with their recording label Silvertone meant that they could not work on a follow-up album until mid 1993. By then, the pressure on the band to produce an album equally as significant was enormous, and led to huge tensions between members of the band. Their new album *The Second Coming*, released in December 1994, was not that well received – and the band fell apart within two years. Brown, Squire and Mani all went on to other musical pursuits, whilst drummer Reni has kept a low profile.

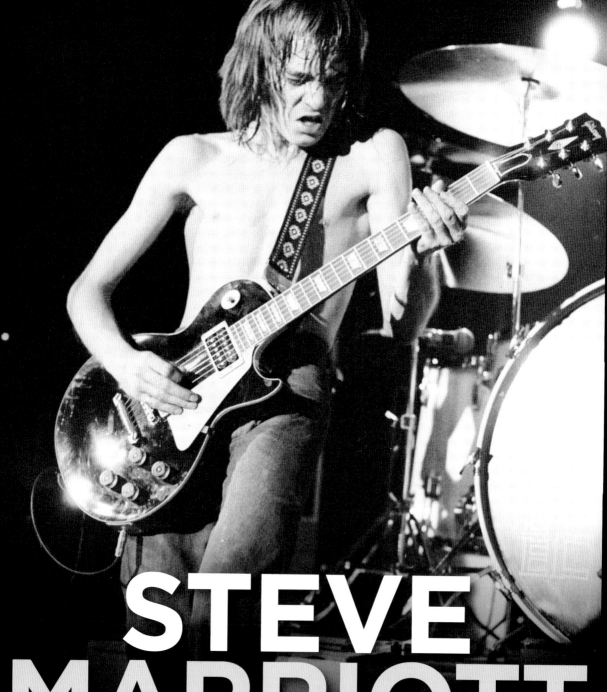

STEVE MARRIOTT

dies in a fire of his own making

DATE 20 April 1991, Arkesden, Essex

They had been arguing badly on the flight home, so badly, in fact, that a stewardess had to come over and remonstrate with them. 'Please, be quiet, the other passengers are complaining,' she told them. Steve Marriott and his third wife Toni stopped and made some grumbling noises. But five minutes later were furiously sniping at each other again. It was pretty obvious that their relationship had come to an end, and Marriott wanted out as soon as possible. The woman was driving him mad.

Marriott and his wife were flying to London from Los Angeles. It had not been a great trip. Marriott had been in LA to work with his former ally, guitarist Peter Frampton. Marriott had first met Frampton in 1968. At the time Marriott was the leader of a fine band called Small Faces, which had enjoyed several chart hits, including 'All or Nothing' and 'Itchycoo Park'. Small Faces

MARRIOTT LOVED A GOOD TIME. HE LOVED TO MIX WORK WITH PLEASURE. THAT WAS THE WHOLE POINT OF BEING A MUSICIAN, WASN'T IT?

fashioned a unique sound based around soul, pop, psychedelia, Britain's music-hall tradition and, most of all, Marriott's amazingly soulful voice.

Although their music was the equal of many of their contemporaries, Small Faces had a huge problem: they were seen as a teenybopper group. Despite all their efforts to shake off the tag, their sharp image, youthful demeanour, use of fashion and ability to craft hit singles made them highly attractive to young girls. At one event they were almost crushed in a Mini car under the weight of screaming fans. Many of their gigs ended with the band having to rush from the stage to the safety of cars waiting to whisk them away from the screaming girl hordes rushing towards them. The band hated their pop-band tag; but their happy-go-lucky characters, raw sense of humour and refusal to take life that seriously tended to rebound against them. In an effort to widen the band's appeal, Marriott asked Peter Frampton to join the band. The band did not want Frampton. The band fell apart.

In 1969 Marriott and Frampton formed Humble Pie, a heavy-rock band whose albums such as *Rock On* and *Performance: Rockin' the Fillmore* won them many fans in the US, and led to sell-out shows at prestigious venues such as Madison Square Garden in New York.

Frampton left the band in 1971, but the two men kept in touch. Now Frampton envisaged the pair working well together again, maybe even re-forming Humble Pie. That is why he had invited Marriott out to America. But Marriott had arrived in LA a man out of time. It was 1991, and the music business there had no tolerance for the kind of rock'n'roll excess that Marriott enjoyed. In this part of the world, musicians tended to be tanned not stoned. Record-company executives worked gyms, not drug dealers.

Marriott loved a good time, loved to mix work with pleasure. That was the whole point of being a musician, wasn't it? After two weeks he was on a flight back home, drinking heavily and wondering how soon he could divorce Toni.

When they landed at Heathrow, Phil Anthony was waiting for the unhappy couple. Anthony had played guitar in one of the several bands that Marriott had fronted in the 80s, and had been looking after Marriott's house in his absence. Anthony was nervous. Whilst he was out one night Marriott's house had been burgled and his favourite Epiphone guitar stolen. Anthony was fearful that suspicion for the burglary might fall on his shoulders. But when Marriott and Toni arrived he quickly forgot that worry.

AS TONI SLEPT, MARRIOTT OUTLINED HIS PLANS FOR THE FUTURE, A NEW BAND BEING HIS PRIORITY. HE ALREADY HAD THE NAME: I SHOULD COCOA

'When Steve first arrived at Heathrow,' Anthony recalls, 'he appeared agitated. There was a definite atmosphere between him and Toni.' After a swift drink at the airport bar, the party of three clambered into Anthony's car. Toni lay out in the back seat, exhausted. Meanwhile, Steve lit up a cigarette. He much preferred to smoke roll-ups, he told Anthony, but the airport did not sell loose tobacco, so he was forced to smoke these.

As Toni slept, Marriott outlined his plans for the future, a new band being his priority. He already had the name: I Should Cocoa. The two men laughed, and Toni

Steve Marriott fronts a re-formed Humble Pie on a New York stage in October 1980. His original band were left penniless in the mid-70s despite breaking America in a significant manner.

woke up. What are you laughing about, she asked goodnaturedly? Instantly, Marriott snapped at her, told her to shut up. 'Every time she would say something, he would shout her down,' Anthony recalled.

They stopped at Anthony's house where they drank tea. Then it was on to the river, where Marriott kept a boat. He wanted to make sure all was fine. With that confirmed, they drove back to Marriott's house, which was situated in a small village called Arkesden in Essex. Marriott

wanted to assess the damage caused by the burglary. Worn down by the couple's arguing, Anthony now said his goodbyes and headed off. It was about five o'clock in the afternoon.

Marriott and Toni took their luggage into the house. Once unpacked, they started arguing again, and this time the vitriol reached such a peak that Marriott smashed the telephone in frustration.

Salvation arrived in the form of a local car dealer and mutual friend, Ray

Newcomb. Ray persuaded the couple to have a meal at one of Marriott's favourite restaurants, The Straw Hat in nearby Sawbridgeworth. It seemed like a good idea, so they moved off. At the restaurant they were joined by Ray's friend Phil, and they all consumed a lot of wine. Unfortunately, the alcohol increased the tension between Steve and Toni, and the arguing got so loud that staff came to their table and asked them to tone it down.

> ## 'AS SOON AS I SAW THE BODY CLEARLY I KNEW WHO IT WAS. I USED TO BE A FAN. IT'S HARD TO PUT MY FEELINGS INTO WORDS'

By the end of the meal Marriott was very drunk. Ray then suggested that they spend the night at his house. He feared that if he left them alone, serious damage would be sustained by one or the other. The couple agreed, and they drove to Ray's house. At about one o'clock Steve and Toni went to bed. Ray and his friend Phil stayed up. Five minutes later, Marriott appeared downstairs and ordered a cab. 'I have had enough of her,' he told the two men. 'I am going home.'

Marriott headed back to his house. He arrived at about one-thirty. Lying on his bed, he thought: I will have one more cigarette before I go to sleep. He lit up, and settled his head on the pillow...

At four o'clock that morning a passing driver noticed flames shooting out of Steve Marriott's house. He drove on to the nearest telephone box and phoned the fire brigade, who dispatched a vehicle immediately. One of the firemen who attended the fire was Keith Dunatis. He rushed round the back of the house and broke in through the kitchen door and rushed upstairs.

His heart skipped a beat. 'As soon as I saw the body clearly, I knew who it was,' he later said. 'I used to be a fan. It is difficult to put my feelings into my words.'

Later inquiries would suggest that after the fire began, Marriott woke up confused after having inhaled inordinate amounts of smoke. He tried to escape through the nearest door but, tragically, picked the cupboard door next to the bed. Before he could rectify his mistake the fire got him. His body could only be positively identified by using dental records. That is how badly Steve Marriott was burnt.

The funeral took place on Tuesday 30 April 1991. Family and friends and large contingents of Marriott fans showed up at the church. Everyone kept a calm demeanour until the record Steve was best known for, 'All or Nothing', came blaring through the speakers. That was when the tears rolled and the impact of his too-soon passing really hit home.

Rick Wills, former bass player with Humble Pie, said: 'When we walked in

EVERYONE KEPT A CALM DEMEANOUR UNTIL THE RECORD STEVE WAS BEST KNOWN FOR, 'ALL OR NOTHING', CAME BLARING THROUGH SPEAKERS. THAT WAS WHEN THE TEARS ROLLED AND THE IMPACT OF HIS TOO-SOON PASSING REALLY HIT HOME

STEVE MARRIOTT
1947–1991

the crematorium and saw this tiny white coffin, I just couldn't believe that Steve was in there. This guy that had always been so full of life and had given so much to the world musically, was gone. I coped pretty well until they played "All or Nothing"...'

It was later revealed that if Steve had been smoking the roll-ups he favoured then the fire would not have happened. Loose tobacco does not have added chemicals to keep it burning. The ciggy in his hand would have extinguished itself, and the man many believe to be one of the greatest British vocalists ever, the man that Keith Richards voted as one of his five favourite artists of all time, would still be with us.

Stephen Peter Marriott was born on 30 January 1947, and grew up in the East End of London. He quickly became obsessed with music, especially Buddy Holly, his first musical inspiration and hero. He helped form Small Faces in 1964. Within a year they were national pop stars, with hits such as 'Whatcha Gonna Do About It' and 'Sha-La-La-La-Lee'. Marriott's amazing voice and songwriting abilities helped propel the band forwards. Their mix of soul, music-hall and psychedelia was an inspired sound. However, Marriott felt the band were not being taken seriously, and left in 1969 to form the heavy-rock act Humble Pie. Their no-nonsense approach won them many admirers, in America especially. In 1976 the band disbanded, and Marriott returned to the UK where he would oversee an unfortunate Small Faces reunion. In the 80s he fronted a number of pub bands such as the Packet of Three. Marriott died in 1991, but his influence can be seen and felt in many different bands, including Oasis, The Jam, Blur, Ocean Colour Scene and others.

KURT COBAIN
is kissed by his bandmate live on TV

DATE 11 January 1992, NBC TV Studios, New York

On the morning of his appearance on the prestigious American TV show *Saturday Night Live*, Kurt Cobain awoke and decided to shoot up heroin. He reasoning was simple. If he fixed himself straightaway, he should be functioning by the time his band Nirvana went before the cameras. The only trouble was that Kurt Cobain was now a serious heroin addict who was injecting more and more of the stuff to get high. He was also performing and scoring in a city where the heroin is stronger than most.

When Cobain arrived for a photoshoot that afternoon he could hardly keep awake, often nodding off as the camera clicked away. At the soundcheck at the NBC studios he looked terrible, his complexion, his clothes, his look, all bedraggled and pale and dishevelled. Recently an interviewer

EVERYONE AROUND HIM WAS WORRIED, NOT LEAST DAVE GROHL AND KRIST NOVOSELIC WHO PRAYED THAT HE WOULD THROW AWAY THE SYRINGE AND RE-ENTER THE WORLD

had said Cobain was 25 years old but he looked over 40. He also said that Cobain had pinpoint eyes and kept falling asleep throughout their interview, the sure sign of someone using heroin.

After the soundcheck, Cobain lay on a sofa in his dressing room and refused to engage with the world. This should have been the happiest time of his life, but he was basically comatose for most of it. He had a woman, Courtney Love, he deeply loved and cared for. His band was selling records at a ridiculous pace, and now came the news that next week the band's second album *Nevermind* would replace Michael Jackson's *Dangerous* at the top of the American charts. It had sold nearly 400,000 copies in the week after Christmas, an incredible amount for what is normally a dead week in record retailing.

Tower Records said they had never seen so many young people swapping Christmas CDs for one particular album. *Nevermind* had struck a chord with America's young; it had restored rock's rebellious spirit with a music characterized by slow verses and angry choruses. Nirvana were now in a category that included their heroes The Sex Pistols.

FEEDBACK ROARED THROUGH TV SETS ALL OVER AMERICA. AND THEN, AS THE CREDITS ROLLED, KRIST WENT STRAIGHT UP TO KURT AND PUT HIS TONGUE IN HIS MOUTH

The Pistols' Sid Vicious had died a junkie, and Kurt looked set to follow in his footsteps. Cobain took drugs, so he liked to claim, because of terrible stomach pains that rendered him so weak he could hardly get out of bed. He saw numerous doctors, took numerous medicines, but nothing worked. Then one day he tried heroin, and the pain went away. So, he reasoned, if these pains are going to make me look like a junkie, I might as well become a junkie. Four years later he was a full-blown addict. Many times friends had to rush to bathrooms and hotel bedrooms and slap

him and bring him back to life. Numerous interventions were staged. Family members and band members and manager all demanded that he recognize his problem and enter rehab. But he would just turn on them, tell them they were all hypocrites, and eventually they would all go away and he would then stick another needle into his arm and head for the darkness.

Everyone around him was worried, not least his band members, drummer Dave Grohl and bassist Krist Novoselic, who prayed that he would throw away the syringe and re-enter the world. By the time they were due on stage, Kurt was sober and in a down mood. He looked annoyed, unapproachable, cut off by an internal anger, either with himself or others. It was always hard to tell with Kurt.

The band opened their *Saturday Night Live* set with 'Smells Like Teen Spirit', the song that would become their anthem. All the band members launched themselves into the song with furious anger, not least Kurt who looked like a demented banshee howling at his demons. They had passed the first test successfully.

They came back later in the show for a song called 'Territorial Pissings', again with the anger and the fury. And then at the song's conclusion Kurt slammed his guitar into his amplifier à la Townshend. Ironic really: in a recent interview Cobain had said he would rather die than get old and be Pete Townshend. Now, he was the young Townshend, and Nirvana were the young Who, gleefully smashing up their instruments. Dave Grohl kicked his drums forwards onto the floor and hurled a microphone at Novoselic, who hurled it back at Grohl.

THIS SHOULD HAVE BEEN THE HAPPIEST TIME OF HIS LIFE BUT HE WAS BASICALLY COMATOSE FOR MOST OF IT

Feedback roared through TVs all over America. And then, as the credits rolled, Krist went straight up to Kurt and put his tongue in his mouth. Later Kurt would say the provocative action was pure punk rock, a way of upsetting the rednecks and the homophobes that they despised so much. But it wasn't. It was a gesture of deep friendship from Krist to Kurt, a way of saying we love you and we care for you. 'I wanted to make him feel better,' Krist said later. 'At the end of it all I told him: it's going to be okay. It's not so bad, okay?'

Cobain skipped the aftershow party. Instead he gave a lengthy interview, and then went back to his hotel. Meanwhile, Courtney Love had just made an amazing discovery. She was pregnant with Kurt's baby. But she couldn't tell him. Kurt had overdosed again.

The band Nirvana hailed from the town of Aberdeen, Washington. It was formed in 1987 by Krist Novoselic and Kurt Cobain. The band had various line-ups, but settled into a dynamic three-piece outfit when drummer Dave Grohl joined. Their collective love of punk rock and couldn't-care-less attitude saw them signed to the independent label Sub Pop. They released an album, *Bleach*, but were soon frustrated by its relative lack of success. They found new management and were signed to Geffen Records in 1990. Their second album, *Nevermind,* hit gold as did the single 'Smells Like Teen Spirit'. Within months they were the biggest band in the world, the leaders of what was termed the grunge sound. Their third album, *In Utero,* was still abrasive but slightly differed from the normal Nirvana sound. Unfortunately, Cobain's increasing heroin addiction meant that the band missed many opportunities to push the album. Nirvana came to an abrupt and tragic end on Friday 8 April 1994 when Kurt Cobain committed suicide. He was 27 years old.

SINEAD
O'CONNOR

tears up a picture of the Pope live on American TV

DATE 3 October 1992, New York

In 1965 John Lennon said that The Beatles were bigger than Jesus Christ. He was not being arrogant or superior, just stating a fact. More people listened to his band than went to church. But all hell broke loose. How dare this upstart even start to compare himself with the son of God? Facing a hysterically hostile media, and with death threats coming in from all sides, Lennon was forced into a public apology the proud man was furious about having to make. Rock stars would think twice before offending the religious sensibilities of Americans again. Most would, anyway – but not Sinéad O'Connor.

After the vilification of John Lennon, a lesson had been learnt. Never mix pop with God. You cannot win. From now on pop would steer as far away from religion as was humanly possible. Apart from the occasional outburst (such as Madonna's 'Like a Prayer' video) artists refused to dip their toes into religion. It was career-ending stuff and no one needed that.

Sinéad O'Connor thought otherwise. On 3 October 1992 she single-handedly created one of the most memorable and captivating moments in musical history. At the time Sinéad had a new album out. It was called *Am I Not Your Girl?* and consisted of inspirational songs from her childhood. It had not been an easy childhood by any stretch of the imagination. As she would later reveal, part of it was spent in an Irish Magdalene asylum, one of a chain of homes for orphaned girls and fallen women that is now well known for the harsh treatment of those in its care.

No wonder her album was filled with covers of songs such as 'Gloomy Sunday' and 'Success Has Made a Failure of Our Home'. It was a difficult album for her audience to take, especially after the goodwill she had engendered with her massive-selling *I Do Not Want What I Haven't Got*, released two years previously.

In 1992 *Saturday Night Live*, the liberal New York entertainment show, invited Sinéad to perform two of her songs. The 26-year-old musician chose to sing her new album's title track and then an *a capella* version of the Bob Marley song 'War'. When rehearsing 'War', Sinéad finished the song by pulling out a picture of a small African baby and showing it to the cameras. This act was okayed by the show's producers who thought it was a great way to bring attention to Third World poverty. Little did they know that Sinéad had something else up her sleeve, literally. She had a picture of the Pope, and she was about to tear it up in front of millions of watching Americans.

The voice she used that night was not sweet, light or likeable. It was husky and raw and intense, and it was absolutely captivating. Dressed all in white, her head shaven, and surrounded by symbolic candles, Sinéad sang with true intensity, just her voice, no instruments. Halfway through the song she replaced the phrase, 'racial abuse' with 'child abuse'. It was the first clue to what was coming.

Sinéad finished the song on the word 'evil'. At which point she pulled out a large picture of the Pope and defiantly tore it up in front of the camera. There was silence, pure silence. Everyone was trying to work out what had just happened. Then the producers – in time-honoured fashion – hit the button. 'Go to an ad,' they screamed.

This act of burning defiance, this extreme provocation was utterly shocking to the watching Americans. That night it was reported that the show received more than 4,500 protest calls in an hour. Then the celebs weighed in. Frank Sinatra, in a decidedly unChristian manner, said he

IN SOME WAYS, THIS WAS AN EVEN MORE COURAGEOUS ACT THAT WHICH PRECIPITATED IT. TO FACE DOWN THOSE WHO HATE YOU IN THE MOST PUBLIC WAY POSSIBLE TAKES TRUE COURAGE

would like to punch the singer right in the mouth. Joe Pesci made similar noises. But the most hurtful condemnation for Sinéad to take came from another woman – Madonna – who said: 'I think there is a better way to present her ideas rather than ripping up an image that means a lot to other people.' Sinéad kept her own counsel on the event, and refused to explain or justify her actions. So the papers filled their pages with the condemnation that her silence made possible.

Yet, in Sinéad's eyes, tearing up the photograph was not some gratuitous act. It was a comment on the child-abuse scandal that had engulfed the Catholic Church in 1992. Some of the abused had come forwards, tried to name and shame their local priest, but there had been little public outcry over the issue. The Church had moved quickly to hush up any scandal. Sinéad was out to change all that because she had been a victim herself.

Two weeks after the scandal, Sinéad appeared at a Bob Dylan tribute show. Introduced warmly by Kris Kristofferson, she walked on stage to be met by a barrage of boos and some cheers, a vocal fight between right and wrong. Sinéad reacted brilliantly. She stood still at the microphone, refused to sing and faced her detractors head-on. In some ways, this was an even more courageous act than that which had precipitated it. To face down those who hate you in the most public way possible takes true courage.

The band attempted to strike up the music but Sinéad cut them short. Then she launched into a quick burst of 'War' – making sure to include the phrase 'child abuse'. As the boos intensified, she walked off, straight into the welcoming arms of Kris Kristofferson. There she sobbed huge tears into that great man's shirt.

Sinéad withdrew from the music business, focusing on rearing her son, choosing when to enter the spotlight and when to leave its harsh glare. In 1997 she apologized to the Pope through the Italian newspaper *Vita*. She said that her protest had been 'a ridiculous act, the gesture of a girl rebel', which she did 'because I was in rebellion against the faith, but I was still within the faith'. Quoting St Augustine, she added: 'Anger is the first step towards courage.' The Church refused to comment. Two years later a rebel Irish priest ordained Sinéad as a priest. The Catholic Church does not recognize women priests.

Sinéad Marie Bernadette O'Connor was born on 8 December 1966, and raised in Ireland as a Catholic. Her parents parted company when she was eight years old, and she and her siblings stayed with their mother. In her teens she was placed in one of Ireland's notorious Magdalene asylums. After leaving the institution, she and friends formed a band called Ton Ton Macoute, and they moved to Dublin in search of a contract. The death of her mother in a car accident in February 1985 devastated the singer, and she moved to London. She was signed by Ensign Records. After months of wrangling she was allowed to produce her own album. *The Lion and the Cobra* was not a massive seller, but it did establish her as a strong-minded artist. Her next album contained her version of Prince's *Nothing Compares to You*. Her take on the song, along with a striking video, catapulted Sinéad to worldwide fame. Sinéad used her fame to speak out strongly on subjects such as child abuse, women's rights and organized religion. This caused huge controversy that damaged her music career.

MADONNA'S
Sex book

DATE 21 October 1992, USA

S he is pictured in the book straddling a dog. She stands between rapper Big Daddy Kane and the model Naomi Campbell, and all three of them are wearing next to nothing, touching each other. She poses with lesbians, and the camera catches her masturbating. The pages are filled with sadomasochistic imagery. Madonna's *Sex* was a groundbreaking book. Never before had an artist of her commercial standing produced such a personal and provocative work.

To explore sexuality, both her own and other people's, took a courage not found in many of Madonna's contemporaries. Her album *Erotica* was also part of this process, and so was the video for 'Justify My Love'. In it we watch as Madonna walks down a hotel corridor, leans against a wall, then unbuttons her coat to reveal her body clothed in just black suspenders and underwear. A good-looking guy (her boyfriend at the time, Tony Ward) walks towards her as other guys and girls dressed just as provocatively, come into view. Madonna and her man go into the hotel room and caress on the bed. He then watches another man kissing her...

Unsurprisingly, MTV and many other channels refused to show the video. Yet Madonna was a huge star at this point. In the preceding five years she had sold more than 30 million albums, toured the world,

played to huge audiences. She was the sassy teenage girl singer. So why was she so fixated on exposing her sexuality at this point, and why was she risking the damage to her career? Maybe the answer lies in the shape of a Pepsi-Cola bottle.

In 1989 Madonna signed a lucrative deal to promote Pepsi. In one of her Pepsi commercials she debuted her new single 'Like a Prayer'. Unbeknownst to Pepsi, the

WHY WAS SHE SO FIXATED ON HER SEXUALITY? WHY RISK THE DAMAGE TO HER CAREER? MAYBE THE ANSWER LIES IN THE SHAPE OF A PEPSI-COLA BOTTLE

video to accompany this song featured Catholic imagery. The *Like a Prayer* album tackled everything from her uneasy relationship with her father to the effect that her Catholic upbringing had wrought upon her.

Madonna was out to confront her past, She had changed, thrown aside the cheeky girl in the lace vest-tops and the funny boots who had brought her fame and replaced her with a woman seeking to express herself artistically – whatever that took. Pepsi suddenly realized that they had bought into the wrong Madonna, and so they killed the deal. Perhaps Madonna now realized that corporate deals are never compatible with true artistic endeavour.

MADONNA LEANS AGAINST A WALL, THEN UNBUTTONS HER COAT TO REVEAL HER BODY CLOTHED IN JUST BLACK SUSPENDERS AND UNDERWEAR

Then Warren Beatty came a-knocking, asking Madonna to co-star with him in *Dick Tracy*. According to biographer Lucy O'Brien, Beatty encouraged Madonna to return to the Monroesque dizzy-blonde image of before. Madonna did so because she and Beatty were tight at that time. But

the experience was dispiriting. Madonna felt she had become a symbol, not a human being. The *Sex* book and the *Erotica* album were her response.

The first signs of this new approach came with her 1990 'Blond Ambition World Tour', a show filled with sexual provocation. The Pope asked all Catholics not to attend any of her shows. She could not have asked for better publicity.

After the tour came an album of greatest hits that she cheekily called *The Immaculate Collection*. It contained two new songs, including 'Justify My Love'. Madonna's response to the criticism of the sex-heavy film was to the point: 'Why is it that people are willing to go and watch a movie about someone getting blown to bits for no reason at all,' she asked, 'and nobody wants to see two girls kissing and two men snuggling?'

Although *Erotica* was one of her most interesting albums, it sold just five million copies worldwide. One big problem for Madonna was that the *Sex* book was dominating the agenda. No one could quite believe how far she had gone with it. It sold more than three million copies, but the consensus was that she had not seriously examined sexuality, instead she had produced a work that was high-class porn. The 'Justify' video had been tasteful; this book, said many, was risible.

Madonna was left as a bit of a laughing stock with a seriously dwindling audience. The only way back was to undergo another tour, but with a far less provocative show. Although 'The Girlie Show' began with a dancer on a rope wearing just a G-string, the theme was high camp. It was a case of Madonna using a lot of circus imagery to get her point across. She was now the ringmaster – no longer the S&M mistress.

THE CONSENSUS WAS THAT SHE HAD NOT SERIOUSLY EXAMINED SEXUALITY, INSTEAD SHE HAD PRODUCED A WORK THAT WAS HIGH-CLASS PORN

A new album, a collection of ballads, followed, and it won her audience back. Madonna then took on the role of Eva Perón in the film *Evita* for director Alan Parker. 'This is the role I was born to play,' she told reporters.

The path she had taken with her *Sex* book and *Erotica* album had been abandoned. She was back doing what was expected of her but struggling once more with two conflicting desires: the urge to explore and push forwards, and her equally strong need to be the most successful female artist of all time, ready to make all kinds of concessions to achieve that aim. It is a conundrum that Madonna still faces every time she walks into a studio.

MADONNA
1958–

Madonna Louise Ciccone was born in Bay City, Michigan, on 16 August 1958. Her mother was French Canadian, and her father an Italian American. In 1977 she moved to New York and formed a band called The Breakfast Club. She came to the attention of Sire Records, who signed her as a solo artist. Her first single 'Everybody' and her debut album *Madonna* were dance hits. Her next two albums, *Like a Virgin* and *True Blue,* brought her worldwide success. A memorable MTV appearance, in which she appeared on top of a huge wedding cake whilst singing 'Like a Virgin', garnered her a huge female teenage audience, cementing her reputation as a sassy girl with attitude. She appeared in the film *Desperately Seeking Susan*, and married her co-star, Sean Penn, who she later divorced. By the end of the 80s she was one of the most popular artists in the world, soon to be named the second-highest-selling female artist (just behind Barbra Streisand). In the 90s she took control of her music, establishing herself as a strong artist and performer.

The disappearance of

RICHEY
EDWARDS

DATE 31 January 1995, London

At about 6.30 p.m. on the evening of 31 January 1995, James Dean Bradfield and Richey Edwards of The Manic Street Preachers sit in a car listening to 'Small Black Flowers that Grow in the Sky'. It is the work of both men, but this the first time Edwards has heard his words set to music. He tells Bradfield how much he likes the tune, and Bradfield thanks him. Bradfield has no idea that this is the last day that he will ever see his bandmate alive.

The two men get out of the car and walk into their hotel, the Embassy in London's Bayswater. James suggests that maybe they catch a film that night. Richey agrees, but when James calls his room Richey says he no longer fancies going out; he wants a quiet night in. James says cool, and arranges to go with a mate instead. James returns to the hotel at about 11.30 and goes

to bed. He gets up early the next morning and goes down to reception, where he is due to meet Richey. They are flying to America that day to promote the band's new album.

James waits. No Richey. He calls up to his room. No answer. Finally he asks the hotel manager to let him into Richey's room, as the guitarist is obviously still fast asleep. He goes with the manager to Room 516. The room is empty save for a tube of Prozac pills, a packed suitcase and a curious-looking box that sits on a table. The box is wrapped with paper that has various literary quotes and pictures, inscribed upon it. It is addressed to Jo, an on-off girlfriend of Richey's. James opens the box. Inside there are books, and videos of the films *Equus* and *Naked*.

James looks at his watch. He has to go. But he is not unduly worried. Richey has gone missing before, and no doubt Richey

JAMES LOOKS AT HIS WATCH. HE HAS TO GO. BUT HE IS NOT UNDULY WORRIED. RICHEY HAS GONE MISSING BEFORE, AND NO DOUBT RICHEY WILL GO MISSING AGAIN

will go missing again. After all, Richey is the loose cannon in the band.

Two years previously, in front of *NME* journalist Steve Lamacq, Richey had taken a knife to his arm and cut the words '4 Real' into his forearm. Lamacq had criticized the band's punk attitude, thinking it out of date. Richey's gesture was designed to show how serious they were.

THE BAND REFUSE TO BELIEVE THAT HE IS DEAD, THAT HE HAS THROWN HIMSELF OFF THE BRIDGE, EVEN IF A NOTORIOUS SUICIDE POINT IS JUST NEARBY

After that incident the band's punk style had grabbed bigger and bigger audiences, whilst the group's ability to produce interesting albums never waned. Richey's part in all this was as a lyricist. His guitar-playing was never going to give anyone sleepless nights, but his talent for memorable metaphors and interesting subjects made him invaluable to the group's art.

Since the band's rise, however, Richey had taken to the bottle in quite a big way. In 1994 he booked into the Priory rehab clinic for treatment. There were other incidents of self-harm, and a tendency towards depression and anorexia nervosa... Amongst his heroes were Sylvia Plath, Tony Hancock and Kurt Cobain – suicides all.

Police officers visit Richey's flat in Cardiff and find his passport. Richey had the document with him in London, which means he must have left the hotel that day and driven home. They also ascertain that he has drawn £2,800 from his account over the last few weeks. His sister, when questioned, says that Richey is fascinated by the idea of a perfect disappearance.

Two weeks later the police issue a public missing-person appeal. The very next day Richey's car, a silver Vauxhall Cavalier, is discovered parked ominously close to the Severn Bridge. The car's battery is dead, and there are signs that Richey spent the night on the back seat.

The band refuse to believe that he is dead, that he has thrown himself off the bridge, even if a notorious suicide point is just nearby. Sightings of Richey now start coming in. He is spotted in Liverpool, Whitby, Cambridge, Brighton and Newport. There is also a report of him sitting on a beach in Goa, strumming his guitar.

The most intriguing story is told by a Cardiff cab driver, who says he picked up a tall, gaunt young man who asked him to drive around town, supposedly looking for his boss's car. The man asked if he could lie down in the back seat as they travelled, which stuck in the cab driver's mind. Equally memorable was the man's accent, which kept switching from bad cockney to pure Welsh. Eventually the man paid his fare – £68 – and got out somewhere in Cardiff city centre. The band point out that Richey could never be described as tall.

They set up a trust fund, however, into which they pay a quarter of their royalties. The money is made available to Richey's parents, who have accepted the inevitable and been granted a court order declaring their son 'presumed dead'.

The band use many of the lyrics that Richey left behind for their tenth album *Journal for Plague Lovers*, considered by many to be one of their best pieces of work.

'HOW CAN YOU ACCEPT THAT HE IS DEAD WHEN THERE IS NO BODY, NO EVIDENCE WHATSOEVER. IT'S IRRATIONAL'

And The Manic Street Preachers still refuse to countenance anything other than Richey's safe return one of these days. 'Personally, I think he is alive,' says the band's bass player Nicky Wire. 'I have got no physical evidence to think that he is, but I do. How can you accept that he is dead when there is no body, no evidence whatsoever. It's irrational.'

And so a great rock mystery continues to entice and baffle minds.

The Manic Street Preachers were formed in Blackwood in 1986. After some personnel changes they settled on a line-up of James Dean Bradfield (guitar, vocals), Nicky Wire (bass), Richey Edwards (guitar) and Sean Moore (drums). In 1992 they released their debut album, *Generation Terrorists*, and were quickly noticed for their androgynous punk-rock glam image and socially aware attitude and lyrics. The album was accompanied by a plethora of literary quotes and sold a quarter of a million copies, establishing a loyal fan base that the band have yet to lose. In 1995 Richey Edwards disappeared and the band continued as a three-piece. They have since released ten chart albums, including landmarks such as *The Holy Bible*, *Everything Must Go* and *Journal for Plague Lovers*, the latter featuring a set of Edwards's unpublished lyrics set to music. The band are also well known for their numerous cover versions, including material from the likes of The Clash, Happy Mondays, The Faces and Rihanna. They remain one of the UK's most popular outfits.

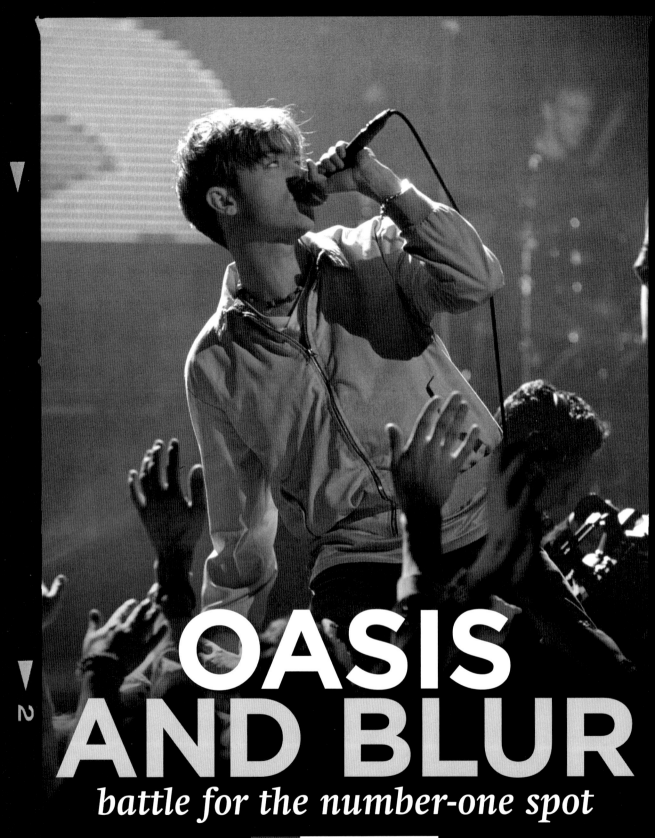

OASIS
AND BLUR

battle for the number-one spot

DATE 20 August 1995, UK

For decades bands have sniped and criticized each other, putting down each other's music or their characters. On the surface it feels nasty, looks nasty. In reality it is a game, a good way of gaining better press coverage. Fights always generate larger headlines. Yet very few arguments have ever matched the intensity generated by Oasis and Blur in the summer of 1995.

In terms of class, origin and outlook, the two bands could not have been more different. Oasis, the cocky working-class band from the north of England, revelling in their ability to cause chaos, talking loudly in favour of drug-taking and the rock'n'roll lifestyle, were up against Blur, a middle-class band from the south of England with college backgrounds and a tendency to talk up their cleverness. Occasionally they acknowledged one another. 'Blur are a good pop band,' Oasis singer Liam Gallagher said, 'but nothing to do with us. We are a great rock band.'

In August 1995 the two bands were preparing to release new material. Blur's latest single, 'Country House', was due to appear before 'Roll with It', the new Oasis offering. Damon Albarn, who has been characterized as 'one of the most competitive men in pop', changed the release date of his band's single so that it came out on the same day as that of Oasis. The race to the number-one slot was on — the winner able to claim the title of most popular in the land.

On 16 August the ITN television news featured an item about the rivalry between the bands. All the national newspapers

AFTER THE BRITISH ROCK MUSIC OF BEFORE, **OASIS WERE THE STORM** BLOWING EVERYTHING AWAY IN A HURRICANE OF OUTLANDISH BEHAVIOUR

jumped on board. For a week everyone in the UK was talking about who would win this extraordinary chart race. 'We had more coverage than the war in Bosnia,' Albarn pointed out.

Both bands were representatives of the movement known as Britpop, which

BLUR
1989–2003

Blur were formed in 1989 with a line-up of Damon Albarn (vocals), Graham Coxon (guitar), Alex James (bass) and Dave Rowntree (drums). They signed to Food Records in 1990. After early success with the single 'There's No Other Way', Blur fell slightly from grace. A two-month American tour, designed to wipe out their debts, persuaded the band to adopt a much more British style and approach in their music. With the albums *Modern Life Is Rubbish*, *Parklife* and *The Great Escape* the band placed themselves at the centre at the Britpop scene. But internal tensions and a desire to move on musically saw the band switch styles once more on the *Blur* album, which adopted a more American, independent sound. Their sixth studio album, *13*, was marked by its sonic experimentations whilst *Think Thank*, released in May 2002, challenged many with its electronic sounds and styles. By now Graham Coxon had quit the band, and Blur were put on hold as Albarn embarked upon a series of solo projects. The band re-formed in 2009 for a highly successful tour.

now became a household word. Ironically, the roots of Britpop lay in America, in the grunge music that had been brought to the UK's shores by bands such as Pearl Jam and Nirvana. Grunge music was specifically American, unable to truly speak to British kids. So Blur wanted to stop emulating American musical influences and forge a very British sound.

IF ONE BAND SUMMED UP THE HEDONISTIC 90S, IT WAS OASIS. AND YET HERE WERE BLUR CHALLENGING THEM, PICKING A FIGHT WITH THEM

It was an artistic conceit taken to its very limit by the band's third album, *Parklife*. Prior to its release Albarn said, 'When our third album comes out, our position as the quintessential English band of the 90s will be assured.' And he was right. 'Parklife' the single, with its jaunty cockney-London atmosphere, and *Parklife* the album placed Blur right at the centre of the Britpop movement. Albarn insisted that the album was a 'loosely linked concept album' that involved lots of different stories: 'It's the travails of the mystical lager-eater, seeing what's going on and commenting on it.'

Oasis were the band of the 90s, their rock'n'roll behaviour capturing the decade's hedonistic spirit and their music creating a blueprint for many bands to follow. Unique at the time, they split in 2010.

In Blur world, grandmas eat pizzas, the high street is always the same, the park is a world unto itself, the young go to Greece and shag anything that moves, the Queen is off her head, and there are characters such as Tracy Jacks who quietly go out of their minds.

Blur pointed to the musical signposts that had inspired them (The Kinks, Small Faces et al.), but they also evoked literary names such as Samuel Beckett and Martin Amis as major inspirations.

For Oasis, such intellectualizing was anathema. For them, rock music should never be inhabited by arty types who read books. Rock'n'roll was about rebellion, not caring a damn, hedonism, glamour and fame. Their attitude was perhaps best summed by the song 'Rock 'n' Roll Star'.

The band had been formed in the early 90s by Noel Gallagher's tempestuous brother Liam, along with guitarist Paul 'Bonehead' Arthurs and bass player Paul 'Guigsy' McGuigan. They were joined by drummer Tony McCarroll. Noel joined later, and it was he who wrote all the songs that Liam sang in his very distinctive voice. The band was absolutely rubbish at first but somewhere along the line turned a corner and began producing a slew of classic songs such as 'Live Forever' and 'Don't Look Back in Anger', which pulled on the 60s and the 70s to present a new sound for the 90s.

'PEOPLE SAY WE'RE THE STONES AND BLUR ARE THE BEATLES THAT'S NOT RIGHT. WE ARE BOTH THE STONES AND THE BEATLES. BLUR ARE THE MONKEES'

Early Oasis records carried the grandeur of a Phil Spector record aligned to a punk attitude. Oasis made no secret of their love for The Beatles. Many of their songs deliberately inserted Beatle melodies or riffs so as to talk up the comparison between the two. 'People say we're the Stones and Blur are The Beatles,' Noel Gallagher once said. 'That's not right. We are both the Stones and The Beatles. Blur are The Monkees.'

What Oasis really represented was a return to the classic rock'n'roll format.

They were a band who looked like a gang, acted like a gang and made no bones about their desire for alcohol, women, drugs and fame. After the introverted British rock music of before, Oasis were the storm blowing everything out of the way in a hurricane of provocative remarks and outlandish behaviour.

This combined with Noel's melodic big-chorused songs made the band an instant success. *Definitely Maybe* was at the time Britain's fastest-selling debut album. The public rivalry between the Gallagher brothers also helped sales and made the band a compelling spectacle.

In an early interview they made their opposing positions very clear. Noel believed people loved Oasis for its music, Liam argued that it was his attitude which brought people to their gigs. Over the next few years the brothers would fight constantly, both grappling for the soul of the band, their fighting and rowing often ending with either one breaking off from touring to return home. Still, the band were unstoppable. In one year, they went from playing a pub in Leeds to selling out the Sheffield Arena and playing to a crowd of thousands.

If one band summed up the hedonistic 90s, when cocaine and lads' magazines proved highly popular, it was Oasis. And yet here were Blur challenging them and their values, picking a fight with them.

On 14 August the singles went to the shops. A week later it transpired that

Oasis had sold 216,000 copies of 'Roll with It', whilst Blur had sold 284,000 copies of 'Country House'.

Although Blur won that battle, it could be argued Oasis won the war. By 1996 their album *What's the Story (Morning Glory)* had shifted some ten million copies worldwide, and their two concerts at Knebworth Park attracted 2.6 million ticket applications. Fourteen years later it was revealed that Oasis had outsold Blur on overall record sales by quite a margin.

ALTHOUGH BLUR WON THAT BATTLE, IT COULD BE ARGUED THAT OASIS WON THE WAR

That said, it could also be argued that Damon Albarn's subsequent career has proved far more interesting than those of the Gallagher brothers. Albarn went on to form a band called Gorillaz, made music with key African musicians, started up his own label and wrote an opera to be performed in Chinese. But what can't be denied is the real excitement that both bands generated during that memorable week in the summer of 1995.

OASIS
1991–2009

Oasis came into being in 1991. The line-up was Noel Gallagher (guitar), Liam Gallagher (vocals), Paul McGuigan (bass), Paul Arthurs (guitar) and Tony McCarroll (drums). In May 1993 they were discovered by Alan McGee at a Glasgow club gig, and signed to Creation Records. Their debut album, *Definitely Maybe*, confirmed them as one of the most exciting bands of the decade, whilst the 1995 follow-up, *What's the Story (Morning Glory)*, became the third-largest-selling album in British history. In 1996 the band played two nights at Knebworth Park. So many people applied for tickets the band could have played for 53 nights. Their third album, *Be Here Now*, was the UK's fastest-selling album ever, clocking up sales of 696,000 in the first week. With the departure of Paul McGuigan and Paul Arthurs in 1999, the band recruited two more members. However, in August 2009 following yet another altercation between Liam and Noel, the latter quit the band for good. Liam instantly formed a new band using the remaining Oasis band members, which he named Beady Eye.

The murders of
TUPAC AND
BIGGIE SMALLS

DATE 13 September 1996, Los Angeles, and 9 March 1997, Las Vegas

After the two rap stars had both been killed, after all the recriminations and investigations and speculations had been concluded, Biggie Smalls's mother sat down in her house, turned her face towards a camera and said: 'Two lives were lost as the result of what? Stupidity?'

It was a good question. The story of Tupac Shakur and Biggie Smalls is a tale borrowed from any one of a hundred gangster films. Two friends come together, get close, fall out and set in motion events they cannot control. As they do so, into their lives step corrupt policemen, organized crime and fatal ideas about honour and respect.

There is one problem: the story of Tupac and Biggie is not a Hollywood gangster fantasy, sold to us through the medium that the rap community so adores. This happened. In real life.

In the 90s there was real animosity between East and West Coast rappers; between New York – home of hip hop – and Los Angeles, the city that created gangsta rap. Los Angeles was home to two rival gangs, The Crips and The Bloods, whose clashes claimed hundreds of lives. Gangsta rap reflected these events, pushed forwards a no-holds-barred approach. No wonder Tupac and Biggie often spoke of violence: death by gunfire was an everyday hazard.

Of the two, Tupac had the more interesting background. His mother, Afeni, was an ex-Black Panther who had fallen into drug use. The family lived in various cities, moved around a lot. Tupac started rapping when he was at school. So no shock that, when the family moved to California in 1998, he should hook up with the band Digital Underground.

NO WONDER TUPAC AND BIGGIE OFTEN SPOKE OF VIOLENCE: DEATH BY GUNFIRE WAS AN EVERYDAY HAZARD FOR BOTH MEN

He worked with Digital before landing a solo deal and releasing *2Pacalypse Now*, an album that showcased his political beliefs. The work did not sell well. Nor did his second solo attempt, *Strictly for My N.I.G.G.A.Z.* Success came about in 1993, when Tupac put together the band Thug Life and began developing a more gangsterish persona.

Two years before he is murdered Biggie Smalls rolls a cigar outside his mother's house in Brooklyn, enjoying the fame and attention that landmark singles such as 'Hypnotize' have given him.

In November 1993 some of his crew were charged with sexually assaulting a woman in a hotel room. Tupac claimed he and the woman had previously met for sex. She claimed that on her second visit Tupac invited in his friends, who assaulted her.

The day before the verdict was announced Tupac was shot five times in a Manhattan recording studio. He received two bullets in the head, two in the groin and one that passed through his arm and thigh. Unbelievably, he survived and came out of hospital spitting fire at the people he believed responsible: Puff Daddy, Andre Harrell... and his old friend Biggie Smalls.

Christopher Smalls came from a middle-class family. His mum took on two jobs to support him, and was outraged when, on his debut single 'Juicy', Biggie talked about growing up in a shack. She went to the press to put the story straight. 'My son had everything,' she said.

At 17 Biggie dropped out of school. In 1991 he was caught dealing crack and spent nine months behind bars. By now he had begun rapping, and a tape he made on his release from jail found its way to Sean Combs, aka Puff Daddy. When Combs started up Bad Boy records, Biggie was one of his first signings. Biggie quickly gave him a hit with 'Juicy' and then hit gold with his debut album *Ready to Die*.

Combs's main rival on the West Coast was Suge Knight. He was raised in the Compton area of Los Angeles, known for its gang warfare. In 1991 he co-founded Death Row Records (later renamed Row Records). His first signing was Dr Dre, whose graphic tales of gang life were early examples of gangsta music. In 1992 Dr Dre's solo album, *The Chronic*, with its lazy beats and rap style, its constant references to smoking weed, went platinum.

If anyone understood that it was garish depictions of street life that sold units, it was Suge Knight. He adored films such as *Scarface* and *The Godfather*. The money and power he had acquired led him to believe that his gangster fantasies could now be re-enacted for real.

When Tupac was arrested for sexual assault, Suge Knight offered to stand bail if he would sign to Death Row. Tupac accepted the offer. Tupac's music now became far more gangsta, far less political. He released 'Hit 'Em Up', an attack on Biggie that went so far as to boast that he had slept with his wife, the singer Faith Evans.

On 7 September 1996 Tupac Shakur and Suge Knight attended the Mike Tyson

TUPAC
1971–1996

Tupac Amaru Shakur was born in East Harlem in Manhattan, New York, on 16 June 1971. Both his parents had been active in the Black Panther movement of the 60s. By 12 he was living with his mother in Baltimore, where he began honing his rapping skills. He got his break in Los Angeles when he hooked up with the band Digital Underground. His work on their 'Sam Song' record brought him to the notice of Interscope Records. His first solo album did not sell well, and in 1993 he formed a band called Thug Life, which raised his profile. Dropped by Interscope after pressure from the company's shareholders and leading politicians who disliked his anti-police stance, Tupac signed with Death Row. In 1995 he was convicted of molesting a young girl, and imprisoned. Shortly afterwards he released his album *Me Against the World* and became the first artist ever to have an album at number one whilst incarcerated. On his release he became one of rap's biggest stars, selling some 70 million records before he was shot dead in September 1996.

BIGGIE SMALLS
1972-1997

Christopher Smalls was born on 21 May 1972 and raised in New York City. His mother, Voletta Wallace, was a schoolteacher and his father, George Latore, was a welder. Latore left the household when the boy was two years old. At school, Biggie was a good student, especially in English, but by the age of 17 he had dropped out of school and turned to drug dealing. He was arrested in North Carolina for dealing crack and was imprisoned for nine months. On his release he returned to New York where he cut a demo tape that fell into the hands of an A&R man named Sean 'Puff Daddy' Combs. Combs worked at Uptown, and he signed Biggie. Soon after, though, Combs left Uptown and launched his own label, Bad Boy Records. Biggie followed him there. In September 1994 he released the four-times platinum album *Ready to Die*. A year later he was involved in a war of words with his former friend Tupac Shakur, who was subsequently murdered. On 9 March Biggie was shot four times whilst sitting in his car. He was dead on arrival at hospital.

versus Bruce Seldon fight in Las Vegas. Why they were out together remains a mystery. According to later reports, the men were now at loggerheads with each other. The day before, aware that Death Row owed him a huge amount of money in unpaid royalties (as much as $10 million some said), Tupac had asked his lawyer to retrieve all the tapes of the music he had been working on.

After the fight – which lasted just 19 seconds – Tupac went backstage and congratulated the victorious Tyson. He was then spotted on a CCTV camera walking through the hotel. Suddenly, he approached a young man and a fight erupted. The man in question was Orlando Anderson who had allegedly stolen a bracelet from one of Knight's henchmen. On the CCTV footage, Knight is seen joining in with the vicious beating administered to the hapless Anderson.

Knight, Tupac and their entourage returned to their hotel to change clothes. They moved on to Suge Knight's Las Vegas residence where they stayed until ten. They then set out for Club 622. Suge and Tupac drove together in Knight's 760 BMW Sedan. As they were cruising down the Strip, police pulled Knight and Tupac over for playing their music too loud and for not displaying proper licence plates. After being let go, they drove off, pulling up at a red traffic light. A car with four girls in it appeared on the left-hand side. Suge and Tupac began chatting to them. As they did so a Cadillac pulled up on the other side, and 13 bullets were sprayed into the car.

Tupac dived into the back seat for protection but took five shots to the body. Shrapnel cut Suge's head. He jammed his foot on the gas and sped away. He then stopped and pulled a U-turn. He later said that he wanted to get Tupac to hospital as fast as possible. That statement mystified many, as the hospital was the opposite way. As a former resident of Vegas Suge would have known this. Others say that Suge was in a state of panic, hence his wrong turn.

The police who had pulled Suge over followed the speeding car. Suge had to stop because his tyres burst. Emergency services arrived at the scene. Tupac was rushed to hospital and straight into surgery. His right lung was removed, and doctors said he might pull through. They were wrong. Tupac Shakur passed away on 13 September, a week after the shooting.

The blame for the shooting fell on New York, but Puff Daddy, Andre Harrell and Biggie Smalls denied any involvement. Six months later Biggie and Puff Daddy attended a party at *Vibe* magazine in LA. They left in separate cars and came to some traffic lights. Puff passed through, Biggie stopped. A black Chevrolet Impala pulled up alongside, a window was rolled down and seven shots were fired. Biggie took four bullets and passed from this earth.

The LA Police Department put a detective named Russell Poole on the case. Poole was old-school, a man of principle.

KNIGHT ADORED GANGSTER FILMS SUCH AS SCARFACE AND THE GODFATHER. THE MONEY AND POWER HE ACQUIRED LED HIM TO BELIEVE THAT HIS FANTASIES COULD BE RE-ENACTED FOR REAL

His investigation revealed that police officers were working out of hours for Suge Knight. The record-company boss also had a district attorney on his books. For Poole, this revelation was absolutely shocking.

Poole focused on two individuals in particular: Rafael Pérez and David Mack. He believed that they were gang members hired by the LA police force. More sensationally, he claimed to have discovered at Mack's home a Black Chevy Impala, a shrine to Tupac and ammunition of the type used to kill Biggie...

Poole was taken off the case and took early retirement. He has since filed a lawsuit against the LAPD for preventing him from revealing his findings to the public. No one has ever been brought to justice for the murder of either rap star.

Suge Knight was later incarcerated for breaking his bail conditions in beating up Anderson. Death Row no longer exists. No gangster film ever ends happily – guess that was one thing Suge Knight forgot.

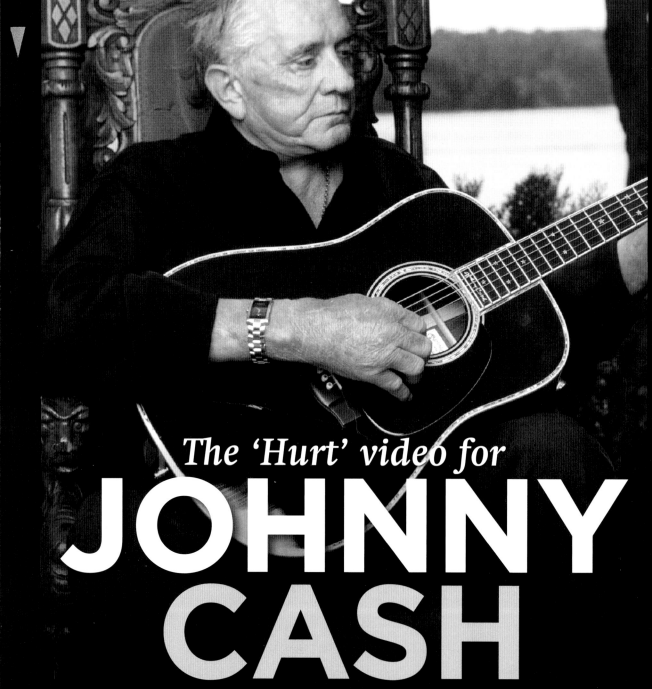

The 'Hurt' video for

JOHNNY CASH

DATE 8 March 2003, Hendersonville, Tennessee

The brief of the pop-music video is simple – sell, sell, sell and always entertain, never inform. That is why they are colourful and fake and smiley and sexy, and why they always feel good. But they are never ever about death. They are never about mortality, the silent burden that rests on all our shoulders.

Not until Mark Romanek's video for the Johnny Cash single 'Hurt' came along, that is. Cash loved this video. After screening it to his daughter Cindy, he enthusiastically asked her opinion. 'I find it deeply disturbing,' she said. 'It is as if you are saying goodbye.' 'That's exactly what I am doing,' Cash replied simply.

IN 1977 HE TRIED TO KILL HIMSELF WITH DRUGS, FAILED, AND THEN SPENT NINE YEARS WRITING A BOOK ABOUT THE APOSTLE PAUL. 'THE MAN IN WHITE' HE CALLED HIS BOOK

The 'Hurt' video was born out of circumstance. The director's original intention was to bring Cash out to Los Angeles and use images of him cut with scenes from a Samuel Beckett play.

But Cash got sick and could not make that journey. So Mark Romanek came to Cash, at his house in Hendersonville, Tennessee. Cash performed the Trent Reznor song for him on guitar and piano, and gave the director some footage he thought he might like. The resulting video is remarkable: Johnny Cash at 77 years of age, his body and soul immersed in the music, cut with images from his past.

The film makes little attempt to hide Cash's physical appearance. He is going bald, his face is beaten, his eyes stare into the distance. All around him is old: old bottles, old chairs, old pictures. He sings a line and then it starts: footage of Cash as a young man, the young Cash in black jacket and white shirt, smiling into the future and riding a train, then the man Johnny striding through a prison yard, and then Johnny peering through the window of his childhood home.

What did he see? What did he think as he viewed those images, this boy from Arkansas with the heavy-drinking father and the loving mother, this boy who grew up on a farm and whose childhood was filled with the sound of trains and the songs of those who worked the fields?

Johnny worked those fields as well, smelt the earth, learnt the turning of the clouds so well that in later life he could predict rain and always be right. Nature made Johnny Cash. 'That's where I think he got a lot of his spirituality from,' says his daughter Cindy, 'from nature.'

'I FIND IT DEEPLY DISTURBING,' SHE SAID, 'IT IS AS IF YOU ARE SAYING GOODBYE.' 'THAT'S EXACTLY WHAT I AM DOING,' CASH REPLIED

In 'Hurt' we understand that his was a childhood hit by the Great American Depression of the 30s, and then torn apart by the tragic death of the 14-year-old brother Jack he adored, a childhood that instilled in him conflicting emotions, the urge to believe and live in God set against the urge for oblivion and self-destruction.

He learnt music through the songs sung to him by his family and the songs played to him by his radio. At 18 he joined the US Air Force, worked some in Germany, and then made his way back to the States. He could play guitar and piano now, and

'Hurt' captures him doing just that, hitting the dramatic chords of the song on the piano, picking out its mournful melody on his guitar, the music of his life.

When Cash came home, rock'n'roll was starting to make itself felt in the lives young white teenagers. Sam Phillips in Memphis was the man behind this new music. So Cash went there, got a deal, met Elvis and Jerry Lee Lewis and Carl Perkins and cut rock'n'roll records. Except that he didn't. His songs were rockabilly rock'n'roll with country tinges, always uncomplicated, records with a chick-a-boom beat and simple riffs and his voice, that dominating voice, placed on top.

Fame brought speed pills and women. Cash was married and had four daughters, but his need to take the upward direction by any means necessary superseded all other considerations. So he overdosed, hallucinated, started a forest fire whilst high as a kite, got arrested on the Mexican border in possession of thousands of pills, kissed a million lips and hurt himself in every way possible as he sought the high that beckons to us all.

His family prayed for him because his mother always said: 'God has his hand on him.' And so began the battle of his life, the fight against drugs, Cash imploring God for relief and then spitting in his face when it was granted to him, chucking down more pills until he was brought once more to his knees. Please God, I won't do it again, I promise.

John Carter Cash and his half-sister Kathy Cash receive three awards, one of which is for the landmark video for the song 'Hurt'. Their father Johnny Cash had died two months previously.

In the 'Hurt' video, June Carter Cash stands on the stairs and looks down on Cash with love deep in her eyes. When they met they were both married, yet one of the first things Cash said to her was: I'm going to marry you one day. She said, don't be so stupid. And now years later the camera proves Cash was right. Within months of the filming, both were dead and holding hands in heaven. 'If June hadn't existed, I don't think my daddy would have made it,' his daughter Cindy said.

In 1955 Cash cut a song called 'Folsom Prison Blues'. That led to concerts inside prisons and to one of his biggest-selling albums, *Johnny Cash at Folsom Prison.*

Prisoners, he told the world, are God's children too – and the incarcerated took him as their own. 'The reaction I got there was far and above everything I had in my life,' Cash once remarked.

In the 70s Cash was given his own TV show ('Johnny Cash! A new way to spend the summer!' is how the network sold it to the country), and again he did away with the boundaries by featuring artists such as Mahalia Jackson, Burl Ives, Kenny Rogers, Joni Mitchell, Neil Young and the young Stevie Wonder. He performed a duet of his song 'Get Rhythm' with Wonder.

In 'Hurt' you see in Cash's face a quiet dignity. 'To me,' said Bob Dylan, 'Johnny

Cash was more like a religious figure. Always has been.' Many of the great and famous were proud to sing with him... 'It's great to work with a real protest singer,' Dylan once said to him.

A CHILDHOOD THAT INSTILLED IN HIM CONFLICTING EMOTIONS, THE URGE FOR COMPASSION FOR ALL, THE URGE TO BELIEVE AND LIVE IN GOD SET AGAINST THE URGE FOR OBLIVION AND SELF-DESTRUCTION

Cash stood up to Nixon, told him he would not sing the song 'Welfare Cadillac' to him. He also stood up for the Native Americans well before Marlon Brando did, cut an album called *Bitter Tears* in 1964 that reminded America of the Wounded Knee massacre of 1890, where 300 mainly defenceless Sioux Indians were slaughtered by the US Cavalry. He stood up for the hippies, and he stood up for the American way of life, the right to say what you like, whatever that might be. He met Reagan gladly, told him he would pray for his presidency. Again, away with the boundaries.

In 1977 he tried to kill himself with drugs, failed, and then spent nine years

writing a book about the apostle Paul. He called it *The Man in White* after his famous song 'The Man In Black'. Which is what he was on so many levels. He directed and produced a film about Jesus called *Gospel Road*, and in the 80s found himself a victim of corporate record-company policies. CBS, his workplace for so long, showed him the back door.

He hit the road with a supergroup called The Highwaymen. It consisted of Cash, Willie Nelson, Waylon Jennings and Kris Kristofferson. But in the 90s the flame of fame began to flicker badly, and Cash found himself playing to audiences of less than a hundred people. That was when God sent Rick Rubin into his life.

Rubin was a producer of heavy metal and of heavy-metal rap. He had started the famous label Def Jam. He loved loud guitars and noise and wearing a ZZ Top beard and sunglasses. But enough was enough. Now he wanted a legend to work with, he wanted damaged goods he could put right. And he found Cash.

The extraordinary albums that Rubin and Cash cut in this period, stark and haunting music that settled on his dark side, presented him as the true man in black, the man now seeking redemption for the sins of his life. And now love was all around him. In 1994 at the Glastonbury Festival he walked on stage and thousands of people rose to their feet and applauded him and his music and his soul with deep, deep love. Tears gathered in Cash's eyes as he gazed out on this sea of love, this boy from the Arkansas farm standing in another kind of field altogether.

Cash's new music showed a man willing to tackle any song from any source, just so long as it told a dark truth. Thus the song 'Hurt', written by a heavy-rock band; thus the man Trent Reznor; thus the extraordinary footage.

'I'M NOT REALLY CONCERNED ABOUT BOUNDARIES. I JUST FOLLOW MY CONSCIENCE AND MY HEART'

The video for 'Hurt' won a Grammy Award and also a Country Music Award. As for Johnny Cash, he died on 12 September 2003. In one of his last interviews he said: 'I'm not really concerned about boundaries. I just follow my conscience and my heart. Kris Kristofferson has a new song called "The Heart"... Follow your heart. That is what I do. Compassion is something I have a lot of, because I have been through a lot of pain in my life. Anybody who has suffered a lot of pain has a lot of compassion. Maybe I don't have enough. Maybe I get jaded sometimes... It's been a long time since I left the cotton fields.'

And now he was back where he belonged, and he no longer hurt.

JOHNNY CASH
1932–2003

Johnny Cash was born on 26 February 1932, the third of seven children. He was raised on a farm in Arkansas. As a teenager he enlisted in the US Air Force. He served in Germany, then returned home to marry Vivian Liberto. They had four daughters before splitting up. Cash married June Carter in 1968, and the couple stayed together for the rest of their lives. In 1954 Cash moved to Memphis and signed with Sun Records. Early hits such as 'I Walk the Line' gave Cash a huge audience, but fame brought its own problems in the shape of various addictions. Cash's biggest-selling albums were the live ones he cut in Folsom and San Quentin prisons. In the 70s he hosted his own TV show, but by the mid-80s he was without a recording contract. He formed a band called The Highwaymen and later hooked up with producer Rick Rubin to cut the 'American' albums. In later years Cash found religion and used the mediums of book and film to promote the word of Jesus Christ. June died in May 2003, and Johnny passed on four months later on 12 September.

PETE DOHERTY

burgles his best friend's flat

DATE 25 July 2003, Harley Street, London

Coming home to find your flat has been burgled is one thing. Discovering that the burglar is your best friend, well, that's another trip altogether. But then this is The Libertines we are talking about, a group that smashed its way into the spotlight and then did everything they could to smash that very same spotlight into little bits.

The Libertines followed right in the footsteps of Oasis, presenting themselves as the ultimate drug-taking, swaggering rock'n'roll band with a couldn't-care-less attitude. Hey, hey, we're The Libertines and we're going to get absolutely wasted. What's more, so are you.

The core of the band was the brotherly relationship between singer and frontman Carl Barât and guitarist Pete Doherty. The two met at Brunel University. Barât was studying acting and knew Pete's sister. One day Doherty arrived on campus.

'He was in London for the weekend,' Barât later recalled. 'There was an audition for the theatre society or something, and I was really rubbish. And he got up and auditioned and got the part! He told them after he wasn't a student, and they were really pissed off. I couldn't believe this kid had got one over on me! He was intelligent and witty. I felt I had competition for once. Somebody I could spark off. We just clicked. Then he moved to London and kept hassling me to write songs with him.

I didn't have any confidence really, and he had no talent for guitar, he was completely out of tune, but he had all the confidence in the world. It really inspired me.'

Barât quit his course, and the two men found a flat in Camden where they began writing songs. They took on menial jobs to pay the rent. After two years of demo tapes and hundreds of gigs, the band finally coalesced. With early support from the *NME*, they signed to Rough Trade Records.

Theirs was a punky sound with snatches of classic 60s pop thrown in, the lyrics rooted in an earthy London

SUCCESS WAS THEIRS FOR THE TAKING, WHICH IS PRECISELY WHEN DOHERTY'S FONDNESS FOR CRACK COCAINE AND HEROIN INCREASED TENFOLD

style. Their debut single, 'What a Waster', was full of profanities, which scared off the radio stations. Didn't matter, their reputation was such that Mick Jones of The Clash agreed to produce their debut album, *Up The Bracket*. On its release, everyone was talking about The Libertines.

BARAT AND DOHERTY HAD THE WORD 'LIBERTINE' TATTOOED ON THEIR ARMS IN EACH OTHER'S HANDWRITING. BUT BARAT WAS EXASPERATED

Success was theirs for the taking, which is precisely when Doherty's fondness for crack cocaine and heroin increased tenfold. Not only did his urgent desire for chemicals affect the band's future, it also cut deep into his relationship with Carl.

In May 2003 the band travelled to New York on a promotional tour, taking with them a new batch of songs. In an attempt to get their friendship back on track, Barât and Doherty agreed to have the word 'Libertine' tattooed on their arms – each in the other's handwriting. But Barât was exasperated by his friend. Everyone in the band liked a good time, but Doherty was spinning out of control. Barât finally walked out of the studio and flew back to London. Doherty then took the tapes and

gave them to a fan with orders to make them available on the internet for free.

On his return to the UK Doherty, wary of his friend's growing disapproval, began organizing his own gigs. He would play people's flats, their front rooms, tiny pubs. He also began posting his musings on the band's website, his moods swinging between anger and tranquillity.

A new song, 'Don't Look Back into the Sun', was slated for release, and the band went back into the studio. Doherty was absent most of the time but in an attempt at an apology organized a gig to celebrate Barât's birthday. The event took place the night before the band started a European tour. Barât did not show up. So the next day Doherty did not show up for the tour.

'I found myself distanced from Pete as soon as the drugs started,' Barât later told *Word* magazine. 'He didn't turn up for the tour... because I didn't come to a shitty gig he organized on my birthday. I told him I was having a birthday party; he told me to end my birthday party really early. I said, I can't really do that. Everyone was like, why are you running off to a crackhouse in the East End on your birthday?'

The band brought in a roadie to play the tour, and Doherty did what all best mates do in such a situation: he burgled Barât's Harley Street flat. Pete was arrested and given six months. He was put in Wandsworth prison, but on appeal had his sentence reduced to two months. When he came out, there was one man waiting for him at the prison gates – Carl Barât. The men hugged, went and picked up the other band members and then drove to Kent to play a gig in a small pub. Thanks to his prison time, Doherty was clean and could now put his energies into the band.

In December they played three sold-out London shows, and the following year completed a highly successful tour. All was well, all was good. And then Doherty began using heroin. Barât had no choice, He told Doherty that until he cleaned up he was out of the band. The end was in sight. Doherty formed a band called Babyshambles, which, despite his drug use, received critical acclaim and success.

WHEN HE CAME OUT OF THE PRISON GATES THERE WAS ONE MAN WAITING FOR HIM – CARL BARAT

Barât closed down The Libertines and formed Dirty Pretty Things. Then he and Doherty began bumping into each other at gigs or pubs. They would hug and talk and drink and then part. Rumours started to circulate, rumours that became fact in 2009 when the band re-formed to play the Leeds and Reading festivals. For their efforts they received a cool £1.5 million. Like their music, their friendship survived, and Barât's possessions are safe. For now.

Peter Doherty was born on 12 March 1979. His father was a British Army officer and Doherty spent his childhood moving around different army garrisons. He excelled at school before going to live in London in his grandmother's house. He worked as a gravedigger, then hooked up with his friend Carl Barât to form The Libertines. The band released two critically acclaimed albums (*Up the Bracket* and *The Libertines*) and undertook an arena tour before Doherty's drug problems caused that band to fall apart. Doherty went on to form Babyshambles, whose popularity would outstrip that of The Libertines. The band released two top-ten albums, *Down In Albion* and *Shotter's Nation*, a series of hit singles and in 2007 undertook a major arena tour. He also published a book entitled, *The Book of Albion* and held an exhibition of his art work.,He famously dated model Kate Moss, and fronted an advertising campaign for designer Roberto Cavalli. As well as serving time for burglary, he has made several court appearances for drug and driving offences.

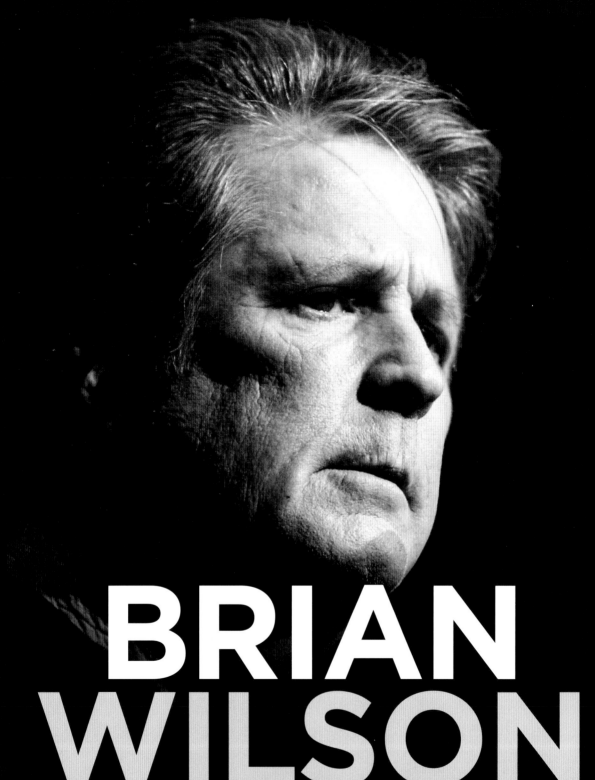

BRIAN WILSON

performs Smile, the album that took 37 years to complete

DATE 20 February 2004, Royal Festival Hall, London

Something remarkable happened on 20 February 2004. Brian Wilson played a concert in London. This was the live premiere of an album called *Smile*, an album that was begun in 1966 and then put away for 37 years. Its journey from a studio in California to one of London's most prestigious concert halls is one of the most mythical and convoluted stories in musical history.

Smile, originally called *Dumb Angel*, was conceived as an album that would celebrate the healing power of laughter. Was there ever an album so ironically named? *Smile* drove Brian Wilson over the edge of reason and into a void that saw the man take to his bed for four years. It would be nearly four decades before he could summon the strength to finish what he had started all those years ago.

Brian Wilson formed The Beach Boys in 1961. They made their name through a succession of catchy songs that extolled the Los Angeles surfing scene. Their early records had titles such as 'Surfin'', 'Surfin' Safari', 'Surfin' USA' and 'Surfer Girl'. Although their drummer Dennis Wilson was the only surfer in the band, The Beach Boys milked the scene for all it was worth.

By 1964 Brian Wilson was bored with surfing music and hated touring. He elected now to stay behind in the studio and write and produce. His ambition was to outdo producer Phil Spector, and that could not be achieved standing on a stage halfway across the world. 'Spector has always been a big thing to me,' he once told reporter Jules Siegel. 'I mean I heard that ["Be My Baby"] and I knew that it was between him and me. I knew exactly where he was at...'

'I LEARNT A LOT OF THINGS FROM LSD, LIKE PATIENCE, UNDERSTANDING. I CONSIDER IT A VERY RELIGIOUS EXPERIENCE'

Wilson now began working towards a much more sophisticated and experimental sound, helped by his use of the drug LSD. He had taken it for the first time in 1965

After 35 years of waiting, the most anticipated album in musical history is given its première in London by Brian Wilson. Paul McCartney was one of the lucky few thousand in the audience.

and told reporter Tom Nolan: 'I learnt a lot of things like patience, understanding. I can't teach you or tell you what I learnt from taking it, but I consider it a very religious experience.' Wilson determined that spirituality would now be an essential element of his future compositions.

Wilson started work on *Pet Sounds* in November 1965. This album placed huge demands on all involved. As Beach Boys singer Mike Love later recalled: 'We worked and worked on the harmonies, and if there was the slightest little hint of a sharp or a flat, it wouldn't go on. We would do it over again until it was right. [Brian] was going for every subtle nuance that you could

conceivably think of. Every voice had to be right, every voice and its resonance and tonality had to be right. The timing had to be right. The timbre of the voices just had to be correct, according to how he felt. And then he might, the next day, completely throw that out and we might have to do it over again.'

At the same time Brian was writing 'Good Vibrations' and 'God Only Knows', two masterpieces that stand as testament to the man's immense musical skills. After *Pet Sounds* was completed in April Wilson refused to rest, taking a further 90 hours in the studio to finish 'God Only Knows'. Incredibly, *Pet Sounds* did not sell well, although its influence was huge. Paul McCartney told reporters the album 'blew me out of the water'. In direct response to *Pet Sounds*, McCartney started on the album that would become *Sergeant Pepper*.

Wilson, meanwhile, was already moving on to the *Pet Sounds* follow-up. 'Good Vibrations' had created the template that Brian would use. 'Vibrations' shifted in tempo, instrumentation and mood with amazing confidence and skill. Wilson's aim was simple – it was to create a brand-new style of pop music... His method was to create wonderful fragments of music. These he then lay aside, the idea being to glue all the pieces together at some later date. He brought in lyricist and musician Van Dyke Parks to work with. One of the first songs they began was called 'Heroes and Villains'. They were still working on it eight months later.

'I am writing a teenage symphony to God,' Wilson told a friend during the making of the album. Given his quest for perfection, his increasing drug-taking, and such grandiose announcements, it is not hard to understand why the recording of *Smile* was far from smooth.

And the working methods were bizarre. Whilst working on a track called 'Fire' Wilson insisted that all the musicians wear firemen's hats. The next day he discovered that as they recorded several fires had broken out in Los Angeles. Convinced that his music had started those fires, he quickly shelved the song.

With some two dozen pieces now finished, Brian set about trying to make the album into a whole. Meanwhile, the other Beach Boys looked on in anguish. For them the *Smile* sessions were an affront. They wanted to make up for the ground lost by *Pet Sounds* with a more commercial approach. Instead, Brian's music had become even weirder.

WILSON NOW BEGAN WORKING TOWARDS A MUCH MORE SOPHISTICATED AND EXPERIMENTAL SOUND, AND HE WAS HELPED BY HIS USE OF THE DRUG LSD

In 1967 The Beach Boys sued their record company over unpaid royalties. *Smile* was caught in the middle of that lawsuit. The Beach Boys used it as bargaining measure, and Capitol responded by saying they would not release the album. A stalemate ensued. Two months later, exhausted by work and drug abuse, Wilson announced he was abandoning the project. The man was now on the verge of a serious breakdown and could go no further.

Brian took to his bed and told The Beach Boys someone else would have to pick up the mess. Without their leader the band were lost. Their first move was logical:

make peace with Capitol. Then they started trying to put together the musical pieces Brian had created. It was hopeless, like five blind men trying to do a jigsaw puzzle.

In July 1967 'Heroes and Villains' was released – but not in the form Brian had imagined. This was followed in September by an album entitled *Smiley Smile*, a patchy

FOR THE ALBUM WILSON BROUGHT IN LYRICIST AND MUSICIAN VAN DYKE PARKS TO WORK WITH. ONE OF THE FIRST SONGS THEY CREATED WAS CALLED 'HEROES AND VILLAINS'. THEY WERE STILL WORKING ON IT EIGHT MONTHS LATER

affair made up of Brian's original tapes with the band's input. Moments of genius stood next to songs taken completely out of their context. The album lacked cohesion and fell between two stools: too weird for a teen audience, and not even on the radar of the hippies who considered The Beach Boys (in the memorable phrase of one of the members of the band) 'a bunch of surfing Doris Days'.

Meanwhile, Brian went into serious decline. His weight ballooned, and his enthusiasm for music seriously dropped. He would only sporadically show up for recording sessions, preferring to stay at home and hide from the world.

In 1975 Brian's wife Marilyn hired a psychologist named Eugene Landy to work with Brian. Using an unorthodox 24-hour therapy that controlled every aspect of Brian's life, Landy managed to curtail Wilson's drug abuse and improve his overall health. However, many felt Landy's programme was isolating Brian, thus allowing the psychiatrist to exert an unhealthy influence on the ailing singer. Landy entered into business deals with his patient as well as making himself a 'creative director'.

But slowly Brian began to recover. He appeared with The Beach Boys at their 1985 Live Aid performance, and in 1988 he issued his first solo album. In 1990 came his memoir, *Wouldn't It Be Nice,* in which he spoke candidly and movingly about his troubled relationship with his father and his subsequent dealings with his children. Within The Beach Boys camp, however, worries about Brian kept surfacing. Although he had stopped taking his illegal drugs and lost much weight, he complained about voices in his head. Many thought that Landy was prescribing too much medication.

In 1989, after several complaints, Landy was called before the California Board of Medical Quality Assurance. Soon after he handed in his licence.

Wilson, meanwhile, had hooked up with a band called The Wondermints, who became his backing band. A young ten-piece outfit full of Wilson fanatics, they toured the world playing key Wilson songs and the whole of the *Pet Sounds* album. The reaction was ecstatic. Buoyed by this success, Wilson was asked to resurrect *Smile*. After much debate, he agreed.

WHILST WORKING ON A TRACK CALLED 'FIRE' WILSON INSISTED THAT ALL THE MUSICIANS WEAR FIREMEN'S HATS

The live version of *Smile* debuted at London's Royal Festival Hall. Everyone came, including Paul McCartney. 'So how good finally is *Smile*, the great lost song cycle that Brian Wilson kept the world waiting 37 years to hear?' asked critic Richard Williams in his review. 'It is better than anyone dared hope.'

It had taken so many years to get there, but get there it did. In April 2004 Wilson and his band recorded *Smile* using the original studio tapes. Again the reviews were ecstatic. The musical vision that Wilson had tried to realize was now a reality. Furthermore, the album was finally able to do what its creator always wanted. It made the world smile.

Brian Douglas Wilson was born in Inglewood, California, on 20 June 1942. By the age of one he was already demonstrating great musical talent. At school he sang with various groups and learned piano. With his brothers Carl and Dennis he formed The Beach Boys, and within a year their songs about surfing culture were chartbound. Wilson became dissatisfied with this style of music and quickly branched out. The band's notable albums and singles throughout this period include *Pet Sounds*, 'God Only Knows' and 'Good Vibrations'. Following a breakdown in the 60s Brian retreated from the public eye for many years. He resurfaced in the late 70s, when he issued solo albums and made sporadic appearances with The Beach Boys. He went solo in the late 80s and, following triumphant years spent touring the albums *Pet Sounds* and *Smile*, he regained his audience. In August 2010 he released his album of Gershwin standards entitled *Brian Wilson Re-Imagines Gershwin*. The album was mauled by the critics.

The death of
MICHAEL JACKSON

DATE 25 June 2009, Los Angeles

The world is never prepared for fate to strike at the gods of our own making. Success seems to guard against all eventualities. And then death proves you wrong – whether that is Elvis Presley or the one they called the Peter Pan of Pop, Michael Jackson. On 25 June 2009 he was discovered dead at his rented mansion in Los Angeles. All attempts to resuscitate him, first by his doctor and then by paramedics, failed.

They had lots in common, Presley and Jackson: the fame, the isolation, the singular behaviour that it triggered. Yet, of the two passings, Jackson's was the more surprising. When the heart of Elvis seized up, he was a virtual recluse, a man hiding from the world, a man who knew he had done it all. Jackson, on the other hand, was a man on the path of a much-publicized comeback, a man ready to engage with the world again, busy preparing for a run of 50 London concerts. He was a relatively young man, 50 years only, attempting publicly to repair a career that had spectacularly fallen off the rails.

In 1985 Michael Jackson was the biggest star on the planet. He had sold 50 million copies of his album *Thriller*, played to huge audiences the world over. He was the all-singing, all-dancing sensation whose songs had swept all before them. His live shows were *tours de force* of modern entertainment and his image clean and innocent, the boy who would spend his money not on drugs and groupies and excess but on a fairground in his backyard where young children could come and innocently play in the sunshine.

SUCCESS CREATES MIRRORS THAT NEVER TELL THE TRUTH, EITHER TO THE PERFORMER OR THE FANS

Success deceives us. It creates mirrors that never tell the truth, either to the performer or the fans. The reality was that at the time of his passing Michael Jackson was addicted to pills that had names such as Percodan, Demerol, Valium, Xanax and Ativan. He had squandered most of his fortune, had debts of millions and, worst of all, there were charges of child abuse hanging uneasily around him.

Michael's own childhood was a nightmare dominated by two terrifying elements: the sheer brutality of his father and the unflinching glare of success. Michael was the eighth of ten children. He was raised in a small house in Gary, Indiana. His father, Joseph, was a guitarist with a band called The Falcons but had to put aside his musical ambitions when he married Katherine Esther Scruse. Instead, he devoted himself to creating a family group that would achieve the success he thought could have been his.

Michael quickly became part of that masterplan. From a very early age he displayed great ability. His grandmother recalls his fine singing at the age of three and his aptitude for dancing. Yet it was not enough to gain the love of his stern father. Joe regularly beat his children with heavy belts and whips as well as subjecting them to verbal assaults on their characters. Later on, in interviews, Michael would talk about these terrible beatings, but he would also reveal his father's eye for what worked for audiences, his talent for putting together a successful band.

Michael drew close to his mother, who remained helpless in the face of her husband's violence. The Jackson Five came together in 1964. Michael was six years old and played the congas and tambourine. He joined brothers Tito, Marlon, Jackie and Jermaine and two years later was promoted to lead vocalist. They won a local talent show in 1966 performing the James Brown classic 'I Got You (I Feel Good)'. Word of this family group fronted by an amazingly young vocalist spread, reaching the ears of singer Gladys Knight, then signed to Motown. She arranged for label executives to see the band in Chicago, but nothing came of her kind actions.

It was when they supported another of Motown's acts, Bobby Taylor and the Vancouvers, that the wheels were put into motion. After their support slot, Bobby Taylor headed for a payphone, called Motown and insisted they audition The Jackson Five. In July 1968 the Jacksons drove to Detroit and were met by Ralph Seltzer and Suzanne de Passe, two Motown bigwigs. When told Berry Gordy would not be at the audition, Joe Jackson very nearly took his boys back home. But he was talked round, and his boys performed James Brown's 'I Got the Feelin'' and Smokey Robinson's 'Who's Lovin' You'.

A film of the audition was sent to Gordy. Three days later The Jackson Five were signed to Motown and later became the first group ever to see their first four singles – 'I Want You Back', 'ABC', 'The Love You Save' and 'I'll Be There' – hit the number-one spot in the Billboard chart.

Ten-year-old Michael led those records, his voice a wonder beyond his years. He knew instinctively how to take the audience with him. Everywhere he went he was mobbed – at airports, at hotels, at gigs. Once two fans grabbed opposite ends of his scarf, nearly choking him to death.

Michael had everything, everything except a childhood. Later he would talk wistfully about looking out of studio windows and seeing children playing happily in parks, and wishing more than anything that he could be there.

MICHAEL HAD EVERYTHING EXCEPT A CHILDHOOD. HE WOULD TALK WISTFULLY ABOUT SEEING CHILDREN PLAYING IN PARKS AND WISHING THAT HE COULD BE THERE

But the demands of his father and his record company came first. For seven years The Jackson Five made records and toured and saw their popularity dip and rise and dip again. On tour, Joe would sleep with other women, often in the room right next to his sons. They would lie in bed and try not to think too much of their mother back home, the mother whom they adored so much.

Katherine would see her husband's shirt collars painted with lipstick, hear his girlfriends calling up the house on the phone, and she would say: that's it, I am leaving. And then he would turn all gentle, all soft, and kiss her fingertips, and woo her back. And she would think this is not the man who treats me and my children so badly, this is the man I love, and she would kiss him back.

In large offices, plans were made. Michael was the moneyspinner, so he was encouraged to make solo albums, appear in dumb films such as *The Wiz*. That film flopped, but there was an upside – through *The Wiz* he met producer Quincy Jones. It was Jones that Jackson turned to when he began planning his first mature solo album *Off the Wall*.

Jones loved working with Jackson. Unlike the other singers he produced, Michael was disciplined, always on the case. Every day he arrived prepared for work. His diligence paid off. *Off the Wall* severed all ties with Jackson's child-star persona and put him in the big boys' league. His vocals were joyful and convincing, and the music was New York sophisticated: disco with soulful overtones. He smiled out from the cover in his tuxedo, a knowing young man of the world now.

Again the distortion. In truth, Jackson was introverted, cripplingly shy. He had hang-ups about his looks, his family, his lack of sexual know-how. He undertook plastic surgery on his nose, isolated himself further by moving out of the family home and began wearing make-up, a courageous act for a black singer.

Only Jackson was neither black nor white, as his new album *Thriller* was about

The Jackson Five in full swing on an American TV show in 1969. Their exuberance and innocence would soon be replaced by business wrangling, family upset and, eventually, huge tragedy.

to demonstrate. Released in December 1982, *Thriller* was a glossy album that touched more on pop than soul, more on attractive shapes than deep meaning. It was the album's second single, 'Billie Jean', that pushed the album into the history books. 'Billie Jean' was a dark brooding dance number that had been inspired by a series of letters Michael had received from a fan claiming he had fathered her child. As he shrank from all female contact at this point in his life, the claim was risible. But it inspired a song that allowed Jackson to cast himself as the star having to deal with troublesome groupies. Again the distortion. A hooker who was mistakenly sent into his dressing room once told of a man who could not touch, who just wanted to talk. 'Oh,' she said, 'you're one of them...'

At the time of *Thriller*, Motown was busy organizing a 25th-anniversary television show. Berry Gordy personally asked Michael to appear with his brothers as The Jackson Five. Jackson refused; he had retreated from them as well. But he made Gordy an offer. He would appear solo but only if he could sing 'Billie Jean'. Do a spot with your brothers, too, and you're on, Gordy replied.

Jackson's performance that night was remarkable. It took Jackson to heights he had never reached before. His dancing was supple, fluid, filled with a passion and trickery. His energy astounded millions of people – including Fred Astaire, who rang him the next day and told him that his performance was that of an angry dancer.

The single shot to number one, and *Thriller* started selling in the millions. Jackson was right at the top of the tree now. Smile for the camera, smile for the fans, all is good, all is bright.

Whilst the world was encouraged to read Jackson as a modern fairy-tale, the strange stories began to emerge. At his Neverland ranch in Encino he had built a fairground. His best friend was a monkey called Bubbles. He took Bubbles with him for his first meeting with Elizabeth Taylor, the actress he formed a close relationship with. He once hired an acting troupe to come and be Snow White and the Seven Dwarves in his living room. He appeared in public with a face mask. His physical appearance began changing: his skin got lighter, many thought as the result of skin bleaching, although he later claimed in an

Oprah Winfrey interview that he suffered from vitiligo, a disease that causes white patches on the skin. It was eyebrow-raising stuff, but it wasn't dangerous or dark. And then came Jordan Chandler.

In 1984 four-year-old Jordan had written a fan letter to Jackson. Jackson replied the next day, and five years later the two met. They became firm friends. Chandler and his mother June spent nights at Jackson's Neverland. Often Michael and Jordan slept together in the same bed whilst Chandler's mother and sister slept next door.

IT WAS EYEBROW-RAISING STUFF, BUT IT WASN'T DANGEROUS OR DARK. AND THEN CAME JORDAN CHANDLER

Eventually, the inevitable occurred. The Chandlers alleged sexual abuse, and after a prolonged period Jackson paid the family $22 million. Not long after he married Lisa Marie Presley, daughter of Elvis, thus joining together music's two grandest families. The marriage lasted barely two years. Despite Lisa's assertion of sexually active behaviour, many thought that the marriage was a sham, there to cover up Jackson's obsession with children. Around this time also, the addiction to

Michael Joseph Jackson was born on 29 August 1958. By the age of six Michael was singing and performing in his brothers' band, The Jackson Five, in their home town of Gary, Indiana. In 1968 they signed to Motown. Their impact was immediate, and their first four singles – 'I Want You Back', 'ABC', 'The Love You Save' and 'I'll Be There' – rocketed to number one, a chart record yet to be equalled. Noting Jackson's huge popularity with the fans, Motown cut solo albums with him, a move that led to fatal internal dissension. The band split, and from 1977 Jackson concentrated on a solo career. His 1982 album *Thriller* became the highest-selling album ever, and follow-ups – *Dangerous* and *Bad* – also sold extremely well. Jackson was dogged by allegations of child abuse. He was arrested in 2005 and appeared before a court where he was judged not guilty. Despite winning numerous awards and accolades, Jackson remained a damaged individual who relied on huge amounts of medication. He died of heart failure on 25 June 2009. He was 50 years old.

pills began. He was still popping them like mad the day he died.

In 1996 Jackson married Debbie Rowe, a dermatological nurse. He had two children with her, Prince Michael I and a daughter Paris. When the priest said you may now kiss the bride, Jackson just gave her a peck on the cheek. He and Rowe separated after three years.

In 2003 Jackson granted an interview to the British journalist Martin Bashir. In the documentary he holds hands with a young teenager and is heard making arrangements to sleep with him. The documentary aired, police raided his house and Jackson was charged with sexual abuse of a minor. In 2005 he stood trial for five months and was cleared of all charges. Yet, before he could get his breath, more bad news. His prized possession, Neverland, was to close down.

Reports of debts totalling millions of dollars began to surface. Despite the huge success of albums such as *Bad*, *Dangerous* and *History,* the tours that would net him more than $100 million at a time, the singer was struggling financially. It was astonishing to think that one man could spend so much money.

Yet Jackson remained unfazed. He was able to raise millions by using assets such as The Beatles' back catalogue as collateral. Only one problem, those assets would soon run out. Hence the announcement of 50 London shows and with them the prospect of enough money to wipe out his debts.

But the discipline that Quincy Jones had so admired was slipping. He missed rehearsal days, claimed illness and took pills for all kinds of ailments from pain to insomnia.

Jackson's personal doctor, Conrad Murray, gave him a drug called propofol. It is used to knock out patients who are about to be operated on. That is how unhappy Michael Jackson was. In the end he craved neither riches or pleasure; he just wanted to be knocked out. For in sleep, the darkest of darknesses, he found a peace he could not find anywhere else...

JACKSON'S DAUGHTER PARIS MOVED THE WORLD TO TEARS WITH HER SHORT STATEMENT THAT HER DADDY 'WAS **THE BEST FATHER EVER'**

When rumours of his passing started to leak out, Google took so many hits it genuinely believed it was under attack. Jackson's televised burial service attracted one billion viewers.

At his funeral, same as it ever was. His father tried to promote his new business venture to the cameras. Stars including Stevie Wonder and Michael's brother Jermaine sang. Berry Gordy and Smokey Robinson gave eulogies and Jackson's daughter Paris moved the world to tears with her short statement that her daddy was 'the best father ever. I just wanted to say I loved him.'

Sony Records waited a decent time and then struck a deal with his estate whereby they reportedly handed over a quarter of a billion dollars for seven posthumous albums. Best thing he ever did, dying, said the wise and the knowing. A point was being made.

The day after Jackson's passing those records of his that had been languishing in bargain bins suddenly flew into the charts. A movie called *This Is It*, filmed as he prepared his comeback tour, did great box office all over the world. Jackson was back on top and six foot under.

*****

This book began with a story about a man called Elvis who was given the keys to the world and coped with it by swallowing pill after pill, which finally took him. Between Elvis's breakthrough single in 1956 and Michael Jackson's death in 2009 there is more than half a century. And in those five decades there are different soundtracks and different characters, but one thing is constant: the song remains the same.

BIBLIOGRAPHY

Last Train to Memphis: The Rise of Elvis Presley
by Peter Guralnick (Little, Brown 1994)

Careless Love: The Unmaking of Elvis Presley
by Peter Guralnick (Little, Brown 1999)

Back to the Beach: A Brian Wilson and Beach Boys Reader
by Kingsley Abbott (Helter Skelter 2003)

He's a Rebel: Phil Spector by Mark Ribowsky
(E.P. Dutton 1989)

Look! Listen! Vibrate! Smile! by Domenic Priore
(Last Gasp, 1995)

The Beatles Recording Sessions by Mark Lewisohn
(Hamlyn 1988)

The Beatles by Bob Spitz (Aurum 2006)

Jimi Hendrix: Electric Gypsy by Harry Shapiro and
Caesar Glebeek (Mandarin 1983)

*Anyway Anyhow Anywhere: The Complete Chronicle of
The Who* by Andy Neill and Matt Kent
(Friedman Fairfax 2002)

Out of His Head: The Sound of Phil Spector
by Richard Williams (Abacus 1972)

The Paul McCartney Story by George Tremlett
(Futura 1975)

Charles Manson: Coming Down Fast by Simon Wells
(Hodder and Stoughton, 2009)

Sid Vicious: No One Is Innocent by Alan Parker
(Orion Books 2007)

Steve Marriott: All Too Beautiful by Paolo Hewitt and
John Hellier (Helter Skelter 2008)

The Wild and Wicked World of Brian Jones
by Anna Wohlin (Blake Books 2005)

Riders on the Storm by John Densmore
(Bloomsbury 1991)

Waiting for the Sun by Barney Hoskyns (Viking 1996)

Return of the Last Gang in Town by Marcus Gray
(Helter Skelter 2001)

Guns, Cash and Rock'n'Roll by Steve Overbury
(Mainstream 2007)

You Send Me: The Life and Times of Sam Cooke
by Daniel Wolff (Quill 1995)

The Love You Make: An Insider's Story of the Beatles
by Peter Brown (McGraw Hill 1983)

*Where Did Our Love Go? The Rise and Fall of the Motown
Sound* by Nelson George (St Martins Press 1985)

*Marvin Gaye: What's Going On and the Last Days of the
Motown Sound* by Ben Edmonds
(Mojo/Canongate 2001)

The Bob Marley Reader by Hank Bordowitz
(Da Capo Press 2004)

Bob Marley: The Untold Story by Chris Salewicz
(HarperCollins 2010)

The True Adventures of the Rolling Stones by Stanley Booth
(A Capella 1984)

Led Zeppelin: When Giants Walked the Earth by Mick Wall
(Orion Books 2008)

Echoes: The Story Behind Every Pink Floyd Song
by Cliff Jones (Carlton Books 1996)

Mick Jagger by Anthony Scaduto (W.H. Allen 1971)

The Who by Numbers by Steve Grantley and
Alan G. Parker (Helter Skelter 2010)

Bowie: Loving the Alien by Christopher Sandford
(Warner Books 1996)

A Man Called Cash by Steve Turner (Bloomsbury 2004)

Madonna: Like an Icon by Lucy O'Brien
(Corgi Books 2007)

Stevie Wonder by Constanze Elsner
(Everest Books 1977)

The Day John Lennon Died by Keith Elliot Greenberg
(Backbeat Books 2010)

Sly and the Family Stone by Joel Selvin
(Avon Books 1998)

Everything (A Book About Manic Street Preachers)
by Simon Price (Virgin Books 1999)

A Bone in My Flute by Holly Johnson (Century 1994)

Take It Like a Man by Boy George (HarperCollins 1995)

Van Morrison: No Surrender by Johnny Rogan (Secker
and Warburg 2005)

The Biography of Kurt Cobain by Charles R. Cross
(Sceptre 2001)

The Beatles Recording Sessions by Mark Lewisohn
(Hamlyn 1988)

John Lennon by Ray Coleman (Futura 1985)

INDEX

ACKNOWLEDGEMENTS

Thank you so much Richard Green, Kim Davies, David Luxton, Vicky Axelson and Wal and Izzy. Big thanks to Mark Lewisohn (WLBE) and Simon Wells (OFR) who are always there when I need some… help.

This book is dedicated to the Yeovil and Balcombe set, Nina and Alan, Suzie and Nick, Tanya and Stu, Francesa, Katie and Pietro, Clyde the Mumper but, especially, Isabella and Millie. Here is the past so you may know your future.

Quercus Publishing Plc
21 Bloomsbury Square
London
WC1A 2NS

First published in 2011

Designed and edited by Therefore Publishing Limited

A catalogue record of this book is available from the British Library

UK and associated territories: ISBN 978 0 85738 503 1
US and associated territories: ISBN 978 1 84866 154 7

Printed and bound in China

10 9 8 7 6 5 4 3 2 1

2–3 Jan Persson/Getty Images; 8 Michael Ochs Archives/Getty Images; 12 Keystone/Getty Images; 15 Astrid Kirchherr K & K/Getty Images; 18 Michael Ochs Archives/Getty Images; 22 Popperfoto/Getty Images; 25 Popperfoto/Getty Images; 28 Richard Chowen/Getty Images; 32 Frank Driggs Collection/Getty Images; 34 Michael Ochs Archives/Getty Images; 38 Michael Ochs Archive / Getty Images; 42 Sony BMG Music Entertainment/Getty Images; 45 Alice Ochs/Getty Images; 48 Keystone-France/Getty Images; 51 New York Daily News Archive/Getty Images; 54 Keystone-France/Getty Images; 58 Michael Ochs Archives/Getty Images; 60 Ray Avery/Getty Images; 64 Keystone-France/Getty Images; 67 Bentley Archive/Popperfoto/Getty Images; 72 John Downing/Getty Images; 74 GAB Archive/Getty Images; 78 Tom Copi/Getty Images; 81 Astrid Kirchherr K&K/Getty Images; 84 Gilles Petard/Getty Images; 88 Michael Ochs Archives/Getty Images; 92 Michael Ochs Archives/Getty Images; 94 Ron Howard/Getty Images; 100 Michael Ochs Archives/Getty Images; 104 Chris Walter/Getty Images; 107 Michael Ochs Archives/Getty Images; 110 Michael Ochs Archives/Getty Images; 114 Keystone/Getty Images ; 117 Popperfoto/Getty Images; 120 Archive Photos/Getty Images; 124 Robert Altman/Getty Images; 129 Robert Altman/Getty Images; 132 Echoes/Getty Images; 136 Steve Wood/Getty Images; 139 Steve Wood/Getty Images; 142 Ron Galella/Getty Images; 146 Michael Ochs Archive/Getty Images; 148 Gijsbert Hanekroot/Getty Images; 152 Evening Standard/Getty Images; 156 Ebet Roberts/Getty Images; 160 Steve Emberton/Getty Images; 164 David Harris/Getty Images; 168 David Corio/Getty Images; 172 Archive Photos/ Getty Images; 174 Central Press/Getty Images; 178 Dave Hogan/Getty Images; 181 Ebet Roberts/Getty Images; 184 Ian Dickson/Getty Images; 188 Michael Ochs Archives/Getty Images; 192 Georges DeKeerle/Getty Images; 197 Georges DeKeerle/Getty Images; 200 Oliver Morris/Getty Images; 202 Dave Hogan/Getty Images; 206 Mike Prior/Getty Images; 210 Debi Doss/Getty Images; 213 Ebet Roberts/Getty Images; 216 Raffaella Cavalieri/Getty Images; 220 Yvonne Hemsey/Getty Images; 224 Time Life Pictures/Getty Images; 228 Paul Bergen/Getty Images; 232 Kieran Doherty/Getty Images; 235 Gered Mankowitz/Getty Images; 238 Ferdaus Shamim/Getty Images; 240 New York Daily News Archive/Getty Images; 244 John Chiasson/Getty Images; 247 Ed Rode/Getty Images; 250 MJ Kim/Getty Images; 254 Mike Marsland/Getty Images; 256 Tim Whitby/Getty Images; 260 Alain Benainous/Getty Images; 264 Michael Ochs Archives/Getty Images

Title page: Roger Daltrey of The Who on stage at the Royal Theatre, Copenhagen, 24 January 1970